104

THE BAROQUE POEM

HAROLD B. SEGEL is Professor of Slavic Literatures at Columbia University. He is the author of the two-volume work *The Literature of Eighteenth-Century Russia* (1967) and *The Trilogy of Alexander Sukhovo-Kobylin* (1969), both of which were published by E. P. Dutton, and *The Major Comedies of Alexander Fredro* (1969). His forthcoming book *Twentieth-Century Russian Drama* will also be published by E. P. Dutton.

THE BAROQUE POEM

A Comparative Survey

*together with 150 illustrative texts from
English, American, Dutch, German, French, Italian,
Spanish, Mexican, Portuguese, Polish, Modern Latin,
Czech, Croatian, and Russian poetry, in the original
languages and accompanying English translations*

HAROLD B. SEGEL

A Dutton Paperback

E. P. DUTTON & CO., INC. :: NEW YORK :: 1974

Published simultaneously in Canada by
Clarke, Irwin & Company Limited, Toronto and Vancouver

Library of Congress Catalog Card Number: 74-95501

ISBN 0-525-47301-7 (DP)   ISBN 0-525-06118-5 (Cloth)

Designed by Mollie M. Torras

Acknowledgments

Grateful acknowledgment is made to the following for permission to quote from copyright material:

TEXTS

English

John Donne: Holy Sonnets, 1, 4, 14; "Elegy 19, Going to Bed," "A Valediction: of Weeping," "The Flea," and "The Extasie," reprinted from *The Poems of John Donne*, ed. Herbert H. C. Grierson. Copyright 1912 by Oxford University Press. Reprinted by permission of The Clarendon Press, Oxford.

William Habington: "*Nox nocti indicat Scientiam*. David," reprinted from *The Metaphysical Poets*, ed. Helen Gardner. Copyright © 1966 by Helen Gardner. Reprinted by permission of Penguin Books, Baltimore.

Edward, Lord Herbert of Cherbury: "To his Watch, when he could not sleep," reprinted from *The Metaphysical Poets*, ed. Helen Gardner. Copyright © 1966 by Helen Gardner. Reprinted by permission of Penguin Books, Baltimore.

George Herbert: "Clasping of Hands," "The Altar," "Easter-wings," "Coloss. 3:3—Our life is hid with Christ in God," "Paradise," "Lovejoy," "Bitter-sweet," "Ana-$\begin{Bmatrix} \text{MARY} \\ \text{ARMY} \end{Bmatrix}$-gram," "Vertue," "Time," and "Death," reprinted from *The Works of George Herbert*, ed. F. E. Hutchinson. Copyright 1941 by Oxford University Press. Reprinted by permission of The Clarendon Press, Oxford.

American

Dutch

Mexican

Sor Juana Inés de la Cruz: "A su retrato," "Yo no puedo tenerte ni dejarte," "Detente, sombra de mi bien esquivo," "Qué es esto, Alcino, cómo tu cordura," and "Rosa divina que en gentil cultura," reprinted from *Sor Juana Inés de la Cruz, Poesías Completas,* ed. Emilio Abreu Gómez. 2d ed., revised and corrected. Copyright 1948 by Ediciones Botas, S.A. Reprinted by permission of Ediciones Botas, S.A., Mexico City.

Miguel de Guevara: "Levántame, Señor, que estoy caído," "Poner al Hijo en cruz, abierto el seno," "No me mueve, mi Dios, para quererte," and "Pídeme de mi mismo el tiempo cuenta," reprinted from *Poetas novohispanos,* Vols. 1, 3, ed. Alfonso Méndez Plancarte. Ediciones de la Universidad nacional autónoma, Mexico City, 1942, 1944. Reprinted by permission of the Universidad nacional autónoma, Mexico City.

Luis de Sandoval y Zapata: "A la materia prima," "Riesgo grande de un galán en metáfora de mariposa," and "A una cómica difunta," reprinted from *Poetas novohispanos,* Vols. 1, 3, ed. Alfonso Méndez Plancarte. Ediciones de la Universidad nacional autónoma, Mexico City, 1942, 1944. Reprinted by permission of the Universidad nacional autónoma, Mexico City.

Portuguese

Luís de Camões: "Mudam-se os tempos, mudam-se as vontades," "O tempo acabo o ano, o mês e a hora," "Transforma-se o amador na cousa amada," "Amor é fogo que arde sem se ver," "De quantas graças tinha, a Natureza," and "Que esperais, esperança?—Desespero," reprinted from *Luís de Camões, Lirica,* ed. Massaud Moisés. Copyright © 1963 by Editôra Cultrix Ltda. Reprinted by permission of Editôra Cultrix Ltda., São Paolo. "—Que levas, cruel Morte?—Um claro dia," reprinted from *Luís de Camões, Rimas,* ed. Álvaro J. Da Costa Pimpão. University of Coimbra Press, Coimbra. Reprinted by permission of Coimbra University Press.

Polish

Stanisław Herakliusz Lubomirski: "Sonet na cała mękę pańską," reprinted from *Poeci polskiego baroku,* eds. Jadwiga Sokołowska and Kazimiera Żukowska. Państwowy Instytut Wydawniczy, Warsaw, 1965.

Jan Andrzej Morsztyn: "Do św. Jana Baptysty," "Cuda miłości," "Cuda miłości," "O swej pannie," "Do tejże," "Do panny," "Na krzyżk na piersiach jednej panny," "Niestatek," "Niestatek," "Do trupa," "Odjazd," and "Pieśń," reprinted from *Poeci polskiego baroku,* eds. Jadwiga Sokołowska and Kazimiera Żukowska. Państwowy Instytut Wydawniczy, Warsaw, 1965.

Zbigniew Morsztyn: "Emblema 39," reprinted from *Muza domowa,* Vol. 1. Państwowy Instytut Wydawniczy, Warsaw, 1954. "Emblema 51," reprinted from *Poeci polskiego baroku,* eds. Jadwiga Sokołowska and Kazimiera Żukowska. Państwowy Instytut Wydawniczy, Warsaw, 1965.

Daniel Naborowski: "Krótkość żywota," "Na toż," "Cnota grunt wszytkiemu," and "Na oczy królewny angielskiej, która była za Fryderykiem, falcgrafem renskim, obranym królem czeskim," reprinted from *Poeci polskiego baroku,* eds. Jadwiga Sokołowska and Kazimiera Żukowska. Państwowy Instytut Wydawniczy, Warsaw, 1965.

go," "Elusive shadow of myself, remain," "Alcino, what is this . . . ," and "O rose divine, with cultivated air," reprinted from *The Pathless Grove: A Collection of Seventeenth Century Mexican Sonnets*, ed. and trans. Pauline Cook. The Decker Press, Prairie City, Ill.

Miguel de Guevara: "Raise me up, Lord, who am fallen down" (two lines) and "Time requires me to give account," trans. Samuel Beckett in *An Anthology of Mexican Poetry*, ed. Octavio Paz. Copyright © 1958 by Indiana University Press. Indiana University Press, Bloomington. Reprinted by permission of Indiana University Press.

Luis de Sandoval y Zapata: "To Primal Matter," "Grievous Peril of a Gallant in Moth Metaphor," and "To a Dead Actress," trans. Samuel Beckett in *An Anthology of Mexican Poetry*, ed. Octavio Paz. Copyright © 1958 by Indiana University Press. Indiana University Press, Bloomington. Reprinted by permission of Indiana University Press.

Polish

Jan Andrzej Morsztyn: "To St. John the Baptist" and "Song," reprinted from *Five Centuries of Polish Poetry 1450–1970*, ed. and trans. Jerzy Peterkiewicz and Burns Singer. 2d ed. Copyright © 1960 by Jerzy Peterkiewicz and Burns Singer. Oxford University Press, 1970 (first published by Secker and Warburg, London, 1960), New York and Toronto. Reprinted by permission of Oxford University Press.

Zbigniew Morsztyn: "Emblem 39" and "Emblem 51," reprinted from *Five Centuries of Polish Poetry 1450–1970*, ed. and trans. Jerzy Peterkiewicz and Burns Singer. 2d ed. Copyright © 1960 by Jerzy Peterkiewicz and Burns Singer. Oxford University Press, 1970 (first published by Secker and Warburg, London, 1960), New York and Toronto. Reprinted by permission of Oxford University Press.

Mikołaj Sęp Szarzyński: "On these words of Job: Homo natus de muliere, brevi vivens tempore etc." and "On the War we wage against Satan, the World and the Body," reprinted from *Five Centuries of Polish Poetry 1450–1970*, ed. and trans. Jerzy Peterkiewicz and Burns Singer. 2d ed. Copyright © 1960 by Jerzy Peterkiewicz and Burns Singer. Oxford University Press, 1970 (first published by Secker and Warburg, London, 1960), New York and Toronto. Reprinted by permission of Oxford University Press.

Modern Latin (Polish)

Maciej Kazimierz Sarbiewski: "Book II, Ode V A Departure from Things Humane," reprinted from *The Odes of Casimire*, trans. G. H(ils). London, 1646.

Czech

Adam Michna of Otradovice: "Disdain for This Transitory World," trans. E. Osers, from an anthology edited by A. French to be published by University of Michigan Press in 1974.

Václav Karel Holan Rovenský: from *Capella regia musicalis*, "Triumph," trans. D. Gosselin and A. French and "Where, where are you, great emperors?," trans. A. French, from an anthology edited by A. French to be published by University of Michigan Press in 1974.

to my teachers
Dmitrij Čiževskij and Wiktor Weintraub,
who kindled the interest

Contents

Preface

For some time, scholars have recognized that between the Renaissance of the fifteenth and sixteenth centuries and the classicism (or neoclassicism, a less apt term still used) of the later seventeenth and eighteenth centuries, the European aesthetic sensibility underwent a development that set it apart from that of both the Renaissance and classicism. *Baroque,* primarily as a period term but also in the sense of a style or a complex of styles and even a way of regarding the world, has become widely accepted to designate that different sensibility intervening between Renaissance and classicism.

Baroque literature, that is, largely the literature of the seventeenth century, may be less known and appreciated than Baroque architecture, painting, sculpture, and music. But it is rich and varied in poetry, drama, and prose and counts within its ranks such important writers as Donne, Herbert, and Crashaw in England, Marino in Italy, Góngora and Quevedo in Spain, d'Aubigné, La Ceppède, and the early Corneille in France, Vondel in Holland, Opitz, Gryphius, and Böhme in Germany, Jan Andrzej and Zbigniew Morsztyn in Poland, Komenský (Comenius) in Bohemia, Lomonosov in Russia, and Gundulić in Croatia. The greatest achievements of Baroque literature came, however, in poetry. Indeed, when we think of the literature of the Baroque, it is the names of poets—Donne, Marino, Góngora—that first come to mind.

The present book deals, above all, with the poetry of the Baroque. Its purpose is twofold. First, to present a comprehensive survey of the Baroque: the state of scholarship in the field, problems in the definition and use of Baroque as a term and concept, the relationship of mannerism to Baroque, the political, religious, scientific, and philosophical background of the age, the possible impact of nonliterary events on the evolution of Baroque taste, art, and outlook, the various types of Baroque poetry and aspects of Baroque poetic style. Second, to illustrate points made in the first, or survey, part of the book by giving a broad selection of representative poems, mostly lyrics, in the original languages and accompanying English translations.

The poems in the second section of the book are divided into two main groupings: religious, mystic and meditative poetry (" The World of the Spirit "), and amatory poetry (" The World of the Senses "). The meditative poetry is further subdivided by theme (mutability, time, death, and so on). The poems have been selected from many literatures, wherever a significant Baroque existed. Since a literary art in seventeenth-century New England and the Spanish colonies in the Americas (Mexico, above all) developed within the context and under the influence of the European, New England and Mexican poets are also included to demonstrate the range of the Baroque literary experience.

The texts part of this book is an anthology, then, of Baroque poetry. It is not the first comparative anthology of Baroque poems aimed at the English-speaking reader, but it is, as far as I know, the first in which Slavic poetry is extensively discussed and represented. And it is also the first in which late sixteenth- and seventeenth-century English, American, and Mexican poetry is brought together with selections from the continental European literatures (including Portuguese).

The translations are meant to be faithful and accurate. Some are my own and some are by other translators whose names appear beneath the English texts. No one pattern of verse translation was followed. My own preference in most cases is for unrhymed verse. The preservation of rhyme in poetry translation is exceptionally demanding and often entails compromises involving a loss of fidelity to the original. However, there have been some very skillful verse translations of Baroque poems and I have tried to incorporate as many of these as possible.

H. B. S.

PART ONE

The Baroque Poem: A Comparative Survey

Introduction

Probably no area of literary study has evoked so much interest and controversy in recent years as the *Baroque* (roughly 1580 to 1680).

In a well-known article, "The Concept of the Baroque in Literary Scholarship," René Wellek reviewed the history of the term "Baroque" in the arts and expressed serious reservations about the definitions assigned it. Yet he acknowledged its usefulness in literary study:

> In spite of many ambiguities and uncertainties as to the extension, valuation, and precise content of the term, baroque fulfilled and is still fulfilling an important function. It has put the problem of periodisation and of a pervasive style very squarely; it has pointed to the analogies between the literatures of the different countries and between the several arts. It is still the one convenient term which refers to the style which came after the Renaissance but preceded actual neoclassicism.[1]

When Wellek's article was being readied for inclusion in a book of his collected essays, *Concepts of Criticism*, he had the chance to revise earlier positions in the form of a postscript dated 1962. In this postscript, he traces the increase of interest in and acceptance of Baroque in Europe and America since his article first appeared and shows, at the same time, the continuing disagreement on the precise definition of the term in literature. However, Wellek again defends the value of it.

> It [Baroque] raises the problem of periodisation, of the analogies between the arts; it is the one term for the style between the Renaissance and classicism which is sufficiently general to override the

[1] Wellek's article appeared originally in *The Journal of Aesthetics*, V (1946), 77–109. I am quoting from the edition of the article in René Wellek, *Concepts of Criticism* (New Haven and London, 1963), p. 113.

local terms of schools; and it suggests the unity of a Western literary and artistic period. The discussion of baroque has contributed enormously to our understanding of a time and art which was for a long time ignored, disparaged, or misinterpreted. This alone is sufficient justification for its continued use."[2]

Although useful, in the ways that Wellek's remarks suggest, the term Baroque itself is imperfect and has not yet won universal acceptance. The greatest problems have arisen with English and French literary historians.

1) Despite Austin Warren's fine study of the seventeenth-century English poet Richard Crashaw published under the title *Richard Crashaw: A Study in Baroque Sensibility* (Baton Rouge, La., 1939), most specialists in late-sixteenth- and seventeenth-century English literature continue to favor the originally disparaging and not quite apt term "Metaphysical" for literary developments that are not, of course, exclusively *metaphysical* in any strict sense and for which most critics on the Continent have long ago accepted the validity of Baroque. In this respect, studies of the 1960s are not much less conservative than those of the 1920s and 1930s, with the apparently unique exception of Warren. For literary scholars of the 1920s and 1930s, John Donne, George Herbert, Richard Crashaw, Abraham Cowley, Henry Vaughan, and Andrew Marvell, among others, were the Metaphysical poets. They so appear in H. J. C. Grierson's (ed.) *Metaphysical Lyrics and Poems* (Oxford, 1921), Joan Bennett's *Four Metaphysical Poets* (Cambridge, 1934), J. B. Leishman's *The Metaphysical Poets* (New York, 1934), Helen C. White's *The Metaphysical Poets* (New York, 1936), Theodore Spencer's and Mark Van Doren's *Studies in Metaphysical Poetry: Two Essays and a Bibliography* (New York, 1939), and Mario Praz's *Studies in Seventeenth Century Imagery* (London, 1939).

Largely unaffected by the outpouring of scholarly works on the Baroque in continental literatures in the 1950s and 1960s, English literary scholarship has been quite content to retain the restrictive Metaphysical, as in Geoffrey Walton's *Metaphysical to Augustan* (Cambridge, 1955), Helen Gardner's (ed.) *The Metaphysical Poets* (Baltimore, Md., 1957), the expanded version of Joan Bennett's earlier book under the title *Five Metaphysical Poets* (Cambridge,

[2] *Ibid.*, p. 127.

1964), J. Hunter's *The Metaphysical Poets* (London, 1965), and George Williamson's *Six Metaphysical Poets: A Reader's Guide* (New York, 1966).

When Metaphysical has been deemed inadequate for one reason or another or a more precise delimitation seemed necessary, English literary historians have operated with the "School of Donne" or the "Donne tradition" in much the same way *gongorismo* and *marinismo* have been used in Spain and Italy, respectively. Thus, George Williamson's early study of seventeenth-century English poetry bore the title *The Donne Tradition* (New York, 1930), while Alfred Alvarez approached the same developments in a book entitled *The School of Donne* (New York, 1961). A good indication of the reticence of English literary historians to accept Baroque in the way the Continent has done is the multivolume Pelican *Guide to English Literature*. The third volume, first published in 1956, carries the title *From Donne to Marvell* and ranges over the great bulk of late sixteenth- and seventeenth-century English literature, both poetry and prose. Yet the only serious consideration of Baroque occurs in a brief article by a European scholar and specialist in French literature, Odette de Mourgues. Even here Madame de Mourgues is willing to make only a partial compromise. The "mood" of the age, which also affected an England whose insularity is a main point in the article, is characterized as follows:

> Some would call it "baroque"—*a dangerously fashionable word in the terminology of literary criticism*—but this term may be helpful if we use it in order to characterize certain manifestations of the sensibility of the late Renaissance.[3]

Elsewhere in the volume, Baroque appears only three times in a few hundred pages: once with reference to the work of Giles Fletcher where the "Spenserian quality is modified by Italian warmth and paradoxical wit in a way that anticipates Crashaw and may be described as 'baroque'";[4] a second time with reference to Crashaw who, before his conversion to Rome in 1645, "was writing in a vein of voluptuous mysticism which suggests Italian and Spanish baroque art";[5] and the third and last time when in an

---

[3] *From Donne to Marvell*, p. 20. Italics mine.
[4] *Ibid.*, p. 54.
[5] *Ibid.*, p. 58.

article on George Herbert "baroque conceit" is mentioned, in quotation marks, as the equivalent of the ornate, decorative image.[6]

One noteworthy recent sign of change in English literary historiography is Frank Kermode's perceptive introduction to his edition of a collection of essays, *The Metaphysical Poets*. Kermode cautiously broaches the matter of the possible relation of Metaphysical to Baroque in this way: "If we grant," he writes, "for the moment that 'metaphysical' is a subdepartment of Baroque and therefore an aspect of a historical phenomenon observable throughout Europe, we had better be sure we are using the word *baroque* sensibly."[7] The emphasis on caution and precision of definition is underscored again, later in the piece.

> Thus metaphysical and baroque come uneasily together again. All one can do is to advise caution. We must not say that the corruption of metaphysical is the generation of baroque. We must not speak at all sharply in these matters. It is enough, perhaps, to remind ourselves that when we think of metaphysical, we do not think at once of St. Ignatius or Bernini or Marino, though we may do so a little later. We think first of a special moment in English poetry, a moment of plain but witty magniloquence, of a passionate poetry ballasted with learning and propelled by a sceptical ingenuity that may strike us as somehow very modern.[8]

2) For a very long time French literary historians declined to apply the term Baroque to French literature from the 1550s to the 1660s. Most insisted that the Renaissance of Ronsard and the Pléiade extended to and was followed by the classicism of the later Malherbe and Corneille, Racine and Boileau. Others were comfortable with "preciosité" in the same way the English were with "metaphysical," aware in some instances that the so-called *précieux* style did not, to be sure, embrace all the literature of the period. Some simply continued and reinforced the neoclassical hostility to a post-Renaissance literature that exhibited many features unacceptable to the aesthetics and "good taste" (*bienséance*) of the new classicism.

As these prejudices gradually diminished in significance and the

[6] *Ibid.*, p. 157.
[7] *The Metaphysical Poets*, ed. Frank Kermode (New York, 1969), p. 13.
[8] *Ibid.*, p. 32.

horizons of French literary history broadened to include works long dismissed as trivial, dissatisfaction with the Renaissance: classicism formula or the all-embracing use of *preciosité* took the form of the reevaluation of forgotten or lightly regarded writers (Jean de La Ceppède, Jean de Sponde, Jean-Baptiste Chassignet, Théophile de Viau, Girard de Saint-Amant, and so on). Among the fruits of this literary archaeology were such persuasive studies as Jean Rousset's *La Littérature de l'âge baroque en France: Circé et le Paon* (Paris, 1954) and Imbrie Buffum's impressive and valuable books *Agrippa d'Aubigné's Les Tragiques: a Study of the Baroque Style in Poetry* (New Haven and London, 1951) and *Studies in the Baroque from Montaigne to Rotrou* (New Haven and London, 1957), or such skilled attempts to introduce greater order into the understanding of the various elements that went to make up the literature of the "Baroque Age" as Odette de Mourgues's *Metaphysical, Baroque and Précieux Poetry* (Oxford, 1953).

Although the newer scholarship in the French field (Buffum, Rousset) has done much to secure the rights of citizenship for Baroque, disagreement still persists. De Mourgues's *Metaphysical, Baroque and Précieux Poetry* strives to distinguish among the three different styles of literary expression mentioned in the title and concludes with a sharply limited vision of Baroque as a relatively minor trend in which form is given precedence over substance. In his lead article, "Common-Sense Remarks on the French Baroque," in *Studies in Seventeenth-Century French Literature* (ed. Jean-Jacques Demorest, Ithaca, N. Y., 1962; Garden City, N. Y., 1966) Henri Peyre goes so far as to disparage the very notion of a French Baroque.

But such dissenting voices, although still heard occasionally in the ranks of French literary historians, are becoming increasingly more isolated as the acceptance of Baroque attracts new adherents willing to find a place for the concept in the terminology of French literary periodization.

For German, Spanish, and Italian literary historians the problem has had small significance for some time and there is general agreement on what the term and concept imply in literary study chronologically, thematically, and stylistically.

In German literature, Baroque was seized on relatively early— in the 1920s—and applied to the literature of the age that intervened between the Renaissance and classicism. In Spain and Italy, the problem was, in a sense, easier. The features now generally regarded as characteristic of the Baroque were associated above all with the influential poets of the seventeenth century—Luis de Góngora y Argote in Spain, and Giambattista Marino in Italy. The style identified with Góngora then came to be known as *gongorismo* and with Marino as *marinismo*. When other writers were found to reveal similar features they were, in turn, "Gongorists" or "Marinists." Once the term Baroque was accepted it was rapidly reconciled with gongorismo and marinismo, which were then perceived to be local variants of a single style cultivated throughout Europe.

As the study of the Baroque has increased, its progress has been horizontal as well as vertical. Students of late sixteenth- and seventeenth-century literature, in England and on the Continent, have gradually become aware of distinct asethetic and cultural parallels in other countries in more or less the same period. The great religious and political conflicts of the late sixteenth and seventeenth centuries engulfed the European continent, so the discovery of parallel developments in the arts and letters should occasion no surprise. However, this awareness of similarities has produced only isolated efforts at comparative scholarship; the emphasis still tends to fall largely on the national literatures.

Two of the most rewarding specimens to date of the comparative method are Frank J. Warnke's study and anthology *European Metaphysical Poetry* (New Haven and London, 1961) and his more recent *Versions of Baroque* (New Haven and London, 1972). Limited only to continental parallels to the poetry of the so-called English Metaphysicals, the earlier book brings together for the first time well-chosen and well-translated Dutch, German, French, Spanish, and Italian lyric poems. Although English poets are excluded from the anthology, they are discussed in the Introduction, particularly as they relate to developments on the Continent. *Versions of Baroque* is a brilliant study of seventeenth-century European literature in terms of specific dominant aspects of the Baroque modality. It is beyond doubt the most valuable comparative study of the Baroque yet to appear in English.

Two other fairly recent comparative studies in English are also worth mentioning: J. M. Cohen's *The Baroque Lyric* (London, 1963) and Lowry Nelson, Jr.'s *Baroque Lyric Poetry* (New Haven and London, 1966). The first seeks to bring out the unity of the Baroque experience through a thematic study of several English and continental poets. Cohen's thematic categorization (indebted partly to the French scholar Rousset) is not precise enough, however, to be truly convincing and the correlation of thematic and stylistic properties is never really attempted in any serious way. Nelson's book is a quite interesting analysis of the manipulation of time by English, French, Spanish, Italian, and German Baroque poets.

A major inadequacy of most comparative Baroque studies has been the relatively limited horizon. Western studies suffer greatly from a near total lack of familiarity with contemporary developments in Eastern Europe, particularly among the Slavs. This is true even of Warnke's splendidly comparative *Versions of Baroque*, though the author does try to give Eastern Europe some representation by mentioning a few Slavic and Hungarian authors *en passant*. Apart from a very few internationally renowned figures of nineteenth- and twentieth-century literature, vast areas of the literary culture of Eastern Europe still tend to be beyond the range of Western comparativists. Conversely, literary scholarship in Eastern Europe has long shunned the broad synthetic comparative technique in favor of deep but narrow studies, generally of a single author, work, genre, or period. Then again, when comparative efforts were undertaken in the East and parallels sought between developments there and in the West, it became apparent that the knowledge of certain Western literatures, particularly English and Spanish, was too limited. However, since most Eastern European literary scholarship freely recognizes that many developments in the evolution of the Eastern European literatures have been responses to Western stimuli, it has been more willing to take cognizance of Western movements than Western scholarship has been inclined to broaden its horizon by considering Eastern European literary events. With notably rare exceptions, however, neither Western nor Eastern European comparative literary study has exhibited any serious desire to range still farther into the non-European cultures of the Middle and Far East. Yet to dismiss the role of the Islamic East especially in the evolution of Baroque art is to neglect a possibly fruitful area of investigation.

The failure of Western literary scholarship to address itself to developments in Eastern Europe has been a decided handicap. Certainly, Eastern European Baroque literature emerged as a response to specific developments in Western culture and thought. But a rather rich Slavic Baroque culture, with some independent features, did come into being between the late sixteenth and mid-eighteenth centuries and merits the consideration of Western scholars, if only to broaden the range of the thematic concerns and stylistic features generally subsumed now under the term Baroque. In the concluding chapters of his fine study *The Poet of the Marvelous: Giambattista Marino* (New York, 1963), James V. Mirollo considers the influence of the Italian poet beyond Italy in the seventeenth century. The review of English, French, and German "Marinists" is detailed and informative. But the world of Eastern European literature lay almost entirely beyond the scope of Mirollo's investigation. Mention is made, in passing, of the Marinist style in Hungarian and South Slavic literature. Yet that part of the book devoted to a survey of Marino's influence outside of Italy would have gained much by a consideration of Marinist echoes in Poland, where Italian culture proved particularly influential in the sixteenth and seventeenth centuries, and in Croatia with its firm cultural links between Dubrovnik (Ragusa) and Venice during the Renaissance. Even that eminent comparativist, René Wellek, who is quite at home in Slavic literatures, barely took notice of the Slavic Baroque in his 1946 article, "The Concept of the Baroque in Literary Scholarship." The updating of the article in 1962 provides some additional information, especially bibliographically, but still does not indicate any serious effort to include Slavic developments in a meaningful reappraisal of the Baroque.

The controversy surrounding the concept of the Baroque in the West is not paralleled in Eastern European scholarship. The Polish literary historian and comparativist Edward Porębowicz (1862–1937) used the term Baroque as early as 1893 in a paper on the seventeenth-century Polish poet Jan Andrzej Morsztyn. Studies in literary Baroque, confined primarily to individual poets, developed extensively throughout the Slavic world in the period between the two world wars, notably in Poland and Czechoslovakia. After World War II and the establishment of Communist regimes in Eastern Europe, there was marked hostility in literary scholarship to the Baroque. This was understandable, but unfortunate. To Communist theorists, the literary culture of the seventeenth century bore the stamp of the Counter-Reformation and the political intrigues and machinations of the Jesuits. If Western scholars long shared the disapproval and indeed rejection of Baroque art passed on to later generations by the arbiters of classicist aesthetics, the Marxist-Socialist-Realist literary scholars of Eastern Europe in the 1940s and early 1950s turned a cold shoulder to Baroque literature because of what they regarded as its distinct Catholic taint.

This imposition of a near total ban on Baroque studies by the Communists had two negative results. It impeded further progress in the promising Baroque scholarship of the late 1920s and 1930s —already, of course, seriously interrupted by the war years. Moreover, it tended to slow, though not completely cut off, the editing and publication of long-forgotten and neglected works of the late sixteenth and seventeenth centuries never published in the lifetimes of their authors and still in manuscript form. As in the West (e.g. France—in connection particularly with the works of Jean de Sponde and La Ceppède), a number of important texts of the Slavic Baroque age awaited discovery.

In the post-Stalinist "thaw," however, the earlier "ban" on Baroque literary scholarship was lifted with the result that since the mid-1950s late sixteenth- and seventeenth-century studies have made rapid strides. The Renaissance and Baroque in Hungary were made the subject of a formidable study, *Reneszánsz és barokk*, published in 1961, by Tibor Klaniczay. Several valuable discussions of general problems in Slavic Baroque scholarship were published in German by the Hungarian scholar A. Angyal,[9] the author of a book on the Baroque in Hungary, *Barock in Ungarn* (Budapest, 1947). These works complement the only other major source of information on the Baroque in Slavic literature in a Western language, the chapter on the Baroque in the Ukrainian scholar Dmitrij Čiževskij's *Comparative History of Slavic Literatures* (Nashville, Tenn., 1971).

Symptomatic of the new post-Stalinist tolerance of the concept of the Baroque in the Communist world is the all-Baroque issue

---

[9] "Das Problem des slawischen Barocks," *Wissenschaftliche Zeitschrift der Ernst Moritz Arndt Universität Griefswald*, VI (1956–1957), 67–77, and *Die slawische Barockwelt* (Leipzig, 1961).

(V, 1960) of the important Polish journal *Przegląd Humanistyczny* (*The Humanities Review*) which includes, in addition to articles dealing with the Baroque in Poland, papers and review articles on Italian, French, English, and German Baroque topics. So productive has the study of the Baroque been in Poland in recent years that besides extensive editing and publication, several major monographic studies of important Baroque poets appeared within the three-year period 1965–67.[10]

The most stubborn resistance to the idea of a literary Baroque in the Slavic world has been in the Soviet Union. The belated emergence of a native Russian secular literary culture in the early eighteenth century and the slight contact historically with the Renaissance and Reformation made for a sharply limited and superficial Baroque. Among non-Soviet specialists in Russian literature, Dmitrij Čiževskij has for some time championed the cause of a Russian Baroque, strongly under Ukrainian and Belorussian influence, in the late seventeenth and eighteenth centuries. But Soviet literary historians for decades vehemently opposed attempts to superimpose a Baroque "character" on any area of Russian literature of the eighteenth century, and showed little enthusiasm for exploring the extent to which the works of the Ukrainian and Belorussian writers prominent in seventeenth- and early eighteenth-century Muscovite literary life reflected the interests and tastes of the Western Baroque.

Within the last few years, however, Soviet literary scholarship has demonstrated a capacity for independence and maturity evidenced in a readiness to discuss Western influences in a considerably more serious and objective way than previously and in a desire to "modernize" criticism and analysis by going beyond orthodox Marxist interpretation and the narrow vision of Socialist Realism. The eighteenth-century studies (e.g. *Poeticheskii stil Lomonosova* [Moscow-Leningrad, 1966] and *Gavrila Romanovich Derzhavin* [Leningrad, 1967]) by I. A. Serman are particularly encouraging in this respect.

The Baroque still remains something of a problem in Soviet

[10] Jadwiga Sokołowska, *Jan Andrzej Morsztyn* (Warsaw, 1965); Lucyna Sieciechowiczowa, *Wacław z Potoka Potocki* (Warsaw, 1965); Jadwiga Sokołowska, Kazimiera Żukowska, eds., *Poeci polskiego baroku*, 2 vols. (Warsaw, 1965); Janusz Pelc, *Zbigniew Morsztyn* (Wrocław-Warsaw-Cracow, 1966); Jan Błoński, *Mikołaj Sęp Szarzyński a początki polskiego baroku* (Cracow, 1967).

scholarship because there is so little *Russian* literature that lends itself to consideration as Baroque; but Soviet literary historians are now at least willing to operate with the concept in their research and to consider the literature of the Ukrainian-Belorussian hegemony of the second half of the seventeenth century and the first two decades of the eighteenth and the works of native Russian writers of the 1730s (e.g. Lomonosov) within the context of a European Baroque. The most important evidence to date of this trend has been the publication of a collective volume of essays on Russian and Western Baroque literature under the title *XVII vek v mirovom literaturnom razvitii* ("The Seventeenth Century in World Literary Development" [Moscow, 1969]).

The rise of Western interest in Slavic culture since the end of World War II has also contributed to the knowledge of Baroque literature in Eastern Europe. Much of this interest has been encouraged by such émigré scholars as Dmitrij Čiževskij, Roman Jakobson, Manfred Kridl, and Wiktor Weintraub.

The cause of the Ukrainian Baroque, in particular, owes much to the efforts of Čiževskij whose booklet *Poza mezhami krasy* ("Beyond the Bounds of Beauty" [New York, 1952]) and chapter on the Baroque in his history of Ukrainian literature (*Istoriya ukrainskoi literatury* [New York, 1956]) comprise the first serious treatment of Ukrainian Baroque literature in any language. Wiktor Weintraub, of Harvard University, and David Welsh, of the University of Michigan, have discussed two highly interesting Polish Baroque poets, Mikołaj Sęp Szarzyński and Zbigniew Morsztyn.[11] John Bucsela, of Emory University, has analyzed Baroque elements in the poetry of the eighteenth-century Russian poet Mikhail Vasilevich Lomonosov.[12] The Belgian Slavicist, Claude Backvis, wrote provocatively on the Polish Baroque in his 1955 paper "Some Characteristics of Polish Baroque Poetry."[13] More recently, he considered the possible Baroque character of the work of Russia's greatest eighteenth-century poet,

---

[11] W. Weintraub, "Some Remarks on the Style of Mikołaj Sęp Szarzyński," *Festschrift für Max Vasmer* (Wiesbaden, 1956), pp. 560–569; D. Welsh, "Zbigniew Morsztyn's Poetry of Meditation," *Slavic and East European Journal*, IX, 1 (1965), 56–61, and "Zbigniew Morsztyn and the Emblem Tradition," *Symposium*, XIX (1965), 80–84.

[12] "Lomonosov's Literary Debut," *The Slavic and East European Journal* XI, No. 4 (Winter, 1967), 405–422.

[13] *Oxford Slavonic Papers*, VI, 56–71.

Gavrila Derzhavin.[14] In 1952, Vsevolod Setschkareff, now of Harvard University, examined the Baroque character of the Croatian poet Gundulić's style in *Die Dichtungen Gundulićs und ihr poetischer Stil.* Nine years later saw the publication of Nikola Pribic's investigation of non-Dalmatian so-called inland Croatian literature, *Studien zum literarischen Spätbarock in Binnenkroatien: Adam Aloisius Baricevic* (München, 1961). And, finally, in 1964 a German scholar, Renata Lachmann-Schmohl, published a carefully prepared monograph on the important seventeenth-century Croatian poet Ignat (or Ignjat) Djordjić (*Ignat Djordjić. Eine stilistische Untersuchung zum slavischen Barock* [Köln-Graz]).

This cursory review of trends in Baroque literary scholarship in both the West and the East should suggest the scope of Baroque scholarship at present and the gradual expansion of horizons. The growth of interest in the Baroque in Western scholarship over the past decade or so is by now an accomplished fact and widely appreciated. The picture of Baroque scholarship in Eastern Europe and the evidence of Western interest in the Slavic Baroque are doubtless less familiar but point up both the broader dimensions of the concept of the Baroque and the ever growing possibilities of fruitful comparative study.

---

[14] "Dans quelle mesure Derzhavin est-il un baroque," in *Studies in Russian and Polish Literature in Honor of Waclaw Lednicki,* ed. Zbigniew Folejewski, *et al.* ('s-Gravenhage, 1962), pp. 72–104.

I

Definitions

1. THE MEANING OF BAROQUE

Disagreement over the meaning of Baroque in literature began with the term itself. It was believed for some time, for example, that Baroque derived from *baroco*, the term for the fourth mode of the second figure in the nomenclature of syllogisms in Scholasticism. Benedetto Croce who, among others, advanced this view in his *Storia della età barocca in Italia* (Bari, 1929) gave the following example of this type of syllogism, considered strained and artificial: "Every fool is stubborn; some people are not stubborn; some people are not fools." (Every A = B; some C does not equal B; therefore, some C does not equal A.) In "The Concept of the Baroque in Literary Scholarship," René Wellek accepted the syllogistic etymology of Baroque, following Croce and Karl Boriński who used it in this way in his *Die Antike in Poetik und Kunsttheorie* (Leipzig, 1914). Wellek rejected the etymology of the Spanish *barrueco*, meaning an odd, irregular-shaped pearl. In his 1962 "Postscript," however, he qualified his earlier position, pointing out that the syllogistic etymology may be correct for Italy but that the English term Baroque, which is a French adjectival form, probably stems from the Portuguese (not Spanish) *perola barroca*, a jeweler's term for the imperfectly shaped pearl. The Portuguese derivation now enjoys the widest acceptance.

The first serious objective use of the term Baroque with reference to the painting, sculpture, and architecture that followed the Renaissance and preceded classicism came in an important study that often serves as a point of departure for any discussion of the Baroque: the German art historian Heinrich Wölfflin's *Renaissance und Barock*, published in Munich in 1888.

Wölfflin's principal task was to trace the transition from Renaissance to Baroque in Roman architecture. That his thinking still reflected at least initially the Classicist assumption that the art of the Baroque marked a period of lapsed taste, of decadence, of fall from the once lofty ideals of the Renaissance, is evident in his preface to the first edition.

> The subject of this study is the disintegration of the Renaissance. . . . My aim was to investigate the *symptoms of decay* and perhaps to discover in the "capriciousness and the return to chaos" a law which would vouchsafe one an insight into the intimate workings of art.[1]

As distinguishing features of Baroque in architecture, Wölfflin singles out the following: (*a*) painterliness, which supplanted a predominantly linear style and achieved an illusion of movement, and a certain impression of transitoriness principally through effects of light and shade (chiaroscuro); (*b*) monumentality, which Wölfflin defines as the love of the grand, the massive, the colossal, the overpowering, the awesome; (*c*) the multiplication of members or units making up a whole or the multiplication of contours, in part to satisfy the demands of the much larger proportions favored by the Baroque, and in part to enhance the "painterly" effect; and (*d*) movement, unlike the permanence and repose in everything sought by the art of the Renaissance, specifically in an upward direction. To quote Wölfflin at this point,

> The Baroque never offers us perfection and fulfillment, or the static calm of "being," only the unrest of change and the tension of transience.[2]

Before proceeding to the realization of the Baroque style in specific architectural types (church, palace, villa, and garden), Wölfflin makes a limited and on the whole unsatisfactory attempt to account for the aesthetic he characterizes as Baroque. He isolates as the major factor the post-Renaissance "solemnity" in all spheres of life (the obsession with religion, the "renewed distinction between the worldly and the ecclesiastical," the disparagement of hedonism) and attributes this in the main to the climate of the Counter-Reformation.

One rarely overlooked contribution of Wölfflin's *Renaissance und Barock* is the link made at one point between developments in

---

[1] *Renaissance and Baroque*, trans. Kathrin Simon, intro. Peter Murray (Ithaca, N.Y., 1966). Italics mine.
[2] *Ibid.*, p. 14.

the visual arts and literature. In discussing the causes behind the dissolution of the Renaissance style, Wölfflin compares the restlessness, solemnity, and *Weltschmerz* (to borrow Wölfflin's term) of Michelangelo's sculpture and painting to the spiritual mood of Torquato Tasso's epic *Gerusalemme liberata* (Jerusalem Delivered, 1575). To point up the differences between Renaissance and Baroque still further, Wölfflin briefly compares two masterpieces of epic poetry, Lodovico Ariosto's *Orlando furioso* (1516) and Tasso's *Gerusalemme*. A reflection of the aesthetics of the Renaissance, according to Wölfflin, Ariosto's epic is, in mood and language, simple, cheerful, and lively; Tasso's, on the other hand, has a world-weary hero, is "heavier" in rhythm and sentence structure, and grander in lexicon and imagery.

Such attempts to broaden the understanding of a style and its evolution by examining contemporary developments in other art forms are now commonplace, but they were much less so in Wölfflin's time and demonstrate the German scholar's concern regarding a precise definition of the Baroque style.

The contemporary art historian no longer, of course, accepts Wölfflin's theses about the Baroque unreservedly. Although he may grant him much acuity of perception in certain areas, the period between the Renaissance and classicism is not seen as a unified whole but composed instead of (at least) two distinct periods: mannerism, a term derived from the Italian *maniera*, "style," that gained considerable currency in the 1920s and 1940s, extending from about 1520 to about 1580, and the second, that of the Baroque, from the last decade or two of the sixteenth century to anywhere from 1660 to the 1680s.

Much of what Wölfflin called Baroque is often recognized now as Mannerist. Beginning in Rome about 1520, artists began concentrating more emphatically on technique. Manner, or style, was becoming a thing unto itself. In their search for novelty, for new ways to create a sense of awe, wonder, and *admiration* in the beholder, painters and sculptors began making freer use of ornament and decoration. Works of art not only became richer in design, but richer in color. To heighten the viewer's appreciation of the skill and ingenuity behind the conception and execution of the work of art, the artist drew attention to the units or parts of the whole. The unity and simplicity of impression sought by Renaissance artists no longer enjoyed the same favor. Quite the contrary, the Mannerist artist constantly sought to divert and distract the eye by making it aware not of the totality of the work, but of the details. The painting, sculpture, building, or even utensil took on the semblance of a spectacle or pageant of technique as artists strove to outdo one another in virtuoso performances. This elevation and embellishment of the segment often at the expense of unity and cohesion acted in a centrifugal way: the viewer's eye was deflected away from the center to the periphery which, instead of contributing to and supporting unity, detracted from it. Centrality of interest was dissipated, dissolved, and the relationship of the parts to the whole became so tenuous that the parts grew in autonomy.

Besides ornamental embellishment, Mannerist artists also achieved novelty through variety of shapes and lines. The twisting serpentine figure, the *figura serpentina*, as in the Michelangelo statue of *Victory* (c. 1527–28) and Giorgio Vasari's *Allegory of the Immaculate Conception* (1540–41), became one of the commonplaces of Mannerist style, endowing a work with fluidity of movement. Another was the *contrapposto*, or the asymmetrical arrangement of the parts of the body in sculpture, which heightens the sense of movement in the overall design.

Although art historians generally agree on the distinguishing features of Mannerist style and the distinctions between mannerism and Baroque, there has been often sharp disagreement over the roots of mannerism. To Wylie Sypher in the *Four Stages of Renaissance Style* (Garden City, N.Y., 1955) the historical factors responsible for the breakup of the Renaissance resulted as well in the appearance of mannerism. Apart from the "disconcerting schematic literal-mindedness"[3] which, according to René Wellek, weakens his argument, Sypher goes much too far in using the political and religious upheavals of the sixteenth and early seventeenth centuries to explain the emergence and nature of the Mannerist *Weltanschauung* and style. The events (e.g. religious crises) to which he attributes the anxiety, tension, insecurity, malaise, and impermanence in Mannerist art were not of the same order or intensity throughout Europe, neither was their impact felt everywhere at the same time and to the same degree. Intellectual and artistic responses varied considerably. Moreover,

[3] *Concepts of Criticism,* p. 125.

the conflicts (above all, the Reformation and Counter-Reformation) Sypher posits for the emergence of mannerism continued in some instances well into the post-1620 period, which he characterizes as Baroque and in which he perceives a reconstitution of values, a reconciliation of spirit and flesh, the restoration of a sense of unity and a reversal of the dissolution from which mannerism ultimately issued. Several of the qualities discovered by Sypher and others in mannerism may, in fact, reflect more the psychology and aesthetics of expressionism during which period the term mannerism first became fashionable in art history. John Shearman makes this point convincingly in his excellent book *Mannerism* in the Penguin-Pelican "Style and Civilization Series" (Baltimore, Md., 1967).

Shearman himself lays greater emphasis on the emergence of mannerism from the "continuation of a refining process begun in the High Renaissance"[4] and on an increasing self-awareness in the creative process. As the sixteenth century progressed, the artist came to feel an ever greater sense of his importance as a creative artist, as, in fact, a creator, free to release his talent in any way he chose, no longer bound to rest content with the mere imitation of nature. Closely related to this was the change in the nature of patronage—from about 1520 the artist appeared to take precedence over the work of art. The execution of a particular commission became secondary to the possession of a work by a particular artist.

Shearman's emphasis on the changing role of the artist in the sixteenth century takes on an added dimension later in his book when he considers contemporary aesthetic theory in both the visual arts and literature. The link connecting Marco Girolamo Vida's *De Arte Poetica* (1527), Paolo Pino's advice to painters in 1548, Sperone Speroni's *Discorsi sopra Virgilio* (c. 1582), Lodovico Dolce's literary "guide" (the *Eleganze*) of 1564, Camillo Pellegrino's *Caraffa* (1584), a discourse on epic poetry, and Thomas Morley's *A Plaine and Easie Introduction to Practicall Musicke* (1597) is an enthusiastic espousal of variety, abundance, ingenuity in conception and execution, and sumptuousness. This is more or less what Sypher had in mind when he defined mannerism as

[4] *Mannerism*, p. 42.

a kind of facile learning, an abused ingenuity, a witty affectation, a knowing pose, a distorting through preciosity, or a play with conventional proportions, images, and attitudes.[5]

The common denominator then is a style of art in which, stated simply, the importance of the subject constantly loses ground before an ever increasing concern with manner. Whatever the disagreement concerning the sources and chronological boundaries of mannerism, there is a fair degree of unanimity on the constituent features of the style.

Scholars have had a much harder time agreeing on a Mannerist period or style in literature than in the visual arts.[6] Part of the problem doubtless stems from the relative newness of the serious application of Baroque to literary study and the difficulties attendant on its universal acceptance as a period term. Now that Baroque as term and concept stands on the threshold of such acceptance, the effort to reach a still more precise periodization of the post-Renaissance pre-Classicist literature of the sixteenth and seventeenth centuries by the interjection of a further subdivision naturally threatens to jeopardize what has already been achieved by sowing new and greater confusion.

In his 1962 Postscript to "The Concept of the Baroque in Literary Scholarship," René Wellek mentions a few scholars who have attempted to discover literary analogues to mannerism in the visual arts: E. R. Curtius, who in his *Europäische Literatur und lateinisches Mittelalter* (Bern, 1948) rejects the whole concept of a literary period in favor of recurrent constants in literary evolution and argues that Baroque be dropped entirely in favor of mannerism, an extreme view with few adherents today; Curtius' pupil, Gustav René Hocke, the author of two books on mannerism published in the late 1950s—*Die Welt als Labyrinth. Manier und Manie in der europäischen Kunst* (Hamburg, 1957) and *Manierismus in der Literatur, Sprachalchemie und esoterische Kombinationskunst* (Hamburg, 1959), in which the chronological value of Mannerist and Baroque is dissipated by their use as designations of universal currents in artistic expression from antiquity to the present; Wylie Sypher, and the authors of two Italian studies on mannerism, Georg Weise and Ezio Raimondi. Wellek's survey

---

[5] *Four Stages of Renaissance Style*, p. 109.
[6] The first chapter of Frank J. Warnke's *Versions of Baroque*, pp. 1–20, defines the problem and discusses the divergent opinions in some detail.

of the scholarship on mannerism is updated and augmented by Frank J. Warnke in the first chapter of *Versions of Baroque*. The name of John Shearman merits more prominent considera- tion in view of his extensive consideration of Mannerist style in literature in *Mannerism*. The roster should also include Daniel B. Rowland whose *Mannerism—Style and Mood* (New Haven and London, 1964) attempts to isolate the Mannerist properties of four works in three art forms (painting: the *Deposition* canvases of Rosso Fiorentino and Jacopo Pontormo; music: the madrigals of Carlo Gesualdo; poetry: John Donne's *The First Anniversary*) by comparing them with Renaissance predecessors and Baroque successors.

Probably the most valuable recent attempt to bring order to the chaos of the Mannerist–Baroque controversy is Warnke's *Versions of Baroque*. In Warnke's view, Baroque must serve as the acceptable term for the literary period intervening between the Renaissance and classicism. Baroque, therefore, becomes solely a period term and concept. Within the Baroque, Warnke identifies two "recurrently perceptible" stylistic trends or options amid the variety of "literary phenomena" of the period. One of these is Mannerist, which Warnke characterizes as the "spare, witty, intellectual, paradoxical trend typified by Donne, Herbert, Marvell, Sponde, Quevedo, Huygens, and Fleming," and the other, the High Baroque, characterized as the "ornate, exclamatory, emo- tional, and extravagant trend typified by Crashaw, Gryphius, Marino, d'Aubigné, Góngora, and Vondel."[7] Hence, for Warnke, there is no Mannerist period coming between Renaissance and Baroque; neither is there a transitional Mannerist stylistic phase "intervening between the two great, fully developed styles of Renaissance and Baroque,"[8] the view advanced especially by Helmut Hatzfeld.[9]

My own approach diverges somewhat from Warnke's. I agree on the usefulness of Baroque to designate the period between Renaissance and classicism and it is so used in this book. But, unlike Warnke, my feeling is that a period term and concept such as Renaissance, Classicist, Romantic, Symbolist, or Baroque connotes not only a time segment but a way of looking at the

---

[7] *Ibid.*, p. 12.
[8] *Ibid.*, p. 6.
[9] See, above all, Hatzfeld's *Estudios sobre el barroco* (Madrid, 1964).

world (*Weltanschauung*) and an aesthetic proclivity characteristic of the period and distinguishable in important respects from those of the preceding and following periods. This world view and stylistic preference naturally cannot always be reduced to what Warnke speaks of as a "single, unified, and simply definable style,"[10] but however complex, their components, their constituent features should in combination produce distinctly recognizable patterns of thought or artistic expression irrespective of the degree of indebtedness to the ideas, tastes, and techniques of earlier epochs.

As a period designation Baroque, in my judgment, is no different in this respect from Renaissance or Classicist and I attempt later to delineate the contours of both a Baroque Weltanschauung and a Baroque aesthetic. In regard to the latter, there is not, it seems to me, a great difference between my view and Warnke's. Warnke states at one point that "the study of seventeenth-century literature has supplied us with a wealth of limited terms which, taken together, make up the Baroque: e.g. *Metaphysical style, préciosité, marinismo, conceptismo, culturanismo.*"[11] I agree that these terms designate techniques of verbal art cultivated in different countries during the Baroque and, in turn, together make up the Baroque and distinguish it from the Renaissance and classicism. But I am also of the opinion, and here I believe that I go farther than Warnke, that Metaphysical, préciosité, and so on, ultimately derive from the underlying sensibility of the Baroque and can be viewed more or less as local variants of the same basic aesthetic. Now mannerism can be added to the others, as Warnke proposes. I accept the desirability, at least for the present, and in literary scholarship, of limiting the view of mannerism to a style rather than a period. However, I do feel—and here I have to part company with Warnke—that mannerism, certainly to a greater extent in the visual arts than in literature, manifested itself earlier than the crystallization of the Baroque and that if it was not precisely a transitional phase stylistically between the Renaissance and Baroque, it was a development in the arts coterminous with the dissolution of the Renaissance and the early formation of the Baroque. But the emergence of the Baroque did not spell the end of mannerism. The Mannerist style was absorbed by the Baroque

[10] Warnke, *op. cit.*, p. 4.
[11] *Ibid.*

and modified by it. Mannerism, then, became an aspect of the Baroque, another component of the Baroque aesthetic, more strongly felt in some works, less so in others. The interrelations between the two are treated more fully in the following pages.

2. BAROQUE AND MANNERISM

Most proponents of mannerism in the visual arts accept the origins of the style in Rome about 1520. Among its earliest masters were Jacopo Pontormo, Francesco Parmigianino (*The Madonna of the Long Neck*, 1534–36) and Giovanni Rosso ("Rosso Fiorentino"; *Mars and Venus*, 1530). In the "middle" phase of its development, from the 1530s or 1540s to 1580 or 1590, marked by an excessive concern with form and an exaggerated use of ornament and symmetry, it produced two outstanding artists, Giorgio Vasari (*Perseus and Andromeda, 1570*) and Francesco Salviati (*The Deposition*, c. 1547 and *The Story of Furius Camillus,* c. 1545–48). Between 1580 and 1590 a reaction against Mannerist excess crystallized and expressed itself in the simpler, warmer, more natural, more academic and High Renaissance works of such artists as the Carraccis (Lodovico, Annibale, Agostino), Santi di Tito, Giovanni Battista Crespi (Cerano) and probably the best known of all, Michelangelo Caravaggio.

Although the Mannerist style had its practitioners in France (Jean Goujon, Philibert de l'Orme, Germain Pilon, Jacques du Cerceau the Elder), the Low Countries (where they were known as Romanists, particularly Marten van Heemskerck, Hendrick Goltzius, and Adriaen de Vries, who went to Prague), Germany (Hubert Gerhard), and to a lesser extent England (Isaac Oliver's miniatures) and Spain (El Greco, partially), Italy was its true home and the place of its richest development.

The call for greater variety and inventiveness in the visual arts to which the Mannerist style responded was heard also in sixteenth-century Italian literature. As early as 1527 Marco Girolamo Vida emphasized the value of variety for the literary artist in his *De Arte Poetica.* Whereas Italian Latin writing of the early Cinquecento strove for a new elegance under the aegis of a revised

Ciceronianism, the vernacular literary culture sought the same
goals but with Petrarch as its model.

In his *Il Petrarca* (1534), Giovanni Andrea Gesualdo observed
that in the sixteenth century Petrarch was hailed as the greatest
Italian poet, but that in the fourteenth this distinction was held
by Dante. "Perhaps," wrote Gesualdo, "they did not yet appreciate the brilliant passages of eloquence, nor the ornaments of the
ideas, nor the figures of speech; it being understood, naturally,
that we always appreciate what is most in conformity with our
own habits, and cannot enthuse over something we do not understand."[12] The new highly cultivated, style-conscious Italian
vernacular writing that paralleled the development of mannerism
in painting, sculpture, and architecture came to be known as
Bembismo, after the most influential practitioner of the style and
literary legislator, Pietro Bembo (1470–1547). Despite certain
strictures against the excesses of artificiality of the new style
expressed by Giambattista Giraldi (1504–73) in his *Discorso*
(1549–54) on the romance, Bembismo had become a fact of Italian
literary life before the middle of the century. It reached its apogee
in the romance *L'Amadigi* (1542–60) of Bernardo Tasso (1493–
1569), which John Shearman[13] sees as an invention of the Mannerist period but which long survived it, and in several outstanding
examples of the dramatic genre of the *pastorale* (or dramatized
pastoral, idyll, or eclogue): Agostino Beccari's *Sacrificio* (Ferrara,
1554), Torquato Tasso's pastoral fable *Aminta* (Ferrara, 1573), and
Giovanni Battista Guarini's *Pastor fido* (Ferrara, 1586). Like the
romance, the *pastorale* was distinguished by rich variety in style
and narrative structure.

Writing of his *L'Amadigi* Bernardo Tasso, the father of a more
talented son, reveals how the tastes of the age impelled him to
revise his earlier plan of the work:

> In the beginning I had decided to make it one unified action and
> on this basis I composed ten books; but then it occurred to me that
> it did not have that variety that customarily gives delight and is
> desired in this century, already attuned to the Romance; and I
> understood then that Ariosto [i.e. in *Orlando furioso*] neither
> accidentally nor for want of knowledge of the art (as some say) but
> with the greatest judgement accommodated himself to the taste of

[12] Quoted by Shearman, *Mannerism*, p. 138.
[13] *Ibid.*, p. 91.

the *present century* and arranged his work in this way. . . . I have followed this example, which I find more beguiling and delightful.[14]

Tasso's mention of the example of Lodovico Ariosto (1474–1533) recalls the controversy touched off in sixteenth-century Italy when *Orlando furioso* (begun 1505, first edition 1516, second edition 1521, definitive edition 1532), a literary masterpiece embodying a number of traits compatible with Mannerist aesthetics, was contrasted with *Gerusalemme liberata* (1575), the great epic by Torquato Tasso.

An extension on a vastly superior artistic level of Matteo Boiardo's (c. 1434–94) unfinished romance *Orlando innamorato* (1483–95), Ariosto's epic returns to the world and conflicts of the *Chanson de Roland*. The adventures of the eighth-century heroes Charlemagne and Renaldo (Orlando, in the Italian) are recounted in a highly complex narrative style in which the Aristotelian virtue of artistic unity was freely sacrificed for the variety, inventiveness, and technical virtuosity so highly prized in Ariosto's time.

The proliferation of character and incident echoed by a dazzling procession of asides, interludes, and diversions (as, for example, Bradamante's visit to Merlin's tomb in Canto III, the description of Alcina in Canto VII, the tale told Rodomonte in Canto XXVIII, and so on), which the Italians called *meraviglie* because of their capacity to excite wonderment, operates in much the same way that intentionally distracting ornaments and imbalancing figures and lines do in Mannerist painting, sculpture, and architecture.

In the execution of the *Orlando furioso*, John Shearman sees an analogy to so markedly Mannerist an edifice as Giulio Romano's Palazzo del Tè (1526–34), erected and decorated for Federico Gonzaga around 1530. The comparison of a literary work with a palace may seem unusual today but it was not so in the sixteenth century. In *Il Caraffa* (1584), a discourse on epic poetry, Camillo Pellegrino expressed a preference for the *meraviglie*-rich but more unified rival of the *Orlando furioso*—Tasso's *Gerusalemme liberata*. Referring to Ariosto's work as a "palace," Pellegrino rejects the artistic foundation on which the epic rests on the grounds that the dazzling variety holds appeal primarily for people of unsophisticated taste:

the palace [*Orlando furioso*] with more numerous, more beguiling

[14] *Ibid.*, p. 139.

and visually richer rooms, gives complete pleasure only to the simple-minded, not to the understanding; where the experts in the art discover in it the faults, the false ornaments and enrichments, they remain dissatisfied, and what gives them greater delight is the architecture of the smaller structure [i.e. *Gerusalemme liberata*], which is a body better conceived in all its parts.[15]

Both works had their detractors as well as enthusiasts. To some, the relative unity of Tasso's poem brought it more into conformity with classical theory (Aristotle), a matter of some importance when we recall that Aristotle's *Poetics*, which gave rise to a considerable body of derivative poetic theory, was rediscovered between the writing of *Orlando furioso* and *Gerusalemme liberata*; to others, *Gerusalemme liberata* seemed poverty-stricken in comparison to the opulence of *Orlando furioso*. This was the position of the prestigious Accademica della Crusca as expressed in the *Difesa dell'Orlando furioso* (1585) of Leonardo Salviati and Bastiano de' Rossi. What mattered in the controversy, the point on which argument turned, was the artistic validity of Ariosto's eschewal of an organic Aristotelian unity in favor of a different sort of unity—not structural but decorative, ornamental, and in large measure achieved by a variety of "free-floating" elements that depended for effect on multiplicity instead of contrast.[16]

The nearly four decades separating the definitive edition of *Orlando furioso* (1532) from the completion of *Gerusalemme liberata* (1575) saw a gradual turning away from the excesses of mannerism, yet it would be a mistake to regard the controversy surrounding the two great Italian epics of the sixteenth century as a conflict between a Mannerist art and one opposed to mannerism. Compared to the dense ornamentation and narrative complexity of *Orlando furioso*, Tasso's *Gerusalemme* creates the impression of a greater overall simplicity and unity of structure. Tasso's work still accords great prominence to the supernatural and to love, although to be sure the love, in its melancholy and sensuality, is of a different sort from that of *Orlando furioso*. But in its style, rather than its structure, it too reflects the Mannerist enthusiasm for novelty, cultivated artificiality, obscurity, and *meraviglie*. Besides a wealth of esoteric allusions, exotic vocabulary (in part lexically continuing the Latinizing trend of Bembo),

[15] *Ibid.*, p. 146.
[16] *Ibid.*, p. 149.

and contrived, difficult figures of speech, the syntax is highly "mannered" in the sense of convoluted, rhymes are irregular, metaphor is used abundantly, and the imagery is opulent. That all of this was a conscious design by Tasso to achieve the loftiness, cultivated artificiality, and desire to provoke wonderment of the Mannerist style is unequivocally stated by the poet himself in his discourses on poetry in general (*Dell'arte poetica*, 1570), and on the epic in particular (*Del poema eroico*, 1594).

In England, Edmund Spenser, whose poetry proceeded from essentially the same Mannerist aesthetic as his Italian sixteenth-century counterparts, echoed Tasso's apologia for ornament and variety in a letter to Sir Walter Raleigh appended to the first part of *The Faerie Queene* (1590), a work that owes much to the *Gerusalemme liberata*.

Apart from romance, epic, and pastoral, the *intermezzo* also came into a prominence in the sixteenth century that it hardly enjoyed previously.

In *Mannerism*, John Shearman convincingly argues the case for the intermezzo as, in many ways, the most comprehensive manifestation of the Mannerist style in literature.[17] Intermedia (or interludia, as they were also known)—intermezzi, in Italian—originally were secular *entr'acte* interpolations in medieval miracle plays. In sixteenth-century Italy, particularly at the theatre-rich court of Ferrara, the intermezzo came to be cultivated to such an extent that it began to assume the status of an autonomous art form. Early in the century the intermezzi appeared as choruses, dances, or short recitations based on fairly simple narrative or allegorical subjects. As the penchant for novelty grew, interest in the fixed texts of the *commedie* that housed the intermezzi gradually shifted to the considerably more variable *entr'acte* pieces. To satisfy the new taste for variety and more elaborate entertainment, those charged with the responsibility of mounting court entertainments so enriched the visual, musical, and linguistic aspects of the intermezzi that they succeeded in transforming them into spectacles that rapidly outstripped the *commedie* in appeal. Shearman mentions among the most outstanding intermezzi-spectacles of Cinquecento Italy the elaborate *mascherata* presented at the wedding of Francesco de Medici and Joanna of Austria in Florence, December 1565, with allegories devised by

[17] Cf. pp. 104–112.

Vincenzo Borghini and floats and costumes by Vasari; a per-
formance of a *commedia* in the Gran Salone of the Palazzo Vecchio
with intermezzi built loosely around the theme of Cupid and
Psyche and employing music by Francesco Corteccia and Alessandro Striggio and impressive stage machinery by Bernardo
Buontalenti; and the entertainments staged in 1589 at the marriage of Ferdinand de' Medici and Cristina of Lorraine. The
machinery for the latter—perhaps the most impressive of all—
was designed by Buontalenti, with music by Luca Marenzio,
Cristofano Malvezzi, Emilio de'Cavalieri, and Giulio Caccini.
Similar if not identical spectacles also delighted the Italianate
courts of England and especially of France (e.g. the Fontainebleau
fêtes of 1564, and such court entertainments as the *Ballet des
Polonais*, 1573, or *Circé: le Ballet comique de la Reine*, 1581).

In considering the relation of Mannerist art to the Baroque, it
would be well to pay heed to a comment made by Joseph Anthony
Mazzeo, in *Renaissance and Seventeenth Century Studies:*

> Many theories have been advanced to explain the emphasis on the
> Baroque in the seventeenth century, but there is little doubt that,
> from the point of view of the historian of culture, it may best be
> understood as the exaggeration of tendencies already present in the
> Renaissance.[18]

Historians of the visual arts and literature would have little
cause to disagree with such a general statement. Each "new"
period in art emerges in some way or ways from its immediate
predecessor and connects in turn with a more distant past.

To the historian of the visual arts, the concern with form, with
style in the Baroque of the seventeenth century, grew out of the
Mannerist enthusiasm for variety, novelty, and decorative
splendor. But the Baroque began crystallizing at a time—in the
late sixteenth and early seventeenth centuries—when a certain
anti-Mannerist reaction set in in the arts. In painting, for example,
the trend brought to prominence the Carracci brothers, Santi di
Tito, Cerano, and especially Caravaggio, who of all of these is
best seen as already marking a transition to the Baroque. The
nature of the anti-Mannerist reaction can be clearly perceived in

[18] Joseph Anthony Mazzeo, *Renaissance and Seventeenth Century Studies*
(New York and London, 1961), pp. 58–59.

even a cursory comparison of, let us say, the Transfiguration canvases of Lodovico Carracci and Giovanni Rosso. In general, the technique becomes simpler, more unified, less artificial but more dramatic, subjective, lyrical, and, finally, more corporeal.

The search for novelty and richer texture led the Mannerists to embrace ornamentalism and deliberate distortion. Mannerist art became highly stylized and, consequently, artificial. In the emergence of the Baroque, the reaction against mannerism resulted in a movement to restore the unity and relative significance of subject that had been diminished by the excessive Mannerist concern with form. This restoration of unity did not carry with it any marked lessening of interest in technique. Style continued to be important, but the hegemony of form in Mannerist art was challenged by a new respect for unity and the use of style to elucidate a particular subject. Variety, ornament, the search for ways of exciting wonderment still had a place in Baroque art, but because of the resuscitated passion for unity they were not used indiscriminately, as was often the case among the Mannerists, but more sparingly and usually to emphasize a particular idea, evoke a particular emotional response or create a single impression. Instead of the Mannerist proliferation of variety merely to arouse wonderment and admiration, the Baroque artist employed a kind of "piling" or cumulative technique. The variety and ornamentalism of the Mannerists may excite wonderment and admiration at the inventiveness and skill of the artist; the technique is artificial, essentially, and the response aesthetic and intellectual. The emotions really have little place—or no place—in mannerism. This changed appreciably with the Baroque. By using variety and ornament cumulatively in support of a central unity, the Baroque artist aimed at responses that could be emotional as well as aesthetic and intellectual. The "piling" or cumulative technique produced a tension that sought—and eventually was rewarded with—release (which is why the technique is not precisely the same thing as the *blason* or "cataloguemaking" of poets of an earlier time).

The greater emotionalism and subjectivity of the Baroque expressed itself not only in a restoration of unity and a cumulative use of variety and ornament, but also through a richer use of color (which became deeper, more saturated than in the practice of mannerism), a more provocative opposition of shades of light and dark (the chiaroscuro), and a heightened sense of drama. The element of drama, which grew in significance as the Baroque matured, realized itself through its most natural means—tension and conflict—and, additionally, through the cumulative patterns, color saturation, and chiaroscuro by which the Baroque artists generally sought to induce emotional involvement.

If the restoration of unity and symmetry signaled at least the apparent return of Baroque art to the "classical," academic style of the High Renaissance, the new corporeality removed whatever doubt remained as to the general orientation of a trend already apparent in the canvases of Caravaggio. The elongated, disproportionate, in a sense, "dehumanized" figures of much Mannerist art gradually disappear, and their places are taken by the full, fleshy, earthier bodies of a Guido Reni, Peter Paul Rubens, Frans Hals, Rembrandt, Diego Velázquez, Bartolomé Murillo, Jacob van Ruisdael, and Jan Vermeer. This Baroque sense of amplitude, reinforced by the cumulative use of variety and ornament, resulted in the massiveness and physical sumptuousness generally associated with Baroque art. The sculpture and architecture of Giovanni Bernini offer superb examples of this, above all the façade of the Barberini Palace in Rome, the colonnade in the piazza in front of the Vatican, and the Fountain of the Four Rivers in the Piazza Navona.

The corporeality and physical emphasis of the Baroque also made for an earthiness and sensuality virtually impossible in Mannerist art by its very nature. Such a "rediscovery" of the world of the flesh was by no means accompanied by a diminution of spiritual concern. The usually clear, sharp division in mannerism between the spheres of earth and spirit faded before the Baroque vision of the indivisibility of man's world and God's. Renaissance unity, balance, and harmony disintegrated, with their anthropocentric self-confidence, and opened the way to the partial union of matter and spirit of the Mannerists. But the circle was completed only with the advent of the Baroque when the divisions between the two spheres were blurred and finally eradicated. A Mannerist treatment of a religious theme may at first glance occasionally *appear* to exhibit involvement in the spiritual. The usual Mannerist treatment of a popular subject—the conversion of St. Paul, for example—manages to include some spiritual apparition in the heavens or beside the stunned, unhorsed figure

of Paul. Now there is no such apparition or vision in Caravaggio's magnificent *Conversion of St. Paul* (c. 1600). The figures
of Paul and the horse dominate the canvas and are so grouped as
to heighten the dramatic impact of the scene. But where heavenly
figures appeared in the Mannerist paintings, Caravaggio has only
the darkness of night. Yet in this darkness is felt the presence of
the spiritual, the mystery of unknowable beings and forces. The
more corporeal Paul and the horse, the dominance of the figures
and the elimination of distracting elements point up the nature
of the transition to the Baroque no less than the heightening of a
sense of drama through the mystery of night and the visual
absence but felt presence of spiritual forces.

The shift in Western Europe from mannerism to the Baroque,
in literature and the visual arts, occurred in the last decade or so
of the sixteenth and the first two decades of the seventeenth
centuries. A mature, full-blown Baroque style dominated the
arts of most of Europe down to at least the middle of the seventeenth century. In some cases, particularly in Central and Eastern
Europe, it extended its sway well into the 1670s, 1680s, and 1690s.
There are some Polish scholars, in fact, who carry the Baroque
in Poland as far as the ascension to the throne in 1764 of the last
Polish king, Stanislaus August Poniatowski, or even to the Con-
federacy of Bar (1768–72), which precipitated the First Partition
(1772). Even if a Baroque style lingered in Poland as late as the
mid-eighteenth century, the matter is of no great importance
because of the low level of Polish art and intellectual life from the
late seventeenth century to the ascension of Stanislaus August.
Until the emergence of a Polish classicism in the 1760s, the last
literary works of any significance date from the 1670s and 1680s.
The late emergence of a secular culture in Russia explains the
faint echoes of Baroque style in Russian art in the first half of the
eighteenth century. In their rush to Europeanize and modernize
the Russians borrowed almost indiscriminately from the West
(selectivity only came much later), telescoping the centuries and
often freely blending Baroque, Classicist, and pre-Romantic
elements.

To all intents and purposes, then, the European Baroque, with
a few exceptions, began to wane within a decade or two after the
middle of the seventeenth century. Determining an accurate

chronology for the emergence of the Baroque is more demanding and inevitably less gratifying than establishing the outer boundaries of its development. For the latter, we are greatly aided, after all, by the unequivocal evidence of the documented Classicist rejection of Baroque aesthetic values. In England, John Dryden's *Essay of Dramatic Poesy* (1668) left little doubt that the tide of taste had turned. When Malherbe wrote a few years after the death of the Baroque poet Jean de La Ceppède in 1623

> J'estime La Ceppède, et l'honore et
> l'admire
> Comm'un des ornaments les premiers
> de nos jours . . .

he was paying tribute to a poet whose style he himself turned away from in his later career and who was in a few decades to be condemned to the neglect of centuries by that arbiter of Classicist standards, Nicolas Boileau (1636–1711). Corneille's Classicist revisions from the mid-1640s to the early 1680s of such early dramatic works as *Clitandre* (1632), *Mélite* (1632), and *L'Illusion comique* (1636) parallel the assaults on Baroque taste taking place more or less in the same period in the arena of literary theory. As Imbrie Buffum shows,[19] the most extensive changes were made in 1660, the year of Corneille's own Classicist "manifesto," *Examen*, a year that marks the lowest ebb in the fortunes of the Baroque style in France.

---

[19] *Studies in the Baroque from Montaigne to Routrou*, pp. 163–211.

II

Historical Background

1. RELIGIOUS AND POLITICAL

Ranging approximately from the 1580s to at least the middle of the seventeenth century, the Baroque era encompassed events of profound significance in European history. Although there is a tendency at times to accord them too much prominence in efforts to disclose the sources of trends in the arts of the period, their impact on art cannot be minimized. These events can be divided into three categories: religious, political, and scientific.

In the realm of religious history, the momentous events of the sixteenth and seventeenth centuries were, of course, the Reformation and the Counter-Reformation. For many students it is these events, above all, that stand behind the emergence of developments in the arts summed up in the term Baroque. This statement in J. M. Cohen's *The Baroque Lyric* is representative:

Certainly the seventeenth century had learnt by bitter historical experience that worldly goods and honours were at best impermanent, and that a man's life counted for little in an era of civil and religious wars. The great nations which had sought to repeat and imitate the grandeur of Rome by spreading their frontiers into other continents had dissolved in internal strife. The Reformation, which had promised a new purity to Christianity, had led to secular warfare and a permanent division between Protestant and Catholic. The Counter-Reformation had saved the Church of Rome, and enabled her to reclaim much of her lost ground, but at the cost of a total suppression of free thought in southern Europe. The optimism of the Renaissance had yielded to a disbelief in the perfectability of man, and a cynical exploitation of his social blindness by a new race of power-politicians, many of whom were churchmen. For the Baroque thinker, poet or religious, life was a flux. What could be observed was no more than an appearance, and in describing these appearances the poet could at best only hint at a reality that he was unable to grasp.[1]

Although not everything in Cohen's assessment need be taken at face value, it conforms, in the main, to a commonly held view of the Baroque as a product of the religious strife of the sixteenth and seventeenth centuries. Indeed, older critics of Baroque art were fond of speaking of it as the art of the Counter-Reformation.

In considering the possible impact of the sixteenth- and seventeenth-century religious upheavals on art it would be well to recall that, with a few exceptions, the main events occurred in the *sixteenth century*, prior to the emergence of the Baroque. The innovations of Luther, Zwingli, and Calvin, the beginnings of Anglicanism, and the extension of the Reform movement to Poland during the reigns of Sigismund I (1506–48) and Sigismund II (1548–72) had taken place—and occasioned reaction—before the middle of the sixteenth century.

Spurred by the vigor and spread of the Reform movement, Pope Paul III (Alessandro Farnese) established a church reform commission in 1536. Two years before, the militant Society of Jesus was formed with the express purpose of spearheading the internal reorganization of the Church and the drive against the Reformation. On September 27, 1540, the Society received the sanction of the Holy See. The Council of Trent, which sponsored a massive program of organizational and doctrinal reform in the face of the Protestant threat, convened between 1545 and 1564. The French religious wars between Protestant and Catholic factions were fought intermittently between 1562 and 1598, and found resolution finally in the Edict of Nantes (April 15, 1598). St. Bartholomew's massacre took place on August 23 and 24, 1572.

If we turn to political and scientific events, we again discover that great changes occurred *before* the crystallization of the Baroque. The long struggle between the Christian nations of Western Europe and the Ottoman Turks, which culminated in the siege of Vienna in 1683, produced in the battle of Lepanto on October 7, 1571, one of the truly great military adventures of the century. Before dissension between the victorious Spaniards and Venetians dissipated the gains achieved at the expense of Turkish power and pride, Europe rejoiced in what almost universally

[1] J. M. Cohen, *The Baroque Lyric* (London, 1963), pp. 15–16.

seemed the end of the greatest menace Christendom had faced since Roman times. No less significant was another great naval encounter, the defeat of the Invincible Armada in 1588. If it did not really decide the war between England and Spain let alone (as some historians were wont to think in older times) herald the disintegration of the Spanish Empire, it did decide, as Garrett Mattingly shows, that "religious unity was not to be reimposed by force on the heirs of medieval Christendom."[2] Although the independence of the Netherlands became an irrevocable fact only in 1648 by the terms of the Peace of Westphalia, the revolt against Spanish authority, which led ultimately to independence, began as early as 1567. Before the first proclamation of independence from Spain in 1581 (following the Union of Utrecht in 1579), the Netherlands had already experienced the havoc and devastation of war and the ruthless expedition of the Duke of Alva in 1567 was not easily forgotten.

The religious, political, and military upheavals of the sixteenth century had their parallels in the world of sixteenth-century science as well. In terms of its impact on the scientific thought of the century, it would not be farfetched to compare the publication, in 1543, of Copernicus' *De revolutionibus orbium coelestium* (*On the Revolutions of Heavenly Bodies*) and its substitution of a heliocentric universe for the geocentric one of Aristotle and Ptolemy to Lepanto or the defeat of the Armada. Antiquated centuries-old opinions concerning the movement of heavenly bodies were not the only ones to crumble in the sixteenth century. The same year that saw the publication of Copernicus' theory also produced another great work of scientific iconoclasm: Vesalius' *De humani corporis fabrica* (*On the Structure of the Human Body*), which upset many erroneous but traditional anatomical ideas, some of which enjoyed the authority of Galen.

As I pointed out earlier, I do not question either the validity of searching for parallel trends in the arts in any given historical period or of finding among them themes, subjects, and even techniques that reflected important religious, political, military, social, economic, or scientific events. However, the Mannerist enthusiasts, in attributing so much to the impact on the sixteenth-century European consciousness of the calamities of the age, seem,

[2] Garrett Mattingly, *The Armada* (Boston, 1959), p. 401.

in my opinion, to neglect its great advances. I have in mind not so much the scientific breakthroughs that aroused as much controversy and antagonism as they won adherence, but the exploration and colonial expansion of the sixteenth century. Columbus' discoveries in the New World came, after all, in the late fifteenth and early sixteenth centuries, in 1492, 1493, 1498, and 1502. Within a few years after the Eastern travels of Vasco da Gama and Pedro Alvares Cabral, Francisco de Almeida was appointed Viceroy of India in 1505 by the King of Portugal. His victory over the combined fleets of India and Egypt off Diu in 1509 broke the Moslem monopoly of the Far Eastern trade and opened the way to the enrichment of Portugal that followed soon after.

The discovery and colonization of new lands proceeded at a spectacular rate in the first two decades of the sixteenth century. Exploring the Gulf Coast, Vasco de Balboa crossed the Isthmus of Panama in 1513 and discovered the Pacific Ocean. Ferdinand Magellan's great circumnavigation of the globe (1519 to 1521) proved that the new lands being discovered by Portugal and Spain in the American hemisphere were not part of Asia but an altogether different region. Although the major English and French explorations and colonizations of the American hemisphere came only later in the sixteenth and seventeenth centuries, the dazzling exploits in the New World and the Orient of the Italian, Portuguese, and Spanish adventurers, above all those of the legendary Conquistadores Hernando Cortes, Francisco Pizarro, and Gonzalo Jiménez de Quesada, had excited the curiosity and admiration of much of Europe and greatly enriched the treasuries of their native countries.

There were then ample reasons for enthusiasm and optimism in Europe in the first half of the sixteenth century despite such events as the Sack of Rome or the spread of religious dissension. If the art historians find that mannerism first made its appearance in Rome in the early 1520s, spread to other Italian cities and beyond, and reached its apogee in the later 1520s, the 1530s, and the 1540s and then declined and became outmoded in the 1570s, the 1580s, and 1590s, the distinctive traits of the style can also legitimately be seen as an aesthetic response, in part, to the great expansion of the European consciousness brought about by explorations and discoveries of new regions and peoples. The aesthetic theories John Shearman cited in his study of mannerism as the sources of the Mannerist innovations in Renaissance style could also be viewed as a manifestation of the ever expanding horizon of the European consciousness in search of new ways of expressing itself in the arts. The highly developed artistic culture of the Italian centers of the Renaissance would naturally have made Italian artists more sensitive to the winds of change, at least initially. Since the art of the Renaissance radiated outward from Italian centers, innovations in and departures from Renaissance techniques would also be expected to have emerged first in Italy, and then to have spread to other cultures to varying degrees within the Italian cultural orbit, particularly Spain, France, Ragusa (or Dubrovnik on the eastern Adriatic coast), the Poland of Sigismund I whose second wife belonged to the Italian Bona Sforza family and, less directly, Germany, the Netherlands, and England.

The tensions and imbalanced proportions of much Mannerist art might well, as Shearman strongly suggests, have sprung from the search for new ways of artistic expression in an age of magnificent discovery. The decorativeness, ornamentalism, and variety of Mannerist art may similarly be viewed as reflecting a new material opulence fed in part by the riches of the New World and the Orient. In time, of course, the search for novelty and variety could become a goal unto itself and lead to the excesses and excessive concern with form characteristic of later Mannerist art of the second half of the sixteenth century. But this need not have been the case in its initial phase in the 1520s.

Many upheavals of the sixteenth century invoked by scholars to explain mannerism either occurred in the second half of the century or did not become important culturally until then. This is true of both the scientific and religious controversies, but above all the latter. Just as the bitter controversy surrounding Copernicus' theory raged long after the publication of *On the Revolutions of Heavenly Bodies* in 1543, so also the upheavals and wars generated by the Reformation and the spread of Protestantism were felt primarily in the later part of the sixteenth century. The official establishment of the Society of Jesus in 1540 and the opening of the Council of Trent five years later initiated the Counter-Reformation, which sharpened the lines of conflict and thrust well into the seventeenth century. The religious wars that ripped sixteenth-century France raged in the second half of the century and were vividly reflected in Agrippa d'Aubigné's epic *Les Tragiques*, a large part of which was composed in 1578, six years after the St. Bartholomew's Massacre. Religious conflict also lay behind the tumult of revolt and war that bloodied the land of what was to become in time Holland and Belgium, from 1567 to the end of the devastating Thirty Years' War in 1648.

Spain and Venice could find only brief glory in the victory at Lepanto in 1571, for two years later Venice was forced to abandon Cyprus, its largest and most important possession in the East, and seventeen years later Spain suffered the humiliation of the defeat of its once proud Armada. Beginning in the late sixteenth century, both states started the movement of decline that was to continue steadily throughout the seventeenth century.

The humiliation suffered by Spain in the defeat of the Armada was, conversely, a victory for an England worried by Spanish power. Spared to a considerable extent the ravages the Continent endured in consequence of the religious upheaval, England during the long reign of Elizabeth I (1558–1603) enjoyed a growth of power and prestige manifest in the ebullient literary culture of the period. Yet it was not entirely free of the tensions and anxieties rife elsewhere in Europe during the second half of the sixteenth century. Spain was an ever-present danger until the defeat of the Armada. Moreover, the dynastic and constitutional issues of the age culminated in the civil wars of 1642–46 and 1648–49. However true it may be that the Renaissance—particularly the works of Italian Renaissance writers—reached England in the Elizabethan age and that the island nation largely escaped the horrors of the continental religious wars, mannerism, at least on the level of style, had entry through translation (e.g. Harrington's *Orlando furioso*, 1591 and Fairfax's *Gerusalemme liberata*, 1600) and before that the direct involvement of English authors in Italian culture such as, Sir Thomas Wyatt (1503–43) and Henry Howard, Earl of Surrey (c. 1517–47), whose poetry was published posthumously in *Tottel's Miscellany* (1557) and who introduced the Italian or Petrarchan sonnet; Spenser, whose *The Faerie Queene*, as we have seen, borrowed freely from Tasso's *Gerusalemme liberata* and antedates the famous Fairfax translation; and George Gascoigne (c. 1525–77), whose *The Supposes* (1566) was a translation from Ariosto. The indebtedness of the Elizabethan pastoral to Guarini's *Pastor fido* was so well known as to produce this bit of dialogue in Ben Jonson's *Volpone* (1606):

> Lady Politic Would-Be: Here's Pastor Fido.
> Volpone (*aside*): Profess obstinate silence;
>   That's now my safest.
> Lady Politic Would-Be: All our English writers,
>   I mean such as are happy in the Italian,
>   Will deign to steal out of this author, mainly;
>   Almost as much as from Montaigne:
>   He has so modern and facile a vein,
>   Fitting the time, and catching the court-ear.
>
> [Act III, Sc. 4]

The taste for things Italian, derided by the Puritan Roger Ascham (1515–68) in *The Schoolmaster*, published posthumously in 1570, but strong enough in late sixteenth- and seventeenth-century England to account for the settings and characters of most Elizabethan and Jacobean drama from Marlowe (1564–93) to John Webster (c. 1570–1625) and Cyril Tourneur (c. 1570–1626), doubtless also brought the two outstanding prose romances of Elizabethan England—the *Euphues* (1579, 1580) of John Lyly (c. 1554–1606) and the *Arcadia* (1590) of Sir Philip Sidney (1554–86)—within the pale of Mannerist aesthetics. The greatness of Elizabethan literature lay, however, in its drama, and if the enthusiasts of mannerism (e.g. Sypher) have erred perhaps on the side of excessive zeal in their blanket generalizations about the mannerism of Elizabethan drama, they have at least performed the useful service of bringing to the study of the style and structure of much of Marlowe, Shakespeare, and Jonson a perception that does not automatically equate Elizabethan and Renaissance.

Despite the calamities visited upon Europe in the sixteenth century from which not even England was entirely exempt, there were still reasons to warrant optimism and a zest for life. The great discoveries of the age not only shored up the enthusiasm for man's capabilities but also brought new vistas, knowledge, and riches. For some countries, for example, England, Germany, and Poland, the age of exploration and discovery in the second half of the century brought with it the rediscovery of classical antiquity. What glorified Italian civilization in the late fifteenth and the first half of the sixteenth centuries became, before the sixteenth century closed, the common heritage of Europe. If some nations suffered temporary setbacks politically and militarily, others reached heights of power never achieved previously. This was certainly true of England, of Spain, of Portugal, of Poland, and of certain Italian city-states (Venice, Genoa, Savoy, Ferrara).

The aristocratic court-centered and court-oriented life-style of the age was also as much responsible for the ornateness, variety, search for novelty, and general concern with the external and superficial that characterized the art called Mannerist as the strife and anxieties that mounted throughout Europe in the second half of the sixteenth century. The religious and political upheavals, particularly in the second half of the century, may have introduced into the arts a greater spiritual concern, but did not, until late in the century when the Counter-Reformation with its political as well as religious ramifications was in full progress, have sufficient impact on the European consciousness to disrupt the balance between an optimistic zest for life and a negativism that tended to stress the illusory, ephemeral quality of terrestrial existence. Perhaps that explains the usually sharp and clear division between the earthly and the spiritual in Mannerist art (e.g. El Greco's *Assumption of the Virgin*, 1577, and *The Burial of Count Orgaz*, 1586).

With the transition to the seventeenth century, however, much of this changed. The calamities experienced fitfully in the sixteenth century multiplied and intensified in the next age and left no country of Europe unscathed.

The Spanish Empire, at its height in the sixteenth century, unmistakably entered upon its decline in the seventeenth. Symbolically, perhaps, the turn of the century was marked by a great plague (1599–1600), which may have wiped out at a single blow the fifteen percent population increase of sixteenth-century Castile.[3] But plague was not the sole catalyst of decline.

The way was indeed well prepared by the lengthy struggle for independence in the Netherlands begun in 1567, by the revolt of the Moriscos (converted Moslems suspected of the clandestine practice of their original faith) from 1569 to 1571, the defeat of the Armada in 1588, and the war with France from 1598 to 1621,

[3] J. H. Elliott, *Imperial Spain, 1469–1716* (New York, 1966), pp. 294–295.

which brought a marked deterioration in Spanish industry and trade, a rise in domestic political corruption, and an overly zealous prosecution of the Counter-Reformation that resulted in the tragic and costly expulsion of over 250,000 Moriscos between 1609 and 1614 and, in part, involvement in the disastrous Thirty Years' War.

Revolts against Spanish rule broke out wherever non-Spaniards found themselves incapable of enduring the Spanish yoke any longer. By 1648, after a protracted and bloody struggle for independence, Holland became a republic free of Spanish control. Conquered by Spain in 1504, and the center of Spanish power in Italy, Naples attempted to cast off Spanish rule by the so-called revolt of Masaniello (Tommaso Aniello) in July, 1647. At first successful, the revolt was quelled and Naples remained a Spanish possession until the War of the Spanish Succession (1701–14). More dangerous, because it was both internal and worsened relations with France, was the Catalonian revolt that broke out, with French support, in 1640 and lasted until 1659 when the Catalonians were granted most of what they had previously possessed. Although the Peace of Westphalia ended the Thirty Years' War, Franco-Spanish conflict raged on until the decisive defeat of the Spaniards in the Battle of the Dunes on June 14, 1658. The Treaty of the Pyrenees, which was signed on November 7, 1659, signaled not only the end of the hostilities, but the end of Spanish power in Europe.

The Treaty of the Pyrenees was a profound reversal of fortune for both Spain and France. While Spain thereafter entered a bleak period of political and cultural decay, France achieved ascendancy as the greatest power on the Continent in the reign of Louis XIV (1643–1715). This greatness which, once consolidated, saw a turning away in French art from the Baroque to the Classicist came after the bitter and costly Protestant Huguenot–Catholic wars of 1562 to 1598, the economic misery resulting from the policies of the Duke of Sully (1560–1641), the conflict with Spain, and the extensive French participation in the Thirty Years' War.

The general decline of Spain—and a Portugal in conflict with Spain throughout the seventeenth century—was paralleled by that of the Italian city-states and the papacy. Spanish rule in Naples, established early in the sixteenth century, continued until the War of the Spanish Succession; Milan also fell under Spanish rule

after the death of the last Sforza (Francesco II) in 1535 and remained dominated by a foreign power until the nineteenth century
wars of independence, unification, and the establishment of the
kingdom in 1870; Tuscany (composed of Florence and Siena)
followed the general pattern of decline under Medici rule until
the extinction of the line in 1737 and the imposition of Hapsburg
authority; the Genoa that had once known greatness as a commercial power succeeded in retaining its independence as a
republic but steadily declined economically through the sixteenth
and seventeenth centuries and faced the constant threat of en-
croachment by France, Austria, and the independent state of
Savoy. Whatever power Genoa possessed in the East disappeared
after the loss of Chios to the Turks in 1566; though strongly
under French influence in the sixteenth and seventeenth centuries,
Savoy clung to its independence and enjoyed a period of prosperity and progress under the rule of Emanuel Philibert (1553–80)
before war and economic mismanagement in the reign of Charles
Emanuel I (1580–1630) eroded the gains. Despite a respite under
Victor Amadeus I (1630–37), civil war followed his reign, and
when Charles Emanuel II (1638–75) was raised to the throne
French and Spanish interests in Savoy followed a collision course,
greatly weakening the ducal power; long an active cultural center
that greatest of Italian city-states, Venice, declined in commercial
and political power after its prosperity was undermined by the
discovery and rapid exploitation of the new route to the Indies.
As Turkish power moved ever westward it inevitably collided with
vested Venetian interests. There were several victories against the
Turks, above all the naval battle of Lepanto in 1571, at the
Dardanelles during the Candian War of 1645–69 almost a century later, and in the conquest of the Morea (the Peloponnesus in
southern Greece), 1685–87, when the Venetians took Athens; but
the sweet taste of victory was usually short-lived as the Venetians
ultimately were forced to yield more and more territory (Cyprus,
Candia—present-day Crete—the Morea). By the early eighteenth
century, Venice's once numerous possessions had shrunk to no
more than the Ionian Islands and the Dalmatian coast. Politically
stagnant and commercially no longer a significant force in European economic life, Venice now was little more than a shadow of
its once glorious self.

The papacy shared the same general decline of the Italian city-states in the seventeenth century. After the vigorous, fruitful reign of Sixtus V (1585–90) and to a lesser extent that of Clement VIII (1592–1605), the papacy appeared to lose dynamism as it moved farther into the seventeenth century. The difficult, uncertain course of neutrality it attempted to pursue during the tragic years of the Thirty Years' War brought it into a position of ever greater isolation. Before long it was rent internally by the Jansenist issue, which divided the Church into opposing factions through much of the seventeenth *and* eighteenth centuries. In his *Augustinus*, published posthumously two years after his death in 1638, Cornelius Jansenius, Bishop of Ypres, advocated the inner revitalization of the Church, a position diametrically opposed to that of the Jesuits who emphasized instead external reform. Initiated by Innocent X's bull of May 31, 1653 (*Cum occasione impressionis libri*), the controversy over Jansenism produced many acrimonious moments for the papacy before the dissolution of the Jesuit order by edict of Clement XIV in 1773, effectively putting the issue to rest for all time. Divided over Jansenism, politically weakened by its course of neutrality during the Thirty Years' War, and the increasing necessity to make concessions to the Hapsburgs, on the one hand, and the Bourbons, on the other, the papacy suffered further loss of power and prestige in the anti-clerical age of the Enlightenment. By the time of the French Revolution, it was a largely discredited and ineffectual institution.

The glories of the Elizabethan age were no guarantee that England, too, would not know something of the unrest rampant elsewhere in seventeenth-century Europe. Providentially spared the anguish of the Thirty Years' War, religious controversy involving "Papist" plots, prohibitions against the Puritans, and the rights of Presbyterians still surfaced from time to time throughout the century. These were overshadowed, however, by a conflict of deeper significance for future English historical development— the contest of wills between king and Parliament, which roused deep passions in the time of the Stuarts and Cromwell and unsettled English political life down to the Convention Parliament (January 22, 1689—January 27, 1690) and the Declaration of Rights. The high point of the struggle was the Civil War fought between 1642 and 1646, and again in 1648. Although it ended with the beheading of Charles I on January 30, 1649, it was one of history's least bloody civil wars, generally free of excesses on both sides.

The second half of the century produced its share of calamities as well. Costly plague and fire in London in 1665 and 1666 briefly diverted attention from the political strife attendant on the establishment of the Cromwellian Protectorate (1653–58), the Restoration of Charles II (1660–85), and the renewed fear of Catholic domination under James II (1685–88), which led to the invitation to William of Orange and his eventual ascension to the throne in 1689 after a flurry of military conflict, James's flight to France, and a brief interregnum punctuated by rioting in London.

Whatever the bitterness, pain, and disillusionment brought on by national conflicts in the seventeenth century, there can be no doubt that both in terms of contemporary reaction and historical perspective the most profoundly moving upheaval of the entire age was the Thirty Years' War. Begun in Bohemia in 1618 as an extension of the conflict between Protestantism and Catholicism, it rapidly mushroomed into a war of European proportions involving Bohemia, the German states, Austria, Sweden, and France, confusing religious and political issues in its escalation. Although hostilities were concluded by the Peace of Westphalia in late October, 1648, the misery, havoc, and devastation left in their wake lingered in the collective memory of Europe for decades afterward.

Among the Slavs, the Czechs alone bore the full brunt of the war. Two years after it erupted in Bohemia, the battle of White Mountain was fought on November 8, 1620. The event is of great significance in Czech history, for it marks the beginning of a long period of decline ended only by the nationalist revival of the first half of the nineteenth century. The defeat suffered by the Bohemians not only resulted in the loss of their royal charter, tantamount to a loss of independence, but the complete suppression of Protestantism, the execution, dispersion, and confiscation of the land of large numbers of the nobility who led the revolt initially, and an intense Germanization of Bohemian culture successfully challenged and overcome only in the nineteenth century.

The most powerful Slavic state in the seventeenth century was Poland. Although Protestantism made considerable gains in the country in the sixteenth century, a successful Counter-Reformation was instituted in the reign of the first Polish king of the Swedish house of Vasa, Sigismund III (1587–1632), a student of the Jesuits and an implacable foe of the Reform movement. By the middle of seventeenth century, few traces of Protestantism remained in Poland and the vanguard of the Counter-Reformation, the Society of Jesus, was extending its activities to the vast Orthodox-populated regions of the Ukraine. Until the revival of the arts and learning in Poland in the reign of Stanislaus August Poniatowski, the richest period of old Polish culture came roughly in the second half of the sixteenth and the first half of the seventeenth centuries. The Thirty Years' War was without much impact in Poland, but this was little cause for complacency. At the beginning of the seventeenth century Poland was at the height of its power politically and militarily and the seat of an impressive cultural Renaissance. When the century drew to a close, Poland, like Spain, was politically weak, a relatively easy prey for other powers, economically bankrupt, and culturally stagnant. The vigorous prosecution of the Counter-Reformation, dynastic rivalries, war and revolt again were the familiar causes. The history of the Church's efforts to stem the tide of Protestantism in Poland was never marred by the excesses that characterized its campaign in the West, but beginning with the reign of Sigismund III Protestants (and Jews) became the victims of repressive measures that increased in the seventeenth century and led in many cases to persecution and exile.

The Polonization and Catholicization of large numbers of the landowning gentry in the Polish-dominated areas of the Ukraine created another religious conflict for the Poles. Not only did it arouse the enmity of enlightened members of the Orthodox population of the region who undertook a series of countermeasures (principally against the Jesuits) to preserve Orthodoxy and the Church Slavonic language, but it also contributed to the great Ukrainian revolt led by Bohdan Chmielnicki in 1648 that sapped much of the vitality of the Kingdom of Poland. By the time the revolt was suppressed in the 1660s, Poland had seen its treasury drained, such once important commercial centers as Lwów sacked and its population massacred, and a substantial portion of the Ukraine slip under the control of Muscovy. The elevation of a Swedish Vasa to the Polish throne in 1587 eventually embroiled

Poland in Swedish dynastic strife and led to a costly war with Sweden (1655–60), which saw much Polish territory overrun and considerable damage wrought. The Polish difficulties with the Ukraine, Sweden, Muscovy, and the ever unruly Cossacks were compounded by a debilitating struggle with the Turks, which nevertheless produced several military successes. Despite these, the country was materially and spiritually exhausted by the end of the century, its strength and unity fragmented by war and the internal dissension aroused by the acquisition of virtually complete political power by the gentry (*szlachta*) at the expense of the Crown and effective parliamentary operation. The groundwork was solidly laid for the disappearance of Poland from the map of Europe less than a century later.

2. SCIENTIFIC AND PHILOSOPHICAL

The perturbations sustained by the seventeenth-century European consciousness in consequence of the occasionally strikingly paradoxical realignment of political, religious, and economic patterns were increased by other factors of no small consequence. In its vigorous prosecution of the Counter-Reformation, the Church of Rome set in motion a dynamic and far-reaching campaign of spiritual revival, of spiritual reaction against the materialism of the Renaissance, productive of the kind of spiritual concern, religious fervor, and mystic ecstasy unheard of in Europe since the Middle Ages. Polemics and open conflicts with Protestantism added fuel to the fire of religious fervor. The political and military calamities of the age, above all the Thirty Years' War, intensified this fervor and broadened its base. So, too, did the contemporary innovations in science and philosophy.

The controversy sparked by the publication of Copernicus' defense of the heliocentric system of the cosmos in 1543 deepened with the work of Johannes Kepler (1571–1630), who simplified and advanced the teachings of his Polish predecessor. The development of the experimental method, which further divorced science from religion, metaphysics, and the antiquated learning of the past, marked the contributions of Francis Bacon (1561–1626) and Galileo Galilei (1564–1642). The latter's famous experiment in gravitation achieved two immensely significant results: (*a*) it demonstrated the value of the mathematical-experimental method, thereby hastening its general acceptance; and (*b*) it dealt a deathblow to Aristotelian physics and cosmology. This convincing repudiation of Aristotle brought down the wrath of the Scholastic philosophers, while Galilei's further support of Copernicus earned him an appearance before the Inquisition at Rome in 1615 where he was forced to renounce the teachings of Copernicus, considered heretical by the Church, and a year later, in 1616, placed on the Index of prohibited books. (It was only in 1835 that they were finally removed.) Galilei's trials hardly ended in 1615. His continuing propagation of Copernican theory (which he was more successful in disseminating than Kepler) and the publication in 1632 (with the approval of the Florentine Inquisitors) of his *Dialogue Concerning the Two Chief Systems of the World, the Ptolemaic and the Copernican*, brought him to another confrontation with the Inquisition in Rome. At his second appearance in 1633, he was again compelled to abjure Copernican teaching and, in addition, was himself condemned for heresy. For the rest of his life he was prohibited from leaving a villa in the vicinity of his native Florence; his works were banned in Italy and had to be smuggled out of the country (e.g. his studies in mechanics) in order to be published. The fettering of Galilei and Italian science generally was not the universal pattern, however, in seventeenth-century Europe, particularly in countries where the antiauthoritarian, empiric, and, to an extent, theological nature (e.g. the "good works" belief of the English Puritans) of Protestantism did much to promote science.

What had begun in solar mechanics and gravity with Copernicus, and had been extended by Kepler, Galilei, and the Dutchman Christian Huygens (1629–95), was completed by the greatest English scientist of the age, Sir Isaac Newton (1642–1727), whose discoveries of the law of centripetal force and the inverse square law made the greatest contribution to the theory of universal gravitation.

Advances were not limited exclusively to the sciences of astronomy, physics, and mathematics. Optical research made rapid strides and the microscope and telescope were used ever more increasingly in scientific investigation. Medicine made further progress when the theory of the circulation of the blood was finally established by the physician of Charles I, William Harvey

(1578–1657), in his *Exercitatio de motu cordis et sanguinis (On the Motion of the Heart and the Blood*, 1628). The foundations of modern chemistry were laid by German or German-influenced iatrochemists, such as Johann Baptist van Helmont (1577–1644) who first distinguished between gases and the element of air, by the Englishman Robert Boyle (1627–91), who discovered that the pressure of a gas varied inversely with its volume, and the German Georg Ernest Stahl (1660–1734), whose studies in the composition of matter lent substance to the "phlogiston" theory of the later iatrochemists, which held sway well into the eighteenth century.

How far science had come in the seventeenth century can be gauged by the number of scientific societies that came into existence. A group of young English scientists led by the Puritan clergyman John Wilkins (1614–72) and calling itself the "Philosophical College" began meeting regularly in London from about late 1644. The same John Wilkins founded a scientific club at Oxford known as the "Philosophical Society." In 1662, Charles II approved the charter of the "Royal Society for the Improvement of Natural Knowledge," which has been in continuous existence to the present day. Four years later, the Paris Academy of Sciences was founded, the second great European society of scientists to be established in the seventeenth century. The first important scientific society in Italy, the Neapolitan Academia Secretorum Naturae, which was active in the 1560s, proved short-lived when it was forced to close its doors as a result of a witchcraft charge. It was followed by the Accademia dei Lincei in Rome, which met from 1601 to 1630. The membership was small (thirty-two), but included Galilei. The last important Italian scientific society of the seventeenth century was the Florentine Accademia del Cimento, which was active between 1657 and 1667 under the patronage of the Medici brothers, Grand Duke Ferdinand II and Leopold. Among its ten members were Vincenzo Viviani (1622–1703), who constructed the first barometer with Galilei's pupil Evangelista Torricelli (1608–47), and Giovanni Alfonso Borelli (1608–79), who modified Kepler's theories on the movement of planets and studied living organisms as machines (e.g. *De motu animalium, On the Motions of Animals,* published posthumously). Despite the ecclesiastical harassment of proponents of the Copernican system in Italy, the Academy managed to continue its activity, concentrating on experimentation. It was dissolved finally in 1667 when Leopold Medici was given the red cap of a cardinal.

Although less significant than those of other countries, several scientific societies were founded in Germany during this period. The Societas Ereunetica was established in Rostock in 1622 by Joachim Jung (1587–1657), a botanist; and the Collegium Curiosum sive Experimentale was founded in 1672 at Altdorf. Neither one, however, succeeded in continuing its activities after the death of its founder. Considering the disruptions caused in Germany by the Thirty Years' War, little wonder should attach to the fact that the first viable German scientific society, the Berlin Academy established by the Elector Frederick I of Prussia at the urging of the philosopher and scientist Gottfried Wilhelm Leibniz, opened its doors only in the year 1700.

The disquieting effects of scientific inquiry and progress reverberated also throughout the halls of contemporary philosophical thought. Where philosophy was indistinguishable from theology in an earlier day, it now derived sustenance from and developed within the context of science. In the *Advancement of Learning* (1605) and *Novum organum* ("New Instrument," 1620) parts of his vast unfinished *Instauratio magna* ("The Great Renewing"), Sir Francis Bacon was among the first who sought to apply the experimental method of the new science to philosophy and championed the cause of induction, which he opposed to the mathematical-deductive technique developed by Galilei and later carried farther by René Descartes. As the inventor of coordinate geometry, Descartes (1596–1650) was a splendid exemplum of the science-oriented philosopher of the seventeenth century. Rejecting the traditional Aristotelian world view and the hierarchical structure of Scholasticism taught him in his student days in a Jesuit lycée (although retaining other elements of Scholastic teaching), Descartes conceived of the world as a vast machine, its parts all equally subject to the same mechanical laws. This mechanically constituted material world created by God has a spiritual counterpart, he taught, in which man alone of all material entities has a place; thus man shares both worlds—the material and spiritual. Descartes' *Discours de la méthode . . .* (*Discourse on Method*, 1637) and *Principia philosophiae* (*Principles of Philosophy*, 1644) influenced men's minds for generations, in both Catholic and Protestant Europe, but his application of principles of mechanics to philosophy earned the hostility of the Church of Rome with the inevitable result that his works were placed on the Index in Rome and Paris in 1663.

Although primarily concerned with problems of religion and ethics, the Dutch Jewish philosopher Baruch Spinoza (1632–77) was also an able mathematician like Descartes, and of sufficiently diverse scientific interests to write a treatise on the rainbow. In his posthumously published *Ethics*, containing his most important thoughts, he argued for a totally pantheistic universe in which every existing thing is an emanation of a Supreme Being, of God or Nature. Taking over Descartes' mechanistic view whereby everything in nature operates according to a fixed system of laws, Spinoza moved beyond Descartes to the complete rejection of free will and chance. Although clearly more mystic than Descartes in his belief in the existence of only one substance, his attempt to support his arguments by extensive "proofs," like Descartes, reflected the extent to which seventeenth-century philosophy had fallen under the sway of science.

I I I

Some Basic Assumptions About the Baroque Age

From the preceding necessarily brief survey of religious, political, scientific, and philosophical trends from the late sixteenth to the late seventeenth centuries, certain basic assumptions can be made about the Baroque.

a) With notably few exceptions, the age was marked by an *intensification* of conflict in virtually all spheres of life. Undoubtedly, the lowest ebb in the affairs among nations in the seventeenth century was the Thirty Years' War, which for its degree of multinational involvement and destructiveness far surpassed earlier conflicts. By the war's end, Protestantism, despite its lack of unity, its fragmentation, was an established fact; dreams of extirpation on the part of the Church of Rome were no longer feasible. The Thirty Years' War, moreover, set into bold relief, if indeed it did not cause in all cases, the reversal of fortune and decline experienced by a number of states. Bohemia, Germany, Italy, and Spain all exhibited signs of decline and decay that became more obvious as the century grew older. Significantly, it was only relatively late in the eighteenth century that these countries gave evidence of emerging from the morass into which they had sunk politically, economically, and culturally.

Although untouched by the ravages of the Thirty Years' War, the only truly powerful Slavic state in the sixteenth century, Poland, was so weakened by foreign wars and internal dissension, that its progress through the seventeenth century moved in a single direction—downward. From the noble gesture of its participation in the relief of Vienna against the Turks in 1683 to the ascension to the throne of Stanislaus August Poniatowski in 1764, Poland presented a wretched picture of weakness and stagnation. The balance of power in Eastern Europe began shifting during this period and has never altered its course. A Muscovy that was so weak and divided in the early seventeenth century as to be virtually helpless before a Polish invasion that saw the occupation of the Kremlin and the brief occupancy of the throne by a Pole, a century later was an empire of rapidly growing power and prestige and the arbiter of the destiny of the Polish nation.

Probably the brightest picture in Baroque Slavdom was presented by the tiny independent maritime Republic of Dubrovnik (commonly known also by the Italian name of Ragusa, the Latin Ragusium) on the Dalmatian coast. Earlier in its history a part of Venice and in the seventeenth century still very much within the sphere of Italian cultural influence, Dubrovnik by a combination of geography and shrewd politics managed to preserve its autonomy from the Venetians, Hungarians, and Turks who dominated the other provinces of Croatia. Its independence in the face of external pressures and its advantageous mercantile situation enabled Dubrovnik to enjoy prosperity and become over the span of the sixteenth, seventeenth, and early eighteenth centuries a remarkable center of culture and literature vaguely reminiscent of seventeenth-century Holland. Yet, as in the case of Holland, negative forces were also at work. Much of the city of Dubrovnik itself was destroyed by earthquake in 1667 and the opening of new sea routes to the East had an adverse effect on the maritime economy of the Republic, leading to its decline as a mercantile power. Still, Dubrovnik succeeded in clinging to its much-prized independence until the French occupation and annexation under Napoleon in 1808.

For England, France, and the Netherlands, the seventeenth century was less generally disastrous than it was for the rest of Europe, but each country experienced convulsions of sufficient severity to send tremors through the body of the entire nation. An England spared the horrors of the Thirty Years' War still knew religious conflict virtually down to William of Orange's acceptance of the English crown in 1689. The conflict between the Monarchy and Parliament generated much bitterness and unrest and culminated in civil war. Occasional soldierly excesses in the time of Cromwell followed by plague and conflagration in London heightened the sense of fatigue with strife and dismay over the loss of Elizabethan buoyancy. Between the great age of Elizabeth and the return to stability and order in the reign of William III after decades of contention, England had cause to consider itself fortunate that the turmoil on the Continent had largely passed it by, but any sense of contentment was quickly checked by consideration of domestic conditions.

The Thirty Years' War involved both France and the Netherlands and by the war's end both were overwhelmed by the exhaustion and frustration born of the conflict, but their wounds were superficial when compared with those of Spain, Germany, and Bohemia. Like England, they too had cause to thank Providence for being spared the devastation and destruction visited elsewhere, but there were also reasons (as in the case of England) that the national mood was anything but ebullient. The religious strife France experienced in the second half of the sixteenth century continued to make internal peace elusive until force wrote a miserable end to the history of Protestantism in France with the revocation of the Edict of Nantes in 1685. The suppression of the Huguenots not only made for "scenes . . . in the French countryside such as Europe had not known since the Thirty Years' War,"[1] but acted very adversely on the country's economic health. The Jansenist heresy also kept the pot of religious conflict boiling in France. Pope Innocent X's Bull of 1653 made the disciples of Jansen heretics. A peace of sorts was worked out in 1669 that spared the Jansenists the fate of the Protestant Huguenots, and when the relations between the Holy See and the State of Louis XIV were under particular strain in 1682, Jansenist bishops supported the Pope. This won the heresy a temporary reprieve. With the worsening of the already strained relations between state and church, the Jansenist issue receded into the background; the settlement of the differences between Louis XIV and the papacy finally reached in 1693, however, enabled the Church in France to return its attention to still unresolved areas of conflict. Once the Quietist issue was laid to rest in 1694, the reemergence of the Jansenist controversy around 1701 could be dealt with. The matter dragged on to 1728, when the defection of Bishop Noailles cost the Jansenist cause its leadership and its structure. Thereafter, Jansenism existed (well into the nineteenth century) more as a matter of private persuasion and family tradition than as an organization.

A France caught in the quagmire of incessant warring, internal religious tumult involving the Huguenots, Jansenists, and Quietists,

[1] David Ogg, *Europe in the Seventeenth Century* (2d ed.; New York, 1965), p. 296.

and the growth of absolutist monarchy contrasts sharply with the image projected by the Netherlands in the seventeenth century. The long struggle for independence against Spain, which continued until the end of January, 1648, made war no less a reality for the Netherlands than for the rest of Europe. But the imminency of independence, coupled with a growing sense of national pride and purpose, created the kind of optimism and dynamism that enabled the people of the Netherlands to score a number of impressive gains before independence became a reality. When the Twelve Years' Truce was signed with Spain on April 9, 1609, the Dutch seized the cessation of hostilities to initiate a regeneration of their economic and political life. Aided by a series of able rulers of the House of Orange—Maurice (1586–1625), Frederick Henry (1625–47), William II (1647-50), and William III (1672–1702)— they greatly expanded their overseas trade at a time when such trade was declining elsewhere in Europe and moved to resolve internal political dissension through a consolidation of the political supremacy of the Orangists. Once the threat of republican separatism was dealt with in an effective but harsh manner, the next outstanding issue, that of religious unity, could be settled. The campaign to achieve political unity was closely linked to the religious issue: when the last barriers to Orangist absolutism were removed, the unchallenged position of Calvinism as the state religion was assured.

The resumption of hostilities with Spain in 1621 followed by a series of defeats in land battles and entry into the Thirty Years' War again brought conflict to the Netherlands. But stunning naval victories and the acquisition of independence finally in 1648 kept spirits from flagging. With peace came a reopening of the old wounds of the Orangist—republican conflict. Before these could be resolved, a worsening of relations with England, now a rival maritime power, led to open conflict in October, 1651, with the passing of the English Navigation Act. Several setbacks forced the Dutch to sue for peace in 1653 on generally disadvantageous terms. But continued rivalry and hostility provoked a new war in 1665. The Treaty of Breda, which was concluded in 1667, won several concessions for the Dutch (including the retention of Surinam and modifications in the English Navigation Act). The rising menace of an expansionist France was temporarily countered in 1668 by the Triple Alliance of Holland, England, and

Sweden. But in 1672, after several successful moves to isolate the Dutch politically, Louis XIV invaded at the head of an army of 100,000 men. The unlikely aid of Spain and the effective leadership of William III weakened the English-French coalition and led to the peace of August, 1678. The last serious threat to the independence of the Netherlands was thus removed. The issue of republican separation was again laid to rest by the great popular support for the hero of the war, William III, soon to receive an invitation to the throne of England. The Netherlands had met enemies capable of eliminating its hard-won independence and had stood up to them with little loss. The great independence struggle of the late sixteenth century and almost the entire first half of the seventeenth (including the period of the Twelve Years' Truce) produced a climate of hope and national purpose that enabled the Netherlands to realize the richest period of cultural growth in its history. In a sense, conditions were such as to enable the Dutch to experience a kind of Elizabethan age of their own. For this reason the seventeenth-century history of the Netherlands appears at first glance defiant of efforts to relate it to general European patterns of decline and decay in the same period. But the undeniable brilliance of Dutch culture in the seventeenth century should not be permitted completely to overshadow the external and internal conflicts that certainly began multiplying from the end of the Twelve Years' Truce: wars with England and France, which saw a number of Dutch defeats; Dutch participation in the Thirty Years' War; internal strife caused by warring among republican-separatist and Orangist-absolutist factions so strong as to lead to the mob execution at The Hague in 1672 of the prominent de Witt brothers, John and Cornelius; and a certain residue of resentment by the remnants of religious groups opposed to the supremacy of Calvinism.

b) The political and economic turmoil of seventeenth-century Europe was intensified by religious, scientific, and philosophical events. Granted that the outbreak of hostilities between Protestantism and Catholicism dates from the sixteenth century, the intensification of the conflict, despite the apparent exception of the French religious wars of the second half of the sixteenth century, clearly comes in the seventeenth century. Not only is the Counter-Reformation pursued with fullest vigor in the age we call the

Baroque but it is in this period that the vanguard of the Counter-Reformation, the Society of Jesus, enjoys its greatest geographical spread, its widest range of influence, and its most brilliant successes. The burning of the Italian thinker, Giordano Bruno, in the Campo de' Fiori in Rome in 1600 by decree of the Inquisition, the condemnation of Copernican theory in 1616 and the trial and imprisonment of Galilei not long afterward, the stifled intellectual life of seventeenth-century Spain and Italy, the paroxysm of religiopolitical strife represented by the Thirty Years' War, and the persecution of Huguenots following the revocation of the Edict of Nantes in France are only the more outstanding illustrations of the intolerance and ferocity attendant on the Church of Rome's frantic efforts to suppress Protestantism and whatever it regarded as the consequences of the antiauthoritarianism of the Protestant heresies in the seventeenth century.

The history of the Counter-Reformation, the activities of the Jesuits, and the Jansenist and Quietist deviations in France, tend occasionally, it seems, to obscure the divisions and antagonisms within the Protestant world itself. The importance of at least an awareness of these for a study of the literature of the period rests on the long-held and still often encountered belief that Baroque art, including Baroque literature, emerged as an expression of the spirit of the Catholic Counter-Reformation. In the light of the prominent role of the Jesuits in the campaign against Protestantism, it is easy to understand why some students of the seventeenth century have even been led to speak of the "Jesuit Baroque." The importance of the Counter-Reformation, and the Society of Jesus, for the culture and thought of the Baroque age is undeniable. But equating Baroque with Counter-Reformation, Jesuit or even Catholic, however tempting for convenience's sake, is simplistic, for to do so fails to consider the Protestant element. In a valuable survey of the German Baroque in *Periods in German Literature*, edited by J. M. Ritchie (London, 1968), J. H. Tisch-Wackernagel also calls attention to the problem: "To equate Baroque with Counter-Reformation has long enjoyed pseudo-historical respectability, irrespective of the factual and chronological fallacies underlying this assumption which in no way takes cognizance of the Protestant Baroque.[2]

[2] *Periods in German Literature*, ed. J. M. Ritchie (London, 1968), p. 29.

The Catholic emphasis on form and ritual—vigorously re-asserted by the Council of Trent but implicitly rejected in virtually all Protestant teaching—expressed itself artistically above all in architecture and specifically in the design of church edifices. Painting and literature by and large conformed to the same standards of taste, but here the possible distinctions between Catholic and Protestant tend to blur. For obvious reasons, architecture offered only limited possibilities to the Protestant artist; painting, however, was a quite different matter, as we can see from the work of seventeenth-century Dutch artists. The Catholic Utrecht School (Dirck van Baburen, Gerard van Honthorst, Hendrik Terbrugghen, and others), most of whose members passed through Rome in the first two decades of the seventeenth century, developed strongly under the influence of Caravaggio and passed on Caravaggesque techniques to other artists in the Netherlands, Catholic and Protestant alike. Among the Dutch Protestant artists influenced by the School were Rembrandt, Jan Vermeer, and Jan Steen. The realism, naturalism, sense of drama, greater corporeality, and eschewal of idealization of Caravaggio became then something of an international style that freely crossed religious boundaries. As Dutch art progressed through the century, the preference of Protestant painters (Jan van Goyen, Salomon van Ruisdael, Willem Claesz Heda) for landscapes, still lifes, genre scenes, and full figure or portrait paintings notable for their introspective quality became marked. Yet the themes (e.g. the ephemerality of the terrestrial life) and techniques (e.g. dramatic lighting effects) of these painters remained essentially the same as those of their Catholic counter-parts, despite the differences in preferences for subject matter.

The central role of Scripture and the special relationship between Scripture and the individual in Protestant thought led to a very high regard for the word among the Protestants. Literature, consequently, was extensively cultivated and, like painting, varied from the general trend of Catholic Baroque writing far more in subject matter than thematically or stylistically. This is apparent, for example, in seventeenth-century homiletic writing. Doubtless a by-product of the religious turmoil of the age, the sermon attained the level of art in late sixteenth- and seventeenth-century literature, Catholic, Protestant, and Orthodox alike. Again allowing for essential theological incompatibilities, a stylistic comparison of sermons by the Protestant John Donne and his counterparts in Spain and the Catholic and Orthodox countries of Eastern Europe discloses far more similarities than differences. To speak then of a *Baroque* sermon style makes much greater sense than to attempt to divide seventeenth-century homiletic literature into a Catholic Baroque school and a Protestant one, substantially different from the Catholic, or to view the Ukrainian Orthodox homily as something unrelated.

The same can be said for mystic literature. At the mention of mystic writing the great Catholic mystics of sixteenth- and seventeenth-century Spain come to mind—St. Teresa de Jesús (1515–82), Fray Luis de León (1527–91), St. Juan de la Cruz (1542–91). Yet Protestantism made major contributions to Christian mysticism—suffice it to mention the German Jakob Böhme (1575–1624) and the Swede Emanuel Swedenborg (1688–1772). In Eastern Europe, the mystical writings of the Ukrainian Orthodox preacher and polemicist Ivan Vyshensky (mid-sixteenth century–c. 1630) represented the most interesting development in this sphere among the Slavs.

The greater conflict between Catholic and Protestant in the seventeenth century overshadows the internal conflicts within Catholicism and Protestantism themselves. The Jansenist sub-heresy—mainly in the French Church—divided Catholics on the matter of predestination, while Protestantism fell subject to still greater division and fragmentation over a number of issues (Lutherans, Zwinglians, Calvinists, Arminians, Anglicans, Puritans, Separatists, Socinians, Arians, Quakers). Within each persuasion there were divisive elements, so that the paramount struggle between the Counter-Reformation and the Protestants need not be considered the sole source of the tensions and antitheses reflected in the literature of the Baroque. The antagonisms within the religions, at times intermingled with political rivalries, themselves generated ample stimuli.

c) The progress of science and philosophical thought in the seventeenth century also intensified rather than allayed the great political and religious conflicts. The rejection of tradition and authority represented by the Protestant Reformation was echoed in the rejection of Aristotelianism and Scholasticism in contemporary science and philosophy. Beginning with Copernicus, scientists cast aside the ancient conception of a universe in which the sun revolved around a stationary earth in favor of a system in which the earth, as all the planets, revolves, in fact, around the sun. Aristotelian logic was the basis of the Scholasticism of the Catholic Church; when Aristotelian cosmology began to be rejected by scientists in the mid-sixteenth century, it appeared to the Church that the entire edifice of Aristotelian thought was threatened. To admit deviation in one area opened the possibility of deviation in another, with the entire system placed in jeopardy. So the Church reacted vigorously to all those who challenged the Aristotelian view of the cosmos.

The retreat of Aristotelian thought in philosophy was no less significant and brought the same reaction on the part of the defenders of traditional Scholasticism. Using the experimental techniques of mathematics and physics, philosophers (e.g. René Descartes) initiated their inquiries by rejecting preconceptions and attempting to achieve certainty through the systematic elimination of doubt. Thus it was that with Cartesianism modern metaphysics had its real beginnings. From the viewpoint of the Church of Rome the danger inherent in such philosophical thinking was not so much in the results obtained as in the encouragement given to the skeptical questioning of established authority. During a period when a dynamic campaign was undertaken upon the conclusion of the Council of Trent not only to hold the line against Protestantism but also to attempt to win back to the fold of the Church what had already been lost, the antiauthoritarianism manifest in the "new" science (which even went so far as to declare the existence of other solar and life systems) and a philosophy that divorced itself from theology only to wed the suspect science called into question from the very outset the success of the campaign. Combating Protestantism on the part of the Church often became inextricably bound up with the attempt to suppress the non-Aristotelian developments in science and philosophical thought. In all three theatres of operation, the efforts were only partially successful.

d) Out of the great contest joined in the late sixteenth and seventeenth centuries between the Catholic Counter-Reformation and the antiauthoritarianism of Protestantism, science and philosophy, emerged the heightened spirituality so characteristic of the Baroque Age. As Hans-Joachim Schoeps writes in *The Religions of Mankind*:

> The piety of post-Tridentine Catholicism was characterized by mystical and crudely superstitious overtones. Many new saints and relics were adopted. The confessional, the Mass and communion acquired intensified importance. Everlasting worship of the Host, frequent enjoyment of the sacrament, the cult of the Heart of Jesus and the Heart of Mary arose. Cultivation of this type of religiosity, with its fondness for the miraculous and its sensual, narcotic features, deepened the gulf between Catholicism and Protestantism.[3]

The Council of Trent reexamined all the traditional teachings of the Catholic Church in the light of the Protestant challenge, reasserted them, then went ahead through the agency of the Counter-Reformation to strengthen them where danger existed and to reimpose them where they had been uprooted.

The emergence of Protestantism, the gradual systematization of its theology in the later sixteenth and seventeenth centuries, and the expansion of its conflict with Catholicism created another source of spiritual concern no less important than the Counter-Reformation. There were, however, essential differences between the spirituality of Catholicism and that of Protestantism. The Catholic emphasis on ritual and faith was opposed by the Protestant appeal to individual conscience and morality. Moreover, the centrality of Scriptures in Protestant teaching was unparalleled in Catholicism, which placed a higher value on the rigorous adherence to traditional ritual and dogma.

Giving even greater relevance to the intensified concern with man's spiritual life flowing from both Catholic and Protestant sources were the great calamities of the age, above all the Thirty Years' War. The terrible loss of life, depopulation, and devastation caused by war and increased by plague aggravated the tensions and anxieties stemming from religious strife. This resulted in many cases in a tendency to reject life as little more than an apparently unending succession of disasters, and to regard worldly pleasures and accomplishments as only ephemeral. There were those whose view of man's condition on earth had become so jaundiced by events that terrestrial existence seemed no more than an empty

[3] Schoeps, *The Religions of Mankind* (Garden City, N.Y., 1966), p. 317.

and bitter illusion, a kind of dream from which the sooner they could awaken in the true life after death the better. These feelings of despair, frustration, alienation, and rejection of the material world accompanied by the belief that man's transitory life on earth was a vain illusion gave way to a concentration on the inner life. What really mattered was the eternal peace man would acquire after death, and until then life on earth was seen as best used in moral and spiritual perfection rather than in the pursuit of illusory pleasures. In the more extreme cases the result was mysticism, among both Catholics and Protestants. To troubled Catholics unwilling or incapable of bringing themselves to the degree of withdrawal from life implicit in mystic belief and practice, devotion to ritual and utter unquestioned acceptance of the power and efficacy of faith presented the most gratifying solutions. To aid them in overcoming their despair and restoring their belief in God's infinite wisdom and mercy, spiritual "handbooks" such as the *Introduction à la vie dévote* of St. François de Sales (1567–1622) and the *Güldenes Tugendbuch* of the German Jesuit Friedrich von Spee (1591–1635) began making their appearance. The Protestant, on the other hand, sought sustenance in Scripture, prayer, and the cultivation of personal morality. Among the more rigorous and ascetic Protestant sects, the rejection of material existence and its vanities resembled that of the mystics (Catholic and Protestant), but the belief that redemption and spiritual perfection could in part be achieved through "good works" represented a measure of involvement in life alien to mysticism. The closer Catholic parallel here would be the program of St. Louise de Marillac (1591–1660) and St. Vincent de Paul (1576–1660) in France.

e) To assume, in view of increased religiosity and spirituality, that rejection of a world perceived as a cruel illusion in favor of withdrawal into the inner life of the spirit was the universal condition of the Baroque age would be grievously erroneous. Besides an obviously heightened concern with man's spiritual condition, Baroque art reflects also—and very distinctly—a feeling for and attachment to life that can best be described as sensuous. We see this not only in the subjects artists treat, whatever the medium, but also in the rich color and texture and in the more insistent presence of the physical. It is the greater corporeality of Baroque art that explains the link often made between the treatment of the body, and mass in general, in the High Renaissance and in the Baroque. Thus, the familiar association of a Raphael, on the one hand, and a Caravaggio, Rubens, and Rembrandt on the other. But this can be somewhat misleading.

Beginning in the late sixteenth century, the anti-Mannerists in the visual arts turned away from the asymmetrical lines and disproportionate shapes of mannerism and attempted to restore the balance and harmony of the Renaissance. In painting and sculpture the figure again became full, robust, "despiritualized" (in contrast to El Greco, for example), and emphatically earthly. But in the transition from late mannerism to the Baroque, elements appeared that had been little remarked previously in the Renaissance: a greater realism and use of naturalistic detail, richer color, more dramatic interplay of light and dark. The texture, so to speak, of Baroque art became more opulent than that of the Renaissance. Thus, Baroque art relates to Renaissance and Mannerist techniques only partially. It is essential to know what it derives from them, but in discovering the similarities the divergences should not be overlooked.

The sources of this Baroque sensuousness and the seeming paradox of such sensuousness in an age of spirituality are not always easy to pinpoint, but certain likelihoods must be considered. The first is very understandable in human terms. The greater the threat to life, the greater the presence of disaster, the more passionate the attachment to life and to the pleasures and things of this world. In an age so troubled and wearied by the strife of religious and political conflict as the Baroque, an age visited on several occasions by the dread of plague and witness to decline and the seemingly fickle workings of fate, it is hardly to be wondered that the desire simply to live and to continue to enjoy earthly pleasures was as great among many as the anguished rejection of the world and withdrawal into a life of piety and meditation was among others for whom only the eternity beyond death was meaningful. Not only the sensuous but also, and perhaps especially, the *sensual* aspect of much Baroque art reflects this attitude. To view the realism and naturalism of Baroque painting, for example, in this light seems entirely valid.

A second major source of Baroque sensuousness doubtless must have been the Catholic Counter-Reformation itself. One direct consequence of the Council of Trent was the very great emphasis placed by the Church on the *visual* aspects of worship. This campaign (and it was that) to present an image of power, majesty, and opulence, to excite awe through mystery and drama and the appeal to the senses of the faithful and strayed alike is aptly summed up by Hans-Joachim Schoeps:

> Everywhere, and especially in South Germany, new pilgrimage churches were founded. Ritual became pompous and was elaborated in many ways. Many of the elements of religion that the Enlightenment later mocked as foolish became popular at this time, such as the practice of displaying effigies of healed limbs in churches. The use of the confessional was greatly increased—all emphasis was placed now on the outward forms of religion.[4]

The reaffirmation of the sacraments, above all the transubstantiation of Communion, was another contributing factor. In the face of increasing Protestant reinterpretation and deviation, the Church firmly upheld the dogma of the Incarnation, that is the full humanness of Christ first asserted at the Third General Council of Ephesus in 431, and then reasserted its traditional teaching that in the sacrament of Communion believers actually partake of the body of Christ. The bread and wine are transformed, transubstantiated, into the flesh and blood of Christ, thus causing the participants in Communion to participate in the divine being of Christ and to experience, or reenact, the death and the resurrection. By promoting the visual and auditory aspects of worship and then vigorously condemning metaphoric or symbolic interpretations of transubstantiation, the Church revitalized the concept of the complete indivisibility of flesh and spirit. The impact on contemporary Catholic thought and art was considerable. Instead of repudiating the flesh, the Church, by its decrees and actions, demonstrated how an accommodation of the flesh and the spirit was possible. The difficulties involved in reconciling the dualism of man's nature, mirrored quite clearly in Mannerist art, were thus overcome making possible the reintegration or unity characteristic of the Baroque.

f) The Baroque is often characterized as an age of antithesis, paradox, and incongruity. The aptness of the characterization can

[4] *Ibid.*, pp. 317–318.

be realized by considering the struggle between Catholicism and Protestantism and within each religious system itself; the momentous conflict between Christian Europe and the Moslem East represented by the Ottoman Empire; the decline of the once great empire of Spain, which for many in Europe at the time assumed almost the value of a symbol of the illusory, ephemeral nature of man's life on earth and the inconstancy of fate; the intense spirituality in a time of sensuousness and the inclination to reject the world paralleled by a passionate attachment to it; the terrible devastation in the midst of considerable scientific progress, and so on. The perception of these apparent irreconcilables gave rise to the antithesis, paradox, and incongruity so frequently encountered in Baroque art and would seem to deny the possibility of reintegration or unity. But the "tension" generated by the coupling of seemingly irreconcilable or remotely related concepts differs in a very essential way from the tensions in Mannerist art. In the latter, the tension results not from the perception of and *attempt* to reconcile the extremes, but from a sense of dissolution, of fragmentation. The Baroque artist worked instead toward unity, toward reintegration; aware of antitheses and paradoxes and incongruities in the world about him, he sought their reconciliation in the same manner that flesh and spirit were reconciled and viewed as essentially indivisible not only in Catholic thought but in much Protestant teaching as well. Baroque painting illustrates this very well, particularly in canvases depicting religious scenes. Instead of the ascetic upward-surging figures and clear division between temporal and spiritual realms of an El Greco, we see instead—in Rubens or Rembrandt, for example—amply proportioned, distinctly earthbound figures in close, even intimate contact with supernatural ones who are similarly proportioned and somehow secularized in terms of corporeality and proximity to earth and earthlings. Wylie Sypher is quite right, following Walter Friedlaender, when he says:

> No phrase (Friedlaender's "secularizing of the transcendental," die Verweltlichen des Transzendenten) could better describe what was happening in baroque art and piety, which often transfused the spirit with the flesh instead of transfusing the flesh with the spirit. Presently the transcendent was to be secularized by accepting the material image, the physical sensation, as sufficient. Then both

religion and art can really terminate in the senses, and thought does really become a physical experience.[5]

Far from detracting from unity, as in mannerism, space and line, variety and novelty in Baroque art are all managed in such a way as to convey a unified vision. The structural massiveness and ornamentation of the Baroque church, for example, realize in architecture the aggressive reaffirmation of dogma of the Council of Trent. Mass and ornament combine to suggest strength, solidity, majesty, opulence, and to evoke a sense of awe. All individual segments, instead of detracting from unity and living autonomously, work together toward a single goal. Compare, for example, the typically Mannerist Gesú Church in Rome (c. 1569 ff.) with such representative Baroque edifices as the Sant' Agnese in Agone (1653 ff.), the Sant' Andrea della Valle (1591 ff.), and especially St. Peter's (completed 1612), all in Rome.

[5] Sypher, *op. cit.*

IV

General Remarks on Baroque Literature

Approaching now the literature of the Baroque, and poetry in particular, certain major topics have to be considered: (1) the general literary trends as they reflect the age itself; types of poetry and national tendencies and (2) the "technical baggage" of Baroque writers, that is to say Baroque poetic theory and style.

1. LITERATURE AS AN EXPRESSION OF AN AGE

The political and religious conflicts of the Baroque age knew no respect for national boundaries. The existence of European empires—the Holy Roman and Spanish—and multinational states on the order of the Venetian Republic and the Polish Commonwealth assured that few significant events could be localized. When an Augustinian monk named Martin Luther posted his now famous ninety-five theses on the portal of the palace church in Wittenberg on October 31, 1517, he committed a personal act of revolt that changed the political and ecclesiastical structure of Europe to our own time. The Counter-Reformation, which sought to extinguish the great Protestant heresy, fought the blaze wherever the Church of Rome lost ground throughout Europe. A society of militant priests known as Jesuits established in 1540 by the Spanish monk Ignatius of Loyola ranged throughout Europe bearing the torch of the Counter-Reformation, polemicizing with the Protestants, founding schools and academies, counseling princes and kings. The naval defeat administered to a superior Turkish force by a combined Spanish-Venetian fleet at Lepanto in 1571 reverberated joyously throughout a Christendom long in dread of the encroachments of the infidel Turk. And the great siege of Vienna in 1683 saw the deepest thrust of Ottoman power into the heart of Europe broken by a Christian army that included a large Polish contingent headed by King Jan III Sobieski. The election of the Protestant Frederick of the Palatinate to the throne of Bohemia, followed by the Hapsburg-instigated repression of Protestant churches in the country, led to the most devastating conflict Europe had known in centuries—the Thirty Years' War—a conflict that raged throughout much of Europe and involved a number of states.

Abstracting the dominant themes of Baroque literature, *conflict* expectedly appears as one of the most prominent. The political and military upheavals of the age provided topics for a vast number of works and, to be sure, the countries visited by the most bitter strife are the richest in such writing. In this respect, German literature is especially noteworthy. The domestic turmoil and devastation endured by the German states in the seventeenth century, notably in the period of the Thirty Years' War, were virtually unparalleled elsewhere in Europe. Their impact on the seventeenth-century German consciousness found clear reflection in the poetry of the first major German Baroque poet, Martin Opitz (1597–1639), above all in his elegiac epic *Trost Gedichte in Widerwertigkeit des Krieges* (1633), in the lyrics of perhaps the greatest writer of the German Baroque, Andreas Gryphius (Greif, 1616–64), in the poetry and drama of Johann Rist (1607–67; e.g. *Irenaromachia*, 1630; *Das Friedewünschende Deutschland*, 1647; *Das Friedejauchtzende Deutschland*, 1653), in a number of patriotic poems by the lyricist Paul Fleming (1609–40) and, somewhat more obliquely, in that great novel of seventeenth-century Germany *Der abenteuerliche Simplicissimus* (1668) by Hans Jakob Christoffel von Grimmelshausen (1621?–76).

What foreign wars and internal upheaval meant for Baroque Poland can be judged by the extent to which the military epic was cultivated. This was perhaps the most significant development in seventeenth-century Polish literature. To be sure, considerable impetus to the cultivation of the epic genre was given by the publication in 1618 of an excellent rhymed verse translation of Tasso's *Gerusalemme liberata* by Piotr Kochanowski (1566–1620), a nephew of the outstanding sixteenth-century Polish poet Jan Kochanowski (1530–80). But the great popularity of the Polish version of Tasso's epic was not due entirely to the qualities of the

Kochanowski translation. Tasso's epic account of conflict between Christian and Moslem had more than a literary interest for contemporary Poles. The Moslem in the form of the Ottoman Turk was a very real and very close enemy to late sixteenth- and seventeenth-century Poland. When Kochanowski's translation of the *Gerusalemme* appeared in 1618, the relevance of the poem for contemporary Polish conditions made it an immediate success and probably the most widely read and imitated foreign literary work in seventeenth-century Poland.

The titles of the Baroque Polish epics are sufficient introduction to the scope of Poland's seventeenth-century political and military involvements. The prolific writer Samuel ze Skrzypny Twardowski (between 1595 and 1600/61) produced three epic poems: *Przważna legacja ... od ... Zygmunta III ... do ... cesarza tureckiego Mustafy w roku 1621* ("The Urgent Mission ... from ... King Sigismund III ... to ... the Turkish Emperor Mustafa in the Year 1621," 1633); *Władysław IV król polski i szwedzki* ("Vladislav IV, King of Poland and Sweden," 1649); *Wojna domowa z Kozaki i Tatary, z Moskwą, potem Szwedami i z Węgry* ("The Civil War with the Cossacks and Tartars, with Muscovy, and later with the Swedes and the Hungarians," 1681). The Polish victories over the Turks in the two battles of Chocim in the Ukraine in 1621 and 1673 were celebrated in the poetry of two important Polish Baroque writers, both Protestants of the Arian sect: Wacław Potocki (1621–96), in his lengthy epic *Wojna chocimska* ("The Chocim War," 1670, first published in 1850), which celebrates the first battle of Chocim, and Zbigniew Morsztyn (c. 1628–c. 1689), in his poem *Sławna victoria nad Turkami ... pod Chocimiem otrzymana ... roku 1673* ("The Famous Victory over the Turks ... at Chocim ... in the Year 1673"). How far-reaching were the ramifications of the Polish victories at Chocim among the Slavs can be seen from the South Slavic literary works commemorating the events. The first battle of Chocim in 1621 served as the subject matter for the drama *Osmanšćica* (1631) by the Croatian Jesuit Ivan Tomko Mrnavić (1580–1637?). But of far greater significance was the important (unfinished) epic *Osman* (1622–38) by the foremost seventeenth-century Croatian poet, Ivan Gundulić (1588–1638). Another still greater victory over the Turks, at Vienna in 1683, in which the Poles played a notable role, was made the subject of a lengthy poem, *Dzieło boskie albo*

Pieśni Wiednia wybawionego ("God's Work or Songs of Vienna Saved," 1684) by the leading Catholic religious writer of seventeenth-century Poland, Wespazjan Kochowski (1633–1700). Echoes of this event also reverberated in South Slavic literature: the late Baroque Croatian poet Petar Kanavelić (1673–1719) focused especially on the Polish contribution to the victory in his long poem *Ivanu Sobieski, kralju poljačkom Osloboditelju Beča* ("To John Sobieski, King of Poland, Liberator of Vienna"; written probably not long after the lifting of the siege but first printed only in 1745).[1]

The sixteenth- and seventeenth-century battles between Magyar and Turk also produced a great Hungarian epic, the *Szigetvár ostroma* ("The Siege of Sziget," 1651), by Hungary's major Baroque poet, Miklós Zrínyi (1620–64). Influenced above all by Tasso and Marino, in addition to the Homeric epic, Zrínyi's 6,272-line work bears roughly the same relation to the historical episode celebrated as Potocki's "Chocim War." Szigetvár, in southwest Hungary, underwent two devastating Turkish assaults, the first in 1556, led by Ali, the *pasha* of Buda, and the second in 1566, led by Suleiman the Magnificent. Zrínyi, the grandson and namesake of the heroic defender of Szigetvár in the second siege, and himself a prominent figure in the campaigns to oust the Turks from Hungarian lands, worked on his epic between 1645 and 1646. This was nearly eighty years after the event (compared to fifty in the case of Potocki) and at a time when the Turkish enemy was no more than 25 miles away.

Although military conflict, above all against the Turks, produced an outpouring of epic writing among the Hungarians and Slavs (the Poles and the South Slavs) whose contact with the Ottomans was the greatest in the late sixteenth and seventeenth centuries, religious conflict lay at the roots of the French epic of the Baroque age. The awful religious wars of late sixteenth-century France, culminating in the St. Bartholomew's Day massacre (1572), overshadowed any of the religiopolitical conflicts France experienced in the first half of the seventeenth century. Although the *results* of conflict are widely mirrored in French Baroque literature, the great religious wars found their most definitive literary expression in one of the earliest manifestations

[1] See Tadeusz Z. Gasiński, "A Croatian Poetic Echo of King John III Sobieski's Victory at Vienna," *The Polish Review*, XV, 1 (1970), 46–53.

of Baroque writing in France, the epic poem *Les Tragiques*
(1577–94, first published in 1616) by the militant Calvinist poet
Agrippa d'Aubigné (1551–1630).[2]

With the exception of the "official" and political poetry of
François de Malherbe (1555–1628) in France and of the Englishman Andrew Marvell (1618–78, the Cromwell poems and *The
Character of Holland* reflecting the Dutch-English War of 1652–
57), the literary reaction among the majority of French, English,
Dutch, Spanish, Portuguese, and Italian writers to the religious
and political upheavals of the late sixteenth and seventeenth
centuries expressed itself less in the *direct* mirroring of political
and military strife than in a religiosity and metaphysical anxiety
closely related to these upheavals.

This religiosity and what I term metaphysical anxiety—the
outcome, in large measure, of the warring, natural disasters, and
religious strife of the second half of the sixteenth and the seventeenth centuries—produced a truly immense body of writing
throughout Europe, qualitatively more significant than the
literature treating of the conflicts themselves. Like conflict,
religiosity must also be considered a major Baroque literary
current.

This Baroque religious literature in itself comprises several
distinct trends. Before considering these, it would be well to bear
certain facts in mind: one, that the two major religious camps, the
Catholic and the Protestant, or three if we include the Eastern
Orthodox, which saw itself in conflict with Roman Catholicism
in the Ukraine especially in the seventeenth century, produced an
impressive body of religious writing; and two, that within the
framework of the Baroque no substantial stylistic differences exist
irrespective of language. Furthermore, although the religious
poetry of the sixteenth and seventeenth centuries is better known
and has attracted more attention than the prose, there was a great
deal of religious prose written during the period. The most widely
cultivated genre of Baroque religious prose was the sermon, the
homily which, as I mentioned earlier, was raised to the level of an
important form of literary art. In an English-speaking context,
the name of John Donne immediately comes to mind as a master-

---

[2] The subject of a study by Imbrie Buffum, *Agrippa d'Aubigné's Les
Tragiques. A Study of the Baroque Style in Poetry* (New Haven, 1951). On
the Baroque epic in general, see Warnke, *Versions of Baroque*, pp. 158–186.

ful writer of sermons in the Baroque age. But to Donne's name should be added, among others, those of the Polish Jesuit, Piotr Skarga (1536–1612), the Ukrainian Orthodox preachers Kyryl Stavrovetsky (d. c. 1646), Ioniki Galyatovsky (d. 1688), Antoni Radyvylovsky (?–1688), Saint Dimitri Tuptalo of Rostov (1651–1709), Stefan Yavorsky (1655–1722), and Feofan Prokopovich (1681–1736)—the last two were active in Russian ecclesiastical and cultural life in the time of Peter the Great—and especially the Bishop of the Czech Moravian Brethren, Jan Amos Komenský (Comenius, 1592–1670).

One reason, of course, for the prominence of the sermon and religious literature generally in the age of the Baroque was the fact that many of the leading literary figures were churchmen or the sons of churchmen. Donne in England, for example, was the Anglican Dean of St. Paul's in London. Richard Crashaw (1612–49), an outstanding Baroque poet, was the son of a Puritan divine and himself apparently took Orders with some official responsibility at Little St. Mary's. (About 1645, he became a Catholic. In 1649, the year of his death, he was given a post at the Cathedral of the Holy House at Loreto, Italy.) Henry King (1592–1669) was Bishop of Chichester. William Cartwright (1611–43) took Holy Orders around 1638. John Cleveland (1613–58) was the son of the Vicar of Hinckley, Leicestershire. George Herbert (1593–1633) was ordained a deacon some time in 1626. Andrew Marvell was the son of a clergyman of Calvinist leanings. Robert Southwell (1561–95) was a Jesuit priest. Jeremy Taylor (1613–67) was the Bishop of Down and Connon. Thomas Traherne (1637–74) was an ordained minister. Prominent Polish and Ukrainian literary figures who were churchmen have already been mentioned, as was the Czech Protestant Komenský (Comenius). Two other prominent Czech Baroque writers, both Jesuits, merit inclusion here: the poet Bedřich Bridel (1619–80) and Bohuslav Balbín (1621–88), a scholar who wrote primarily in Latin. Among German Baroque authors, Jakob Bidermann (1578–1639), Abraham a Sancta Clara (Hans Ulrich Megerle, 1644–1709), Nicolaus Avancini (1612–86), and Friedrich von Spee (1591–1635) were all ordained Jesuit priests; the well-known seventeenth-century mystic Angelus Silesius (Johann Scheffler, 1624–77) converted to Catholicism in 1653 and eight years later took Holy Orders. On the other hand, Andreas Heinrich Buchholtz

(1607–71), Paul Gerhardt (1607–76), Johann Klaj (1616–56), Johann Rist (1607–67), and Johann Balthasar Schupp (1610–61) were Protestant (Lutheran) clergymen. Siegmund von Birken (1626–81), Daniel von Czepko (1605–60), Paul Fleming (1609–40), Philipp Nikodemus Frischlin (1547–90), Eberhard Werner Happel (1647–90), Magnus Daniel Omeis (1646–1708), David Schirmer (1623?–1685?), Justus Georgius Schottel (1612–76), and Philipp Zesen (1619–89) were the sons of Lutheran pastors. Two poets of some significance in seventeenth-century Dutch devotional literature were clerics: Johannes Stalpaert van der Wielen (1579–1630), a Catholic priest and rector of the convent of St. Agatha at Delft and Jacobus Revius (1586–1651), a minister of the Dutch Reformed Church and the author of a number of highly regarded religious and patriotic poems.

The number of clerics prominently active in literature in the Romance countries during this period is proportionately somewhat smaller. The best known are the Spanish mystics of the second half of the sixteenth century: St. Teresa de Jesús (1515–82), Fray Luis de León (1529–91), and St. Juan de la Cruz (1542–91). To these names might be added those also of the prose writer Baltasar Gracián (1601–55), the Mexican poets Miguel de Guevara (1585–1646) and Sor Juana Inés de la Cruz (1651–95), and such lesser figures in the history of the Baroque as José de Valdivielso (1560–1638), Francisco de Medrano (1570?–1607?), Fray Gabriel Téllez Tirso de Molina (1571?–1648), and Fray Jeronimo de San José (1587–1684). The French and Italian are still fewer: Jacques Davy (Cardinal du Perron, 1555–1618), a relatively minor writer; Pierre Le Moyne (1602–72), a Jesuit; Martial de Brives (?–before 1655), a Capuchin friar; and perhaps also, because he was long a Protestant theologian before his conversion to the Roman Catholic faith, the excellent poet Jean de Sponde (1557–95); Cardinal Guido Bentivoglio (1579–1644), a historian of the struggle of the Netherlands against Spain from 1559 to 1607; and the Marinists Maffeo Barberini (1568–1644), who became Pope Urban VIII in 1623 and Francesco Balducci (1579–1642), who took Holy Orders late in life.

Turning now to the European religious poetry of the sixteenth and seventeenth centuries, the major trend, perhaps better known than others, is the mystic. In this area, without a doubt, the most impressive achievements came in Spain and Germany. Although, strictly speaking, the great Spanish mystics of the second half of the sixteenth century are not Baroque writers in terms of style, they were the fount of later Spanish religiomystical writing and were highly regarded and influential in the seventeenth century. Moreover, they reflect, as religious writers were to do elsewhere in Europe in the late sixteenth and seventeenth centuries, the fervor of post-Tridentine Catholicism. Yet in the intensity and passion of their faith they were as uniquely Spanish as the founder of the Society of Jesus, Loyola. In mentioning the influence of the Spanish mystics, I have in mind not only their relevance for later Spanish literature (e.g. Francisco de Quevedo y Villegas [1580–1645], who first published Fray Luis de León's poems in 1631, Sor Juana Inés de la Cruz, Miguel de Molinos, whose *Guía espiritual*, published in Rome in 1675, had an immense influence on the development of French quietism, the great Spanish Baroque dramatist Pedro Calderón de la Barca [1600–81], and in the late eighteenth century, Fray Diego González [1732–94]), but their influence *outside* of Spain, above all on Richard Crashaw in England. Among Crashaw's poems there is a "Hymn to Sainte Teresa"—referring to St. Teresa de Jésus—one of his finest poetic works, which was included in the collection *Steps to the Temple* (1648). Although a Protestant, the German writer Georg Philipp Harsdörffer (1607–58) was sufficiently interested in Spanish devotional literature to translate works by St. Teresa.

Within the world of sixteenth- and seventeenth-century Protestantism, the only literary development at all comparable to that of the great Catholic mystics of Spain was the Silesian mystic school that grouped around the Görlitz cobbler Jakob Böhme (1575–1624). On the basis of his *Aurora oder Morgenröte im Aufgang* (written 1612, but prohibited from publication until 1618), an exposition of his own theosophical system, Böhme gained adherents to his views among a number of writers in Silesia in the first half of the seventeenth century. These included Abraham von Franckenberg (1593–1652), whose most important contribution was the dissemination of Böhme's ideas; he published Böhme in Holland and in 1651 wrote a biography of the mystic under the title *Gründlicher und wahrer Bericht von dem Leben und Abschied des in Gott seelig ruhenden Jakob Böhme*; Daniel von Reigersfeld Czepko (usually referred to just as Daniel von

Czepko), whose major work was *Sexcenta Monodisticha Sapien-tum* (1647); and Angelus Silesius, a Lutheran who later joined the Catholic Church and was the author of an impressive collection of religiomystic poetry, *Der Cherubinische Wandersmann* (first published 1656). In a later work, *Heilige Seelenlust* (1675), he moved formally and imagistically closer to Catholic mysticism in contrast to the more obvious Protestant inclinations of the *Wandersmann*.

Although influential above all in Germany, Böhme also had admirers and followers elsewhere. Doubtless the most important from a literary viewpoint was the Dutch Anabaptist and mystic Jan Luyken (1649–1712) of Amsterdam. An etcher and engraver by training, Luyken wrote mainly amatory poetry (first published in 1671 in the collection *Duytse Lier*) before he fell under the sway of Böhme's thought. After the death of his wife, he left bustling Amsterdam for the small Zuyder Zee village of Hoorn, where he devoted himself entirely to a life of contemplation. The collection *Jesus en de Ziel* (1678) contains some of his best religious and mystic poetry.

Nonmystic Baroque religious poetry falls into three main groupings: religious or devotional poems, embodying personal expressions of faith; hymns, intended primarily for congregational use; and poems on biblical subjects including verse paraphrases of the Psalms.

Of the three, the first, the religious or devotional lyric, was by far the most common among both Catholic and Protestant writers. In England, its practitioners included William Alabaster (1567–1640), the author of a number of religious sonnets written about the time of his conversion to Catholicism around 1596 or 1597 (he later reconverted to Protestantism) and published only posthumously; Richard Crashaw (major collection: *Steps to the Temple*, published in two editions, the first in 1646, and the second, revised, in 1648); John Donne (main collections of religious lyrics: *The Litany*, 1609, and *Divine Poems* and *Holy Sonnets*, the greater part of which was written when he was Dean of St. Paul's from 1621 to 1631); Giles Fletcher the Younger (c. 1588–1623), whose most important poem, "Christ's Victorie and Triumph," was published in 1610; George Herbert (1593–1633), an exclusively religious poet; Henry King, whose poems were published anonymously in 1657, without his consent, re-published, again anonymously, in 1664, and a third time in 1700 with a title page ascribing them to Ben Jonson; Andrew Marvell ("A Dialogue between the Soul and Body," "A Dialogue between the Resolved Soul and Created Pleasure"); John Milton (1608–74), particularly in view of his ode "On the Morning of Christ's Nativity" (1629), though the work exceeds the bounds of the lyric; Francis Quarles (1592–1644), known above all for his book of *Emblemes*, first published in 1635 and immensely popular throughout the century; and Henry Vaughan (1621/2–95), the author of two volumes of religious poetry published in 1650 and 1655 under the title *Silex Scintillians*.

Among the German Baroque religious poets were: Paul Fleming, a Lutheran, considered by some the best German lyric poet of the seventeenth-century, the author of a number of religious poems in German and Latin; Andreas Gryphius, a Lutheran, the finest German dramatist of the Baroque age; Johann Klaj, a Lutheran, the bulk of whose often highly interest-ing religious poetry is contained in the collections *Weynacht-Liedt* (1644), *Auferstehung Jesu Christi* (1644), *Höllen und Himmel-fahrt Jesu Christi* (1644), and *Der leidende Christus* (1645); Siegmund von Birken, a Lutheran whose religious verse, culti-vated later in his career, appears in *Todesgedanken und Todten-Andenken* (1670) and the illustrative text on poetics, *Teutsche Rede-bind und Dicht-Kunst . . . mit geistlichen Exempeln* (1679); Justus Georgius Schottel, a Lutheran, also an important writer on the German language and metrics with his *Teutsche Sprach-kunst* (1641), *Teutsche Vers- oder Reim-Kunst* (1645), and the *Ausführliche Arbeit von der Teutschen Haubt Sprache* (1663); Angelus Silesius, whose first book of poetry (dating probably from the early 1650s) included translations of Catholic mystics and earned him the hostility of Lutheran orthodoxy; Friedrich von Spee, a Jesuit, whose major collection of religious poems was the *Trutz Nachtigall, oder Geistlichs-Poetisch Lust-Wäldlein* (1649); Christian Weise (1642–1708), a Lutheran and headmaster of the Zittau Gymnasium for which he wrote a number of plays, two of which, *Der niederländische Bauer* and *Die böse Catharina*, are derived from Shakespeare's *Taming of the Shrew*; Philipp Zesen, a Lutheran, extremely productive in verse and prose, a translator of Komenský, and the author *inter alia* of a popular book of devotions for women; and Quirinus Kuhlmann (1651–89), a would-be prophet eventually burned to death in Moscow where his unorthodox religious views brought him into conflict with the German Protestant churchmen in the city's so called Foreign Suburb (*nemetskaya sloboda*); the author of two very interesting collections of religious verse, *Himmlische Libes-Küsse* (1671) and *Der Kühl-Psalter* published in three volumes from 1684 to 1686.

Apart from the religious verse of such clerics as Johannes Stalpaert van der Wielen and Jacobus Revius, and the mystical writings of Luyken, the devotional literature of the Dutch Baroque was also enriched by the poetry of several other luminaries of late sixteenth- and seventeenth-century Dutch letters: Daniel Heinsius (1580–1655), a classical scholar at Leyden (Leiden) University, writer in Latin and Dutch, and the author of the epic-lyrical *Lof-sanck van Jesus Christus, den eenigen ende eeuwigen sone godes* (1616); Gerbrant Adriaenszoon Bredero (1585–1618), a painter and poet of amatory verse and a cycle of twelve religious sonnets; Dirck Rafaelszoon Camphuysen (1586–1627), whose mystically oriented religious verse appears in the two-part volume *Stichtelycke Rymen* (1624), a work so popular that it went through fifty editions by 1750; Joost van den Vondel (1587–1679), a convert to Catholicism and the greatest Dutch Baroque dramatist; Constantijn Huygens (1596–1687), the father of the distinguished scientist Christian Huygens and a cultured polyglot who knew the English poet Donne; and Heiman Dullaert (1636–84), a student of Rembrandt and an able poet whose works were published for the first time posthumously in 1714. Dullaert's "discovery," however, had to wait until the later nineteenth century and the work of the Dutch poet Albert Verwey.

The Classicist hostility toward and rejection of the literature of the post-Renaissance pre-Classicist period we refer to as Baroque was so complete that it succeeded in condemning to near oblivion for a few centuries several fine French poets "discovered" only in the twentieth century. The most outstanding was the Catholic religious poet Jean de La Ceppède (c. 1550–1622), the author of the two-part *Théorèmes spirituels* (1613–21) containing some five hundred religious sonnets. Another was Jean-Baptiste Chassignet (c. 1570–c. 1635) whose major collection, *Mépris de la vie et consolation contre la mort* (1594), comprises four hundred and thirty-four sonnets on the theme of human mortality. The Protestant theologian and scholar who later converted to Catholicism, Jean de Sponde (1557–95), was another; his religious verse appears in the *Essai de quelques poèmes chrétiens* (1588). Other French religious poets of the late sixteenth and seventeenth centuries were: Du Bois Hus (dates unknown), whose major poem "La Nuit des nuits et le Jour des jours, ou la Naissance des deux Dauphins du Ciel et de la Terre" was printed in 1640; the Capuchin Martial de Brives, whose *Oeuvres poétiques et saints* appeared in 1655; Jean Ogier de Gombaud (1570?–1666); Antoine Godeau (1605–72); Georges de Brebeuf (1618–61); and Laurent Drelincourt (1628–81), the author of a cycle of *Sonnets Chrétiens*.

The writings of the sixteenth-century Spanish mystics appear to be the characteristic manifestations of Iberian spiritual ecstasy. But their accomplishments should not cause us to forget that many fine religious poems were written by some of the greatest talents of Spanish Baroque literature: Luis de Góngora y Argote (1561–1627), the most illustrious name in seventeenth-century Spanish poetry; Lope de Vega Carpio (1562–1635), whose plays too often obscure the fact that their author wrote a number of moving religious sonnets; Pedro Calderón de la Barca, the renowned dramatist; and the Mexican Sor Juana Inés de la Cruz. Apart from these major figures, several minor writers contributed to the development of the Spanish Baroque religious lyric, among them the priest José de Valdivielso (e.g. "Letra de Navidad, descubierto el Santísimo Sacramento"), Bartolomé Leonardo de Argensola (1561–1631), the posthumously published Francisco de Medrano, and Pedro Espinosa (1578–1650), known primarily for his Gongoresque river poem *Fábula del Genil* and an anthology he prepared of the poetry of his own time.

Compared to other literatures in the Baroque age, the Italian offers little of exceptional interest in the area of devotional writing. Towering over the poetry of the Seicento like a giant is the figure, of course, of Giambattista Marino (1569–1625), whose style set a fashion in Italian poetry and indeed extended far beyond Italy. Known above all as an amatory poet on the basis of his *L'Adone* ("Adonis"; Paris, 1623), Marino also wrote many religious poems. In his Roman period, 1610 to 1615, for the sister, a nun, of his Roman patron Monsignor Melchiorre Crescenzio, a papal chamberlain, he wrote two *canzoni*, one on the *Stabat mater* theme, which was later set to music, the other on *La pietà.* The third part of his collection *La lira* (1614), dedicated to Cardinal Doria, Archibishop of Palermo, contains a variety of poems including a number of pious lyrics grouped under the heading *Divotioni.* His genuine interest in devotional literature is evident not only in these poems but also in the prose work *Dicerie sacre,* which also came out in 1614, and in his polemical response, *La sferza, invettiva a quettro ministri della iniquità* (published first in 1625), to an anti-Catholic letter to the French king by a group of Huguenots. Marino's major contribution to Italian religious poetry rests, however, on his posthumously published and very popular *La strage degli innocenti* ("The Massacre of the Innocents"), begun as early as 1605, but brought to print for the first time only in 1632. This widely translated work (English, Latin, German, Dutch, French, Serbo-Croatian, Russian) has as its subject one of the most popular themes of post-Tridentine art (e.g. Guido Reni's painting, *The Massacre of the Innocents,* c. 1611).[3] Marino's many imitators in seventeenth-century Italy (Artale, Della' Valle, Dotti, Gaudiosi, Meninni, Preti, and Sempronio) generally followed the secular, amatory path of their master. Yet they also essayed the religious poem, concentrating in the main on two themes particularly favored by Marino: the Magdalen and Christ crucified.

Besides Marino and his imitators the only other notable Italian writer of religious poetry in the Baroque age was the much harassed author of the famous utopian work *Città del Sole* (1643, *The City of the Sun*), the friar Tommaso Campanella (1568–1639). Essentially a philosophical writer, Campanella wrote a number of religious sonnets ("Gli uomini son giuoco di Dio e degli Angeli," "Dalla' Orazioni tre in salmodia metafisicale congiunte insieme") and madrigals ("Della' Lamentevole orazione profetale dal profondo della fossa dove stava incarcerato," "Dispregio della Morte," "Canzone a Berillo di pentimento desideroso di confessione ecc. fatta nel Caucaso").

Devotional poetry was extensively cultivated among the Slavs during the Baroque age. In the case of late sixteenth- and seventeenth-century Bohemia, the religiopolitical conflict that culminated in the Battle of White Mountain in 1620 created a climate of

---

[3] See James V. Mirollo, *The Poet of the Marvelous* (New York, 1963), p. 95.

anguish and frustration that expressed itself best in religious, moralistic, and didactic writing. The literature of the period is dominated by clerics; the Protestant Komenský (Comenius), an author in Latin and Czech, whose major work was the didactic novella *Labyrint světa i ráj srdce* ("Labyrinth of the World and Paradise of the Heart"), a deprecation of man's material existence; the Jesuit Bedřich Bridel, the author of a number of devotional works including the popular hymn "Co Bůh? Člověk?" ("What Is God? What Is Man?") and *Rozjímání o nebě . . .* ("Thoughts on Heaven"), in which the world is presented as a book written by God, and the Jesuit Bohuslav Balbín, who wrote exclusively in Latin. Lay writers who contributed to the devotional literature were Jiři Třanavský (1591–1637), a Lutheran who settled in Slovakia after White Mountain and the author principally of *Cithara sanctorum, Písně duchovní staré i nové* (1636), a collection of ecclesiastical songs including a number of his own still used among Slovak Protestants, and the Catholic Adam Michna of Otradovice (c. 1600–62), a composer who set much of his own religious lyric poetry to music.

The great Croatian epic poet Ivan Gundulić also distinguished himself in the genre of spiritual poetry; two very well-known poems are the elegiac "Suze sina razmetnoga" ("Tears of the Prodigal Son," 1620) and "Od veličanstva božijeh" ("Ode to the Glory of God," published in Rome in 1621). Three other important poets of the Croatian Baroque who wrote religious works were Dživo Bunič-Vučić (Ivan Bunič-Vučićević, 1594–1658), the author of the lengthy poem *Mandaljena pokornica* ("Magdalen Repentant," 1630); Junije Palmotić (1608–57), one of the best dramatists of the period, whose attempt at a Christian epic, the twenty-four-canto *Christiade* (or *Kristiada*) *to jest život i djela Isukrstova* ("The Christiad, Being the Life and Deeds of Jesus Christ," 1670), was a kind of Baroque reworking of the *Christias* by the Renaissance writer, Marco Girolamo Vida (1485–1566); and Ignjat Djordjić (1676–1737), a Jesuit priest and the author in Latin, Italian, and Croatian of many religious works in prose and verse, including a Croatian version of the Psalter and the epic-lyrical *Uzdasi Mandalijene pokornice* ("The Sighs of Magdalen Repentant," an expanded eight-canto version of which was completed in 1716 and printed in Venice in 1728), considered his most impressive piece of original poetry.

Polish Baroque literature, the richest and most varied of the Slavic, produced a substantial body of devotional literature, some of it of particular interest. A rather large number of religious poems are anonymous and include not only Catholic works but also songs and hymns of the most prominent Protestant group in Poland, the Arians. Several collections of devotional poems published in the late sixteenth, seventeenth, and early eighteenth centuries bore the names of minor writers: Olbrycht Karmanowski (late sixteenth century and first half of the seventeenth), probably an Arian and the author of *Pieśni pokutnych* ("Songs of the Penitent," first published in 1890), reflecting the influence of the Psalms and the Psalter paraphrases of the outstanding Polish Renaissance poet Jan Kochanowski; Szymon Starowolski (late sixteenth century–1656), a priest and prolific author of verse and prose works in Latin and Polish, his major piece of devotional literature was the *Świątnica Pańska zamykająca w sobie kazania na uroczystości świąt całego roku* ("The Lord's Temple Comprising Sermons for the Celebrations of Holy Days Throughout the Entire Year," 1645); Kaspar Twardowski (c. 1592–before 1641), the author *inter alia* of *Kolebka Jezusowa* ("The Cradle of Jesus," 1632), a collection of religious lyrics; Samuel Przypkowski (c. 1592–1670), an Arian who wrote a number of devotional poems and religious-polemical prose tracts in Latin and Polish; Łazarz Baranowicz (c. 1595–1693), a convert to Eastern Orthodoxy, rector of the famous Kiev Academy from 1650 to 1658, thereafter Bishop and Archbishop of Chernigov and an important figure in eastern Slavic political and cultural life in his time, his religious poetry includes "Apollo chrześcijański" ("The Christian Apollo," 1670) and the "Nowa miara starej wiary . . ." ("The New Measure of Old Faith," 1676), both written in Polish; Walenty Odymalski (c. 1620–?), a priest and the author of two devotional works: *Wizerunek doskonałej świętobliwości . . .* ("The Image of Perfect Piety," 1660) and *Świat naprawiony od Jezusa Chrystusa prawdziwego Boga i Człowieka . . .* ("The World Reformed by Jesus Christ the True God and Man," 1670, in ten books); Jan Malina (?–1672), a Protestant minister known for the hymnal *Kancjonał, to jest Pieśni chrześcijańskie . . .* ("Hymn Book, or Christian Songs," 1671); Adam Jan Michał Kępski (first half of the eighteenth century), whose major work was the long poem *Myśli o Bogu i człowieku w mowie człowieka i ducha wyrażone* ("Thoughts on God and Man Expressed in the Speech of Man and Spirit," 1756); and Elżbieta Drużbacka (c. 1695–1765), one of the last significant representatives of the Baroque in Poland and author of spiritual, panegyric, moral, and secular lyrics collected together in a large volume published in 1752. The most valuable devotional poetry came from the pens of four major Polish Baroque writers: Wacław Potocki, known above all for his epic on the first battle of Chocim; Potocki was an Arian who converted to Catholicism when all remaining Arians in Poland were ordered expelled in 1658. His religious poetry includes a collection of songs and a dialogue on the Resurrection (both published for the first time only in 1949), as well as a verse paraphrase of the Evangelium published in 1698; Zbigniew Morsztyn, the most outstanding Arian poet of Baroque Poland whose foremost religious poetry is contained in the *Pieśń w ucisku* ("Song in Embrace," 1661) and a cycle of emblematic poetry published for the first time only in 1954; Wespazjan Kochowski (1633–1700), a Catholic historian and poet (in Latin and Polish) whose religious epic *Psalmodia polska* ("Polish Psalmody," 1695; abbreviated title) ranks as one of the outstanding monuments of seventeenth-century Polish literature and an early manifestation of the messianism that was to become so important an aspect of nineteenth-century Polish romanticism; Stanisław Herakliusz Lubomirski (1642–1702), a distinguished man of state and prolific writer in Latin and Polish whose devotional poetry consists in the main of verse paraphrases of books of the Bible, e.g. *Tobiasz wyzwolony* . . . ("Tobias Liberated," 1683), *Ecclesiastes* . . . (1702).

Written by clerics and laymen alike, religious *hymns* and biblical paraphrases in verse also represented well-developed forms within the general context of Baroque religious poetry. Hymns, of course, were sung throughout the Middle Ages in Latin and the vernacular languages, but the rise of Protestantism and the direct role of the congregation in Church service, so fundamental in Protestant practice, infused new life into the genre. The hymn became the means by which this direct participation in the service was achieved. Verse translations and paraphrases of the Psalms and other parts of the Bible also relate to the prominence of Scriptures in Protestant worship. Often, these versifications were used as hymns and sung in churches. The congregational hymn became the cornerstone on which Protestant worship rested. Initially, in the sixteenth century, in the first era of Protestantism, the revival and spread of hymn writing originated in Protestant circles. Luther himself composed hymns, the first authoritative collection of which was printed in 1529 under the title *Klugsches Gesangbuch*. Some were translations of Latin hymns, others adaptations of folk songs, a number so-called *Leisen* or versifications of the Psalms and other biblical passages.[4] Given this impetus, the composition of hymns increased considerably with the result that by 1571 some 187 hymnbooks were published.[5]

Catholic religious writers lost little time in following the Protestant example. In Germany, the first Catholic hymns were composed by M. Vehe in 1537; some were no more than translations and adaptions of hymns by Luther and other Protestant authors. Because of their quite central place in divine worship, Protestant hymns tended to be conservative in style and imagery and less susceptible to innovation. Yet with the advent of the Baroque, hymns reflected the changes in style taking place in other poetic genres, although rarely as completely or as intensely as in the obviously less restricted secular genres. The kind of impact the aesthetics of the Baroque age had on hymnody can be appreciated by comparing, for example, the hymns of the two outstanding German Lutheran hymn writers of the seventeenth century—Paul Gerhardt and Johann Rist—with those of earlier composers. Gerhardt's very popular and often reprinted early hymns, *Praxis pietalis melica*, the first complete collection of which was published in 1667, and those of Rist to be found in the three-volume collection *Himmlische Lieder* (1641, 1642, 1651), show a more marked personal element, a richer palette of colors, more elaborate imagery, wider use of antithesis, and an intensification of elements of drama and mystery capable of inspiring awe. Rist's "O Ewigkeit, du Donner Wort," which still survives in Lutheran hymnals albeit in abbreviated form, is a particularly good example. Very much the same Baroque tendencies inform the religious oratorios, written for declamation in church accompanied by instruments and chorus, by the poet Johann Klaj, and in

---

[4] See Roy Pascal, *German Literature in the Sixteenth and Seventeenth Centuries* (London, 1968), p. 47.
[5] *Ibid.*

some respects, in a more original and idiosyncratic way, the biblically inspired *Himmlische Libes-Küsse* (1671) and three-volume *Kühl-Psalter* (1684–86) of the visionary Quirinus Kuhlmann. Prior to Kuhlmann's work, the most important German Protestant versifications of the Psalms and other biblical passages were the formally interesting and innovatory translations by Martin Opitz published in 1637 and the Petrarchian poetic versions of the Song of Solomon by the important Pietist thinker and author Gottfried Arnold (1666–1714). Because of its imagery, allegory, and majesty, the Song of Solomon held a distinct appeal for Baroque taste and proved especially popular in verse paraphrases.

The well-known French verse translation of the Old Testament Psalms by the Huguenots Clément Marot (1496–1554) and Théodore Beza (1519–1605), which appeared around 1540, expanded the horizons of contemporary French poetry with the result that many French poets throughout the second half of the sixteenth and seventeenth centuries attempted their own poetizations of particular psalms: Jean de La Ceppède, François de Malherbe, Pierre Motin, Honorat de Bueil, Seigneur de Ragan, Claude de Malleville, Pierre Corneille, and Jean Racine. The original Latin story of the three young men in the furnace added to the apocryphal Book of Daniel also attracted the attention of poets and inspired two verse paraphrases in the seventeenth century: the *Paraphrase du cantique des trois enfants* by Antoine Godeau and the version by Martial de Brives. The Jesuit Pierre Le Moyne found subject matter in the Bible for his collection of sonnets on biblical and other heroines published in 1647 under the title *La Galerie des femmes*.

Although the first complete English versification of the Psalms appeared in London in 1562 (an "official" Scottish version appeared only in 1631), it was not until the seventeenth century that hymnody really occupied the attention of English poets. However, apart from such collections as *Hymnes and Songs of the Church* (1622–23) and *Hallelujah* (1641) by the minor Stuart poet George Wither (1588–1667), a Puritan officer, and George Sandys's *A Paraphrase upon the Divine Poems* (second edition, 1631), which inspired the hymns in Jeremy Taylor's *Golden Grove* (1655), the majority of hymns composed by late sixteenth- and seventeenth-century English poets were above all poetic exercises and not intended for singing. This provides a marked contrast to seventeenth-century German hymnody, for example. For the English poet, the hymn was not much more than another type of sacred or meditative poem. This can be said, in the main, of Milton's hymns on the Nativity, Passion, and Circumcision, written about 1629; those of Donne included in *Poems* (1633) and *Poems* (1635)—"A Hymne to Christ, at the Author's last going to Germany," "Hymne to God my God, in my Sicknesse," "A Hymne to God the Father"; William Habington's (1605–54) "Nox nocti indicat Scientiam. David," included in *Castara: The Third Part* (1640); Crashaw's "An Hymne to the Nativity, sung as by the Shepheards," and "Hymn to Sainte Teresa" (*Steps to the Temple*, 1646; 1648); Abraham Cowley's "Hymn to Light" (*Works*, 1668); Henry Vaughan's (1622–95) "The Night" (based on John 11:3); and John Norris of Bemerton's (1657–1711) "Hymn to Darkness" (*Poems*, 1687). As elsewhere in Baroque Europe, a number of poems were based on biblical sources other than the Psalms. This was true of Francis Quarles's biblical paraphrase *A Feast for Worms* (1620), "Wherefore hidest thou thy face and holdest me for thy enemie?," and "My beloved is mine, and I am his; He feedeth among the Lillies," included in *Emblemes* (1635); George Herbert's "The Pearl" and "Aaron" (*The Temple*, 1633); and Abraham Cowley's biblical epic *Davideis*.

Hymnody and biblical translations and paraphrases in verse also busied both Protestant and Catholic writers in the Netherlands, Poland, Croatia, and Bohemia. Seventeenth-century Holland knew several major collections of Protestant hymns and Bible translations: The *Liedtboek* (1604) by Hans de Ries (1553–1638), containing a variety of devotional works including versions of the Psalms; the *Boeck der Gesangen* (1618) by Vondel, influenced by de Ries's work; the *Over-ysselsche Sangen en Dichten* (1634), containing a number of hymns and Psalm versions in a great variety of stanzaic forms by the greatest Dutch Calvinist poet of the first half of the seventeenth century, Jacobus Revius; and the *Stichtelycke Rymen* (1652) by Dirck Camphuysen, which was very popular among Dutch Protestants as a psalm book. Of the collections of hymns and Bible translations that preceded these in the later sixteenth century, the following should be mentioned: the *Schriftmetige Gebeden* (1573) with verse versions of the Psalms by the Calvinist Jan Fruytiers (15?–c. 1580); the hymnal *Gheestelijcke Liedekens* (1582) by another Calvinist poet, Joris Wybo (Silvanus, c. 1530–76); and the *Schriftuerlijcke Lofsangen* (1591), containing verse translations of parts of the Old and New Testaments, by Philips van Marnix van Sint-Aldegonde (1540–98), also a Calvinist and poet of above ordinary talent.

Poland is usually thought of as so devout a Catholic country that without any initiation into Polish history one would tend to think that it must have presented a solid front against the tide of Protestantism. This was anything but the case. It is true that Protestantism failed to sink roots in Poland as deeply as it did elsewhere; it lacked leadership, became badly fragmented, did not enjoy the determined support of the landowning gentry who used it for their own political purposes as long as they needed it, and withered before the massive assault hurled at it by the Counter-Reformation. But the range of Protestant influences in Poland was far from slight. The Socinian, Arian, and Unitarian groups were particularly active in various parts of the country and engaged in extensive publication. Moreover, the town of Leszno in southern Poland became an active center of Bohemian Protestant scholarship once the Thirty Years' War and its aftermath sent large numbers of Czech Protestants into exile. Protestantism produced a substantial literature of its own in Poland from the mid-sixteenth century to the mid-seventeenth (the first important vernacular writer in Polish, Mikołaj Rej [1505–69], was a Calvinist) and left its traces in the works of writers who although not Protestant, apparently at one time or another, in various ways, had contact with Protestant groups in the country. This was the case, for example, of Poland's greatest Renaissance poet, Jan Kochanowski, whose deservedly renowned collection of verse paraphrases of the Psalms (*Psalterz Dawidów*) was the first of its type in the history of Polish vernacular literature and an influence on later Polish psalm translations. Protestant hymns and biblical versifications in the Baroque period were mainly the efforts of Polish Arians. The first of any importance was the collection of religious songs by Samuel Przypkowski included in the *Kancjonal* ("Hymnal," c. 1625) of Stanisław Lubieniecki (1558–1633), although Przypkowski's several polemical tracts in Latin represented more significant contributions to the contemporary religious literature. In addition to the hymnal published in 1671, Jan

Malina also translated a number of hymns from German collections. Wacław Potocki, the epic poet, completed a verse adaptation of the *Evangelium* under the title *Nowy zaciąg* in 1680; the work appeared for the first time posthumously in 1698.

The epigram writer Stanisław Serafin Jagodyński (end of the sixteenth century to the first half of the seventeenth) was one of the first Polish Catholic writers to turn his attention to hymnody in the Baroque period. His collection *Pieśni katolickie nowo reformowane* . . . ("Catholic Songs Newly Revised") included original compositions as well as translations from Polish into Latin and Latin into Polish. Like so much of Polish, and European, Baroque literature, the collection remained in manuscript form until the twentieth century when it was published in Czesław Hernas' *Hejnały polskie* ("Polish Heynals," 1961). The prolific Catholic writer and statesman Stanisław Herakliusz Lubomirski wrote verse paraphrases of books of the Bible: *Tobiasz wyzwolony* ("Tobias Liberated," 1683) and *Ecclesiastes* . . . (published in 1702 erroneously as the work of one G. K. Hadziewicz). A younger contemporary, Wojciech Stanisław Chróściński (c. 1665–c. 1722), also a Catholic, published a collection of prayers, psalms, saints' lives, and songs about the Virgin Mary in 1711 under the title *Krótki zbiór duchownych zabaw* ("A Short Collection of Spiritual Entertainments"); in 1745 his thirteen-canto poem *Jożef do Egiptu od braci przedany* ("Joseph Sold into Egyptian Bondage by His Brothers") appeared. That Polish Catholic biblical versification continued well into the eighteenth century is illustrated by the work of the Ukrainian Polish writer Jan Kajetan Jabłonowski (c. 1700–64). In 1747 he published verse versions of the Old Testament books of Esther, Judith, and Susannah (*Księgi Ester, Judyt, Zuzanny z Pisma św. wybrane, na polski wiersz przetłumaczone*). This was followed two years later by a curious verse comparison of the Old and New Testament accounts of the life of Joseph (*Paralele dwóch świętych Jozefów Starego i Nowego Testamentu . . . wierszem polskim krótko objaśniona*).

Following Italian models for the most part, at least initially, Croatian Catholic writers in Dalmatia began composing versifications of the Psalms in the sixteenth century. A version of five psalms by a writer with an inclination toward classical Greek and biblical subjects, Mavro Vetranić (1482–1576), was one of the earliest. A somewhat less poetic collection of seven psalm translations by Nikola Dimitrović (d. 1554) was published in Venice in 1549 under the title *Sedam psalama pokornijeh kralja Davida*. This was followed by a very free handling of several psalms by Šime Budinić (1535–1600) printed in Rome in 1582 under the title *Pokorni i mnogi ini psalmi Davidovi*, a work of some interest for the way in which allusions to contemporary events are woven into the adaptations. The two principal seventeenth-century collections were the ones again comprising versifications of seven psalms published in Rome in 1621 by Ivan Gundulić and the version, also of seven psalms (*Sedam psalama pokornieh kralja Davida*), by Stijepo Djordjić (1579–1632), which appeared in Padua in 1686. A Croatian translation of the complete Psalter appeared for the first time in Venice in 1703. It was the work of Andrija Vitaljić (1642–1725) and bore the title *Iztumačenje pisnih Davidovih u spivanja slovinska složeno*. It was surpassed, however, by the masterful version published in Venice in 1729 by one of the foremost Croatian Baroque poets Ignjat Djordjić. Poetically superior to Vitaljić's work, Djordjić's collection also has an excellent scholarly apparatus. It includes the texts of the Latin originals on which the translations were based and extensive philological commentaries attesting to Djordjić's command not only of previous Croatian versions but also of such Western adaptations as the Latin one by Eobanus Hessus (1542) and the French version by the Huguenots Clément Marot and Théodore Beza, which appeared in 1562, and of the fine poetic version by the Polish poet Jan Kochanowski dating from 1587.

In regard to hymns and psalms and other biblical adaptations, the situation in Bohemia differed considerably from that of the other Slavic countries where such developments had any importance for literary culture in the sixteenth and seventeenth centuries (Poland, Croatia). Such pre-Lutheran reform societies as the Hussite and the Unity of the Czech Brethren had already given considerable encouragement to vernacular usage and had promoted a hymnody much indebted to folk sources and translations and adaptations of various parts of the Old and New Testaments. These works continued to be reprinted and enjoyed use in the sixteenth and seventeenth centuries. Perhaps the best known was the definitive hymnal of the Czech Brethren, *Písně duchovné evanjelistské* . . . also known as the *Šamotulský kancionál* from the name of the shop in Poznań (Poland) where it was printed in 1561. Another edition appeared in 1615, five years before the Battle of White Mountain. The advent of Lutheranism in the country brought several new hymnals in the second half of the sixteenth and early seventeenth centuries. Among the latter were the *Písně chval božských* . . . by the Moravian priest Tobiáš Závorka Lipenský published in Prague (1606, a second edition appeared in 1620) and the *Písničký pěkné a starožitné nyní pospolu sebrane* (1610) by Henyk z Valdštejn.

After White Mountain, with its grave consequences for Bohemian Protantism and Czech vernacular culture, large numbers of Protestants left the hapless country and established new centers of Bohemian Protestant culture. One of these, probably the most famous, was Leszno, just over the Czech border in southwestern Poland. The Czech Brethren located themselves here and it was here that the great Czech writer and thinker Komenský was active from 1628 to 1656 (with two interruptions —1641–48 and 1650–54). Komenský's hymnal (*Kancionál* . . .), published in 1659 in Amsterdam (where Komenský lived from 1656 to the time of his death), was one of the major seventeenth-century Czech Protestant hymnals dating from the post–White Mountain period. Émigré Czech Lutherans organized a strong colony in Perno, in the Dresden district of Saxony, which was under the protection of the Kurfürst of Saxony. Several hymnals were published here by members of the colony, the most important being the *Knížka ruční zpevův a modliteb* (1629) by Samuel Martinius (d. 1634) of Dražov, and one by Jan Ctibor Kbelský published first in 1631 and again in 1634. When Perno became a battleground between Saxons and Swedes, and eventually fell to the Swedes, the colony moved to the town of Žitava in Slovakia. New hymnals came from this center: one by Jan Milesius in 1668, another by Jan Novák in 1685, and a quite popular one by Václav Kleych (1678–1737), published in 1717 and reprinted in 1722 and 1727. The most successful poetically, however, was the *Cithara Sanctorum* . . . (1636), containing some 414 hymns of which 90 were original the rest from Czech, Latin, and German sources by the important devotional writer Třanavsky, and the Třanavsky-influenced *Nábožné písně s modlitbami* by the Slovak Protestant dignitary Juraj Zábojnik (1608–72), published posthumously in 1686 by Štěpán Francisci.

The resurgence of Catholicism in Bohemia that accompanied the imposition of Hapsburg rule after the Battle of White Mountain and the Peace of Westphalia in 1648 created a need for Czech Catholic hymnals. The need was handsomely filled through the second half of the seventeenth and the first few decades of the eighteenth centuries. Actually, the first important Catholic hymnal was the *Mariánská muzika radostna i žalostna* (1647) by Adam Michna of Otradovice. This was followed by his *Loutna česka* (1653) and *Svatoročna muzika anebo sváteční kancionál* (1661). The Jesuit poet Bedřich Bridel's hymnal appeared in 1658; a well-known *Kancionál český* by the Prague priest Matěj Václav Šteyer (Štajer, Štyr, 1630–92) in 1683; the *Kancionál* of the Augustinian monk Jan Rozenplut of Schwarzenbach (?–1602) in 1601; the Czech-language *Capella regia musicalis* of Václav Karel Holan Rovenský (1644–1718) in 1693; and the *Slavíček rajský ...* of Jan Joseph Božan (1644–1716) in 1719. The famous German religious poems of the *Trutz Nachtigall, oder Geistlich-Poetisch Lust Wäldlein* (1649) by Friedrich von Spee appeared in a Czech translation (*Zdoroslavíček v kratochvilném hájičku postavený*) by the Jesuit Felix Kadlinský (1613–75) in 1665 and enjoyed wide popularity.

On reading much Baroque religious and meditative poetry, one is often struck by the emphasis on conflict and, related to this, the extensive use of *military* imagery. The soul "wars" with the body (the spirit with the flesh); man is in conflict with himself, torn between spiritual yearnings and temporal pleasures; heaven (God and the angels) is ever in combat against relentless forces of hell (Satan and the devils), and so on. In the light of the actual conflicts of the age, the role of conflict in the devotional and philosophic literature and the preference for an imagery of martial conflict become an expression of the age itself. This is even more apparent in the religious epic, the one strong area of Baroque epic poetry.[6] Here poets found not only what they considered the most appropriate genre in which to treat of forces and conflicts that they saw as of inherently epic dimensions (Protestantism vs. Catholicism, Reformation vs. Counter-Reformation,

[6] The Baroque epic, its relation to the Renaissance epic, and the reasons for its few notable achievements are discussed in Warnke, *Versions of Baroque*, pp. 158–186.

European Christendom vs. Islam), but also one that could satisfy the Baroque proclivity for the exalted and the massive.

As a fundamentally important part of the literary heritage of the classical antique past, the epic enjoyed a new favor during the Renaissance. The more each nation developed its vernacular literary culture and moved farther away from Latin, the greater was the desire to possess that crowning achievement of a literary coming-of-age—a national vernacular epic. The model, of course, was Vergil, for long a more esteemed epic bard than Homer, largely because of the centuries-old hegemony of the Latin language in much of Europe. Apart from such direct imitations of the *Aeneid* as Ronsard's *La Franciade* (1572), an unfinished poem in four books, the more interesting and valuable Renaissance epics applied the machinery of the Vergilian epic to contemporary events. Two prime examples, both in Romance languages, are: *Os Lusíadas* ("The Sons of Lusus," 1572) by the Portuguese poet and adventurer Luís de Camões (1524–80), dealing with the African and Far Eastern explorations of Vasco da Gama; and *La Araucana* (complete edition 1590), a poem in thirty-seven cantos devoted principally to the Spanish conquest of Chile, by the conquistador Alonso de Ercilla y Zuñíga (1533–94). The popularity of Camões' epic outside of his native Portugal is evident from the translation into English by Sir Richard Fanshawe (1608–66) in 1655.

As the Renaissance began to wane in Italy and a Mannerist style came to the fore, the discovery of affinities with the literature and art of the later Middle Ages attracted poets to the traditions of chivalry and romance. The greatest of the new epics—Ariosto's *Orlando furioso* (1516) and Tasso's *Gerusalemme liberata* (completed 1575, published in an unauthorized edition in 1581 and in a revised form in 1593)—wove into the texture of the classical epic threads of the romances and chivalric tales of earlier ages. As different in spirit as they are in style, the Italian epics gave rise to a number of imitations throughout late sixteenth- and seventeenth-century Europe. In his projected twelve-book but unfinished *The Faerie Queene* (three books published in 1590, three more in 1596), Edmund Spenser chose to follow the path of Ariosto bringing to the Mannerist style of the *Orlando* an element of moral didacticism, present but less developed in his model. A Poland ocked in seemingly endless conflict with the Ottoman Turks found a stronger attraction in Tasso's *Gerusalemme*. Although that remarkably talented translator Piotr Kochanowski rendered both epics into his native language, it was no accident that the acclaim accorded his version of the Tasso work forced the *Orlando* translation into relative obscurity. To contemporary Poland, Ariosto was little more than poetic exercise and entertainment. But Tasso was the reality of their own world to them. With the Kochanowski translation of the *Gerusalemme* ever in view, Polish Baroque poets set about attempting to translate the great military struggles of their age into the stuff of epic (Potocki and Twardowski, above all).

When Tasso began singing "The sacred armies and the godly knight/ That the great sepulchre of Christ did free," a conflict of greater immediacy than the First Crusade was tearing at the heart of Europe: the emergence of Protestantism and the campaign of Rome to stifle it through a Counter-Reformation before it succeeded in forever altering the religious map of Europe. Out of this conflict emerged still another permutation of the classical epic—the Christian religious epic of the Baroque. Its traditional techniques enriched by the stylistic preferences of the Baroque, this new epic sang no longer of crusades and chivalric adventures of Christian knights and Moslem warriors, but of the religious upheavals of a contemporary Christianity, or of the Creation, or of doomsday, or of man's fall from and eventual return to Grace, or of the central figures of the Old and New Testaments.

France and Germany, which knew, together with Bohemia, the most bitter moments in the great Christian religious struggle, produced epics reflecting that struggle. In the seven cantos of his *Les Tragiques* (written between 1577 and 1594 and first published in 1616), the French Calvinist warrior-poet, Agrippa d'Aubigné, immortalized the religious wars of sixteenth-century France and the nightmare of the St. Bartholomew's Day Massacre. His German counterpart, Martin Opitz, a Calvinist by choice after a Lutheran upbringing, transformed the grim reality of the Thirty Years' War into the epic-like poetry of his *Trost Gedichte in Widerwertigkeit des Krieges* (begun in 1621, the year of his conversion to Calvinism, and published in 1633).

La Semaine, ou Création du Monde (begun around 1574, published in 1578), by another French Protestant poet, Guillaume de Salluste du Bartas (1544–90), of more modest gifts than d'Aubigné (to whom he showed a part of his epic), endeavored to tell the story of Creation in verse. A continuation of the work, which was destined to remain unfinished (the fate, fortunately, of so many Baroque epics), appeared in 1584 under the title *Seconde Semaine, ou Enfance du monde;* for its subject, the poet chose the progress of mankind from Eden. Like Camões' *Lusíadas* and Tasso's *Gerusalemme,* du Bartas' poems also had their admirers—and imitators—in contemporary England—and America. Translated by Joshua Sylvester from 1605 to 1607, they won the praise of no lesser personages than Milton and Dryden, and exerted considerable influence on America's first important woman poet, Anne Dudley Bradstreet (c. 1612–72), whose poetry much in the manner of du Bartas, *The Tenth Muse Lately Sprung up in America,* appeared first in London in 1650 and again, posthumously, in a much augmented and revised edition in Boston, Massachusetts, in 1678.

In the sterner world of seventeenth-century English Puritanism man's beginning held less significance as the subject of a religious epic than man's fall and the Day of Judgment. It was to the fall that John Milton addressed himself, producing the greatest epic in the English language, *Paradise Lost* (published in ten books in 1667 and in twelve in 1674). While Milton was completing the work of over twenty years that was to sing in the rich cadences of English blank verse

> Of Man's first disobedience, and the fruit
> Of that forbidden tree whose mortal taste
> Brought death into the World, and all our woe,
> With loss of Eden, till one Greater Man
> Restore us, and regain the blissful seat. . . .

the Puritan Reverend Michael Wigglesworth (1631–1705) in the New England on the other side of the Atlantic was readying for publication in 1662 the most popular literary work of Puritan America, *The Day of Doom,* subtitled *A Poetical Description of the Great and Last Judgement,* a two hundred and twenty-four-stanza poem in seven-foot ballad lines (far easier to commit to memory than Miltonic verse). A deliberately unadorned reaffirmation of traditional Puritan doctrine, the work is the diametric opposite of the loftiness and intricacy of Milton's "cosmic" poem. Not content, like Wigglesworth, to remain only with the vision of man's fall, Milton returned to the Christian epic to create in the unfinished *Paradise Regained* (published in 1671, the same year as *Samson Agonistes*) the hopeful vision of man at last triumphant over sin.

Steeped in the literature of classical Greek and Roman antiquity and conversant with the Italian epics of the sixteenth century, the Croatian poet and dramatist Junije Palmotić sought to create a Christian epic in his native Croatian to rival the secular military epic *Osman* of his greater countryman Gundulić. With the Latin *Christias* of M. Girolamo Vida as his point of departure, and using the metric scheme canonized by Gundulić in the *Osman*, he published his twenty-four canto *Kristiada* (1670), the most noteworthy Croatian Baroque Christian poem after Ignjat Djordjić's *Uzdasi Mandalijene pokornice*.

The religious epic built around a single "hero" appeared also in France and England. The Jesuit theologian Pierre le Moyne chose a saint as his subject and in 1653 produced a huge epic bearing the title *Epopée de Saint Louis ou la Sainte-Couronne reconquise sur les Infideles*. Reaching back to biblical history, the varied talent of the soldier and courtier Antoine-Girard de Saint-Amant (1594–1661) found material for an epic in the life of Moses, *Moïse sauvé* (1653), a poem as quantitatively impressive as Le Moyne's and no more worthy of anything but brief recall. Saint-Amant's laborious exercise was followed a few years later by an English effort to transform biblical history, this time the story of David, into epic—the unfinished *Davideis* (only four books were completed), begun in 1640 by the late Metaphysical poet Abraham Cowley (1618–67). Perhaps the only noteworthy aspect of the poem (in which, in the words of Samuel Johnson, "we find wit and learning unprofitably squandered") is the author's use of decasyllabic couplets, a reflection of his desire to cast his epic in what he considered to be the true mold of classical poetics.

Very closely related to the religious poetry of the Baroque, at times indistinguishable from it and often subsumed under it, was the poetry, by Catholics and Protestants alike, clergy and laymen, of meditation, or reflection. In contrast to the abundant devotional literature, the meditative or reflective poetry progresses from a philosophical rather than a theological base. The meditative poets sought not the celebration of Christian divinities and doctrines, or the poetization of biblical passages, but the personal, individual, distinctly lyrical expression of their reflection upon the theme of man in God's world. Unlike so much of the non-religious, nonphilosophical secular poetry of the Baroque, which is often little more than a relatively emotionless exercise in form for the sake of displaying ingenuity, the meditative poetry explores depths of emotion contained only by the discipline of form. In the amatory poetry of the Baroque, for example, the subject frequently serves the poet as a platform on which to mount a pageant of the conceits prized in contemporary literary practice. In the meditative poetry the conceits serve to heighten and intensify the emotions verbalized.

So voluminous was the meditative poetry of the Baroque throughout Europe, that only the most prominent poets and their works need be mentioned before the poetry itself is brought under closer scrutiny. Although "Metaphysical" in the context of seventeenth-century English poetry certainly embraces more than meditative poetry and is used primarily to indicate a particular "school" or style, the poetry usually classed as Metaphysical is preponderantly meditative. It should include, above all, many of the poems of John Donne, the greatest of the English Metaphysicals, Henry King, George Herbert, John Milton, Richard Crashaw, Abraham Cowley, Andrew Marvell, and Henry Vaughan. Also in the current of the English Metaphysicals was the poetry of several of the American Puritan poets, particularly Anne Bradstreet, Edward Taylor (c. 1642–1729), the author of the long-forgotten *Preparatory Meditations* (written 1682–1725, first published 1939), and the less significant Philip Pain (c. 1647–c. 1667), whose *Daily Meditations* appeared in 1668.

Although separating the strands of religious and meditative poetry in German Baroque literature is often quite difficult, three names stand out prominently in the meditative genre: Simon Dach (1605–59), the founder of the prominent Königsberg literary circle known as *Die Kürbis-Hütte*, and including additionally Heinrich Albert and Robert Roberthin; Paul Fleming, now highly regarded for both his love poetry and such reflective lyrics as "Gedanken über der Zeit" ("Thoughts on Time"), "An Sich" ("To Himself"), "Zur Zeit seiner Verstossung" ("In Time of His Rejection"), and others; and the dramatist Andreas

Gryphius, the author of a number of poems in the meditative vein ("Menschliches Elende," "Human Misery"; "An Sich Selbst," "To Himself"; "An die Welt," "To the World"; "Einsamkeit," "Solitude").

The Dutch Baroque meditative lyric began with the very European and Italianate Pieter Corneliszoon Hooft (1581–1647), whose technically impressive reflective poetry of his middle years included several important works such as the *Noodlot* stanzas and a pen portrait of the French writer Montaigne. It continued in lyrics by the predominantly religious poet Jacobus Revius and in the poetry of the cosmopolitan Constantijn Huygens, the dramatist Joost van den Vondel, and the posthumously published Heiman Dullaert.

The Romance countries produced several particularly interesting reflective poets. Whereas Jean de La Ceppède's impressive sonnet collection *Théorèmes spirituels* more appropriately deserve to be considered religious rather than meditative or reflective poetry, the "death" lyrics of Jean de Sponde and Jean-Baptiste Chassignet contained in the collections *Essai de quelques poèmes chrétiens* and *Mépris de la vie et consolation contre la mort*, respectively, are among the best specimens of Baroque meditative poetry in any language.

In Spain and Spanish America, the foremost writers of the Siglo de Oro also essayed the meditative lyric: Luis de Góngora, Lope de Vega, Pedro Calderón de la Barca, and the Mexican Sor Juana Inés de la Cruz. Their efforts were paralleled on a less brilliant level of poetic art by Juan de Arguijo (1565–1623), Juan de Jáuregui (1583–1641), Francisco de Rioja (1583?–1659), Luis de Carrillo y Sotomayor (1583?–1610), and Antonio Enríquez Gomez (1602–60).

Influential throughout Europe as well as the most imitated poet in seventeenth-century Italy, Giambattista Marino is generally regarded as the most outstanding amatory poet of the European Baroque. The reputation is justly deserved, but such compositions as "La canzone dei baci" ("The Song of the Kisses") and *L'Adone* ("Adonis") dwarf the number of religious and meditative poems that he also wrote. The most consistently meditative poet of the Italian Baroque, however, was the philosopher Tommaso Campanella. In a sense, Camões' place in Portuguese Baroque literature is like Marino's in Italian. If Marino is associated with a single subject—sensual love—Camões is associated with a single work, the epic *Os Lusíadas*. Yet, like Marino, Camões wrote much other poetry and experimented with a variety of forms. His lyrics include a substantial number of sonnets addressed to the central concerns of Baroque meditative poetry.

Among the Slavs, only the Poles and Croats produced any significant meditative poetry during the Baroque age. Reflective lyrics of Baroque stamp appeared in Polish literature as early as the 1570s in the work of the recently rediscovered poet Mikołaj Sęp Szarzyński (c. 1550–81), whose collected poems were printed posthumously in 1601 under the title *Rytmy abo wiersze polskie* ("Rhymes or Polish Verses"). Although the general tendency of Polish Baroque poetry inclined more toward the epic, moralistic, religious, and satiric, meditative poetry continued to be cultivated throughout the seventeenth century, and indeed in the first two or three decades of the eighteenth when Polish culture was already suffering from a numbing parochialism. The outstanding Polish Baroque meditative poet was the Protestant Zbigniew Morsztyn, whose major literary undertaking was a cycle of 114 emblematic poems (*Emblemata*) of both devotional and reflective character (written between 1658 and 1680 but first published only in 1954).[7] Wacław Potocki and Daniel Naborowski (1573–1640), the first complete edition of whose poetry appeared for the first time in 1961, also made several interesting contributions to the genre.

Following in large measure the lyrical path of their late Renaissance predecessors, the markedly Italianate poets Dinko Ranjina (1536–1607) and Dominko Zlatarić (1558–1613), the prolific and highly regarded Dubrovnik writers Horacije Mažibradić (1566–1641) and Dživo Bunić-Vučić (Ivan Bunič-Vučićević), the latter a prominent Slavic Marinist, made the most enduring contributions to the South Slavic reflective lyric.

Apart from expected differences of language and national temperament and divergence in terms of greater or lesser complexity both intellectually and imagistically, there is considerable con-

---

[7] See David J. Welsh, "Zbigniew Morsztyn and the Emblem Tradition," *Symposium*, XIX (1965), 80–84.

sistency in the thematic emphases as well as stylistic techniques of Baroque meditative poetry. In using the term "thematic emphases" instead of simply "themes," I want to avoid the impression that the themes of the Baroque meditative poets were in any way unique to the age. Most certainly they were not. But it is the *prominence* of certain themes in the Baroque, the "thematic emphases" of the period, that enable us to speak of a certain Baroque complex of themes. I have in mind specifically the following:

a) The mutability and brevity of man's life on earth. This connects with another great theme of Baroque meditative poetry;

b) The impermanence, ephemerality, and transience of all material or worldly vanities and pleasures;

c) The related theme of man's terrestrial existence as something illusory, dreamlike because of its mutability, brevity, and ephemerality. An outgrowth of these concerns is the almost obsessive preoccupation of Baroque poets with;

d) Time, which becomes one of the central concerns of Baroque literature and the point on which a very large number of poems turn;

e) Following logically from these reflections is the shift in emphasis from man's earthly life to his spiritual one. The temporal reality is only transitory, dreamlike; therefore, man would do better to think instead of the eternal life beyond the grave, the immortal life of the soul. This gives rise to a great many poems on the subject of *death* as well as, to be sure, the expected poetry of religiosity and mysticism.

f) But the nature of the Baroque age, with its profound calamities, on the one hand, and its pervasive sensuousness, on the other, lent new immediacy to the familiar conflict of flesh and spirit. Poets expose the hollow vanity of attachment to the ephemeral, illusory pleasures of material existence, yet these pleasures are often presented in concrete, sensuous, naturalistic terms that underscore man's passionate yet futile attachment to them and the pain he experiences in contemplating his separation from them. Distinguishing the Baroque treatment of this eternal dichotomy, however, are (*i*) the political and cultural conditions of the age that *intensify* the paradoxical aspect of the dichotomy, and (*ii*) the widespread use of *military* terminology to elaborate the dichotomy and to reflect the prominence of war and physical violence in the culture of the period.

The degree of sensuousness of Baroque art can readily be appreciated by examining the love poetry of the age. The object of the poet's feelings is no longer (or rarely) celebrated in the exalted platonic idiom of the Renaissance, notable for its generally meticulous avoidance of the specific and naturalistic. The celebration of the corporeal, so striking in Baroque painting and sculpture, informs as well virtually the entire body of Baroque amatory poetry. Stripped of its Renaissance idealism and spiritual associations (through love man ascends and gains entry into spiritual realms), love in a Baroque context becomes essentially physical. It may take the form of the poeticized eroticism for which Marino earned justified fame in his *L'Adone,* "La canzone dei baci," and "La pastorella" ("The Shepherdess"); or it may appear as a poet's witty urging of a lady friend to bed (e.g. Donne's "Elegie: Going to Bed," Marvell's "To his Coy Mistress") in quite unequivocal terms; or the sensual enumeration of a woman's charms (e.g. the Marinist Francesco della Valle's "Particolari belleze della sua donna" ["The Beauties of His Mistress"], Hofmannswaldau's "Beschreibung vollkomener Schönheit" ["Description of Perfect Beauty"], Heinrich Mühlpfort's "Sechstinne" ["Sestine"], Jan Andrzej Morsztyn's "O swej pannie" ["On His Mistress"] and "Do tejże" ["To His Mistress"], and Ignjat Djordjić's *Raninin Zbornik* collection of lyrics). So corporeal indeed was the proclivity of the Baroque that poets could even find physical imperfections and improportions as fit subjects for verse. There are a number of examples of this by Marino's followers in Italy, such as Sempronio's sonnets "La bella zoppa" ("The Beautiful Cripple") and "La bella nana" ("The Beautiful Dwarf"), Morando's "Bellissima donna cui manca un dente" ("The Most Beautiful Lady Missing a Tooth"), and by the German translator of Adimari and Guarini, Hans Assmann von Abschatz (1646–99): "Die schöne Blatternde" ("The Pimpled Beauty"), "Die Schöne mit hohem Rücken" ("The Humpbacked Beauty"), "Die schöne Hinckende" ("The Beauty Who Limps"), "Die schöne Gross-Nase" ("The Beautiful Great-Nose "), and "Die schöne Schwangere" ("The Pregnant Beauty").

But for all the sensuousness—and often frank sensuality—marking the treatment of love in Baroque poetry, concerns paramount in both the religious and meditative literature of the age also touch it. In a number of lyrics, love functions as little more than a metaphor for the pleasures and vanities of the world. Góngora's sonnet beginning "Mientras por competir con tu cabello..." ("While in a competition with your hair...") and Hofmannswaldau's sonnet, "Vergänglichkeit der Schönheit" ("Beauty's Transitoriness") are two well-known examples. Then, the Baroque preoccupation with the passage of time intrudes in the love lyric as well. Fretted by a heightened awareness of the swift passage of time and the brevity of man's sojourn on earth, poets often express impatience with the formalities of courtship and beseech their ladyloves to spurn time-consuming conventions and hasten to share with them the pleasures of physical love. A fine example of this is Marvell's often-anthologized poem, "To his Coy Mistress." Many, many analogues can easily be found in other languages.

The spirit-flesh dichotomy touched on by so many Baroque meditative poets appears prominently in the amatory poetry in the transmogrified form of painful separation between lovers. The separating factor may be time and/or space, but the key element of *apartness* or *division* is retained from the meditative tradition. Not only are the lovers separated from each other but neither can function as a complete entity without the other, in the idiom of Baroque amatory verse. The poets bemoan the separation because to them it appears a *division of the self*. Only when the lovers reunite can the whole self again be reconstituted. The lyric "Odjazd" ("Departure") by the Polish poet Jan Andrzej Morsztyn is a splendid example of a Baroque love poem built on this theme, the more so in view of the verbal play in the original (e.g. the poet's internal rhyme, in one place, of *siebie*, self, and *ciebie*, you). The motif of loved ones as but halves of a whole appears in Anne Bradstreet's verse "Letter to Her Husband, Absent upon Publick Employment," in which she implies through the opening question the impossibility of any *total* separation of lovers.

My head, my heart, mine Eyes, my life, nay more,
My joy, my Magazine of earthly store,
If two be one, as surely thou and I,
How stayest thou there, whilst I at *Ipswich lye*?

Marino also turned to the theme of the separation of lovers in his sonnet "Dipartita" ("Leave-taking") in which, through a series of analogies, he argues that the eventuality of reunion should preclude remorse.

Another thematic bond linking the amatory poetry of the Baroque to both the religious and meditative is that of mutability. The sense of impermanence, and change, so poignantly and vividly expressed in religious and meditative lyrics, is echoed in the love poetry in the repeated emphasis on *inconstancy*. Through the lyric hero the poet may yearn for the emotional security of constancy in love, yet he recognizes that despite the fervor of his desire it is an elusive good, all too rarely grasped. The natural condition of love, alas, is pain, pain caused much of the time by the inconstancy of the beloved. The number of poems on constancy and inconstancy is considerable and only a few of the most representative need be mentioned in passing: Thomas Carew's "To my inconstant Mistris," Sir John Suckling's "Song" ("Out upon it, I have lov'd . . ."), Sidney Godolphin's "Constancye," Richard Lovelace's "The Scrutinie," John Wilmot's "Love and Life," Daniel von Czepko's "Angst und Hohn der Liebe Lohn" ("Scorn and Dismay the Lover's Pay"), Johann Christian Günther's "Als sie an seiner Treu zweifelte" ("As She Doubted His Faithfulness"), Johann Rist's "Sie rühmet ihre Beständigkeit" ("She Boasts of Her Constancy"), Agrippa d'Aubigné's "Sonnet pour Diane," Georges de Scudéry's "Sonnet" beginning "Aimez ou n'aimez pas, changez, soyez fidele . . . ," Vincent Voiture's "A une demoiselle qui avait les manches de sa chemise retroussées et sales" ("To a Young Lady Who Wore the Sleeves of Her Shift Rolled up and Dirty"), Marino's "Fede rotta" ("Broken Vows") and "L'amore incostante" ("Inconstant Love"), Francisco de Trillo y Figueroa's "A un retrato de una dama, hecho de cera, aludiendo a la inconstancia de las mujeres" ("On the Portrait of a Lady Done in Wax, Alluding to the Inconstancy of Woman"), Camões' sonnets "Este amor que vos tenho, limpo e puro . . ." ("This love of mine, so pure, so chaste . . ."), "—Que esperais, esperança?—Desespero . . ." (—"What do you hope for, Hope?—

I hope for naught . . ."), "Sempre, cruel Senhora, receei . . ." ("Ever, cruel Lady, did I fear . . ."), "Quem pudera julgar de vós Senhora?" ("Who could believe, my Lady . . ."), and several poems by Jan Andrzej Morsztyn titled "Niestatek" ("Inconstancy").

Baroque secular poetry included in addition to epic, meditative, and amatory works, a substantial amount of "official" poetry (primarily in the form of panegyric odes) celebrating state events and court personages, and many poems addressed to various aspects of the world of nature notable, I think, particularly for the anticipation of the nineteenth-century Romantic affinity for a dynamic nature of turbulence, change, and mystery. It is, however, the meditative and amatory poetry that—together with the religious and mystic—rightly command our attention for it is here that the greatest confluence of the thematic and stylistic preferences of Baroque literary art occurs. Establishing the boundaries between the religious, religiomystic, and meditative poetry can often be, as I have said, a trying and occasionally impossible assignment. The amatory verse itself, moreover, frequently echoes central concerns of both the religious and philosophical poetry with which it would seem—at first viewing—to have little in common. Yet perhaps the very cultivation, simultaneously, of ecstatic religious and searching philosophical poetry, on the one hand, and a richly sensuous and sensual love poetry, on the other, reveals something vitally significant about the Baroque age—its quintessentially paradoxical and antithetical nature.

2. BAROQUE POETIC THEORY AND STYLE

Despite the seeming contradictions in Baroque art, the opulent, dazzling structure rested on the foundation of a basically cohesive aesthetic system. Prominent in the system were the following:

a) The creative talent or genius of the poet (the *ingegno*, from Latin *ingenium*, of contemporary Italian aesthetic theory). This is stressed in such representative seventeenth-century treatises on poetry as the Italian Pierfrancesco Minozzi's *Gli sfogamenti dell' ingegno* (Venice, 1641), the Spaniard Baltasar Gracián's *Arte de ingenio* (Madrid, 1642; revised and republished in 1649 under the title *Agudeza y arte de ingenio*), and the Italian Cardinal Sforza-Pallavicino's *Trattato del dialogo e dello stile* (Modena, 1646). This genius reveals itself chiefly in the (*b*) facile perception (*arguzia, argutezza, acutezza*; English *acuity*) of the (*c*) paradoxical, antithetical, incongruous, contradictory, unusual, and marvelous (in the sense of being capable of provoking wonderment, awe), and in (*d*) the resolution, reconciliation, linking of (knowable) extremes (*discordia concors*) through the discovery of correspondences realized poetically by means of metaphors verbally elaborated as (*e*) striking word pictures, or images. The term most frequently encountered in reference to the striking Baroque concept or word picture is the Italian *concetto* (the English *conceit*).[8]

So important was the conceit considered to poetry in the Baroque age, that several books on the theory and practice of conceits appeared as, for example, Giulio Cortese's *Avertimenti nel poetare* (1591), Camillo Pellegrino's *Del concetto poetico* (1599), and Emanuele Tesauro's *Il cannochiale Aristotelico* (1654), the most important of all.[9]

The faculty for *concettismo* (creating *concetti*, conceits) became so intimately associated with the name of Marino in seventeenth-century Italy, for example, that his "school," that is the Marinesque technique of concettismo, frequently was, and still is, referred to as *marinismo* and his followers *marinisti*. Very much the same occurred in Spain. There the concetto style reached its peak in the work of the poet Góngora; to write in "Góngora's style," to follow the poetic path of Góngora, meant therefore to practice the art of *gongorismo*. Subsumed under gongorismo in the lexicon of seventeenth-century Spanish poetic theory are two other frequently met terms representing different aspects of the same phenomenon: *conceptismo*, which is more or less the Spanish equivalent of the Italian "concettismo," and *cultismo*, from *culto*, meaning an erudite, complex, and often obscure, Latin-derived syntactic and lexical style (reminiscent of Italian *Bembismo*).

---

[8] For a good little book on the conceit, see K. K. Ruthven, *The Conceit* (London, 1969).

[9] These works, and seventeenth-century poetic theory in general, are discussed in Joseph Mazzeo's *Renaissance and Seventeenth-Century Studies*, pp. 29–59. There is also much helpful material in James V. Mirollo's *The Poet of the Marvelous*, pp. 141–161, 166–174.

Considering the Baroque "cult" of form and the esteem in which it held inventiveness and novelty in art, one can readily understand the temptation of poets to seek unusual lexical items and bold, unexpected syntactical arrangements. The practice of cultismo sprang directly from the very nature of Baroque verbal art and was by no means a unique Spanish development, despite the impression that the widespread use of the Spanish term may convey.

The English and French terms "metaphysical" and "précieux," respectively, must be viewed in the same light. Both designate schools of poetry in which inventiveness, conceptually or technically, defines the measure of creative genius and in which content is often subordinate to concept and/or form. Too frequently the courtly-aristocratic and *salon* associations of the French précieux poets (e.g. Claude de Malleville, Théophile de Viau, and Vincent Voiture) and the English Cavalier poets (Robert Herrick, 1591–1674; Thomas Carew, c. 1595–c. 1639; John Suckling, 1609–42; Sidney Godolphin, 1610–43; Richard Lovelace, 1618–58), among whom poetry was principally a *social activity*, tend to blur their common attributes and their affinities with the Baroque poetry of the rest of Europe. Like marinismo and gongorismo, and their Germanic and Slavic equivalents, metaphysical and précieux located poetic genius in the wit (or inventiveness) capable of discovering bold and unusual correspondences and of producing novel, striking conceits. In terms of these common denominators, the metaphysical and précieux schools can (and in fact should) be regarded as local variants of a single (Baroque) aesthetic widely cultivated throughout Europe primarily in the seventeenth century. Naturally, in circumstances (courts, salons) where poetry functioned above all as entertainment, manner far outweighed substance in importance and led to a kind of highly artificial exhibitionism of wit and word. But the techniques favored by the court and salon poets were those enjoying the greatest popularity among poets at the time, and the very desire to display wit, to dazzle by inventiveness and verbal dexterity, merely reflected the values of contemporary poetic tastes. Not surprisingly, when these values changed in the course of time, the qualities for which poets were most admired in the age of the Baroque—their inventiveness, their bold and startling metaphors, their skill at creating spectacular images, their facile handling of form—came to be looked upon as defects, imperfections, and the poetic style of the Baroque in general was regarded as excessively mannered, artificial, strained, often illogical, needlessly complex, and esoteric, and for these and other reasons—in bad taste. The ornamentalization of frequently trite and banal subject manner was condemned as the result of an exaggerated, hyperbolic concern for style, manner, technique, form, at the expense all too often of content. Only in the nineteenth century did a partial rehabilitation of the Baroque begin, and only in the twentieth has the poetry of the late sixteenth and seventeenth centuries been at last approached in the context of the aesthetic norms of the age itself.

To appreciate the Baroque poetic style best, we have to examine it in terms of its most important components. Given the key position of correspondences in Baroque poetic theory, metaphor is an appropriate point of departure. Poetic correspondences can be perceived in two ways: as similes (conveying likeness) and as metaphors (conveying identities). Similes, to be sure, were often used by Baroque poets, but were less favored than metaphors for two reasons. The metaphor allowed the poet a richer, more provocative use of his imagination, his *inventiveness*, and the metaphor, because it establishes *identity* rather than merely likeness, is bolder, more difficult, and potentially more successful poetically in view of its greater capacity to excite wonderment. Certainly, no other feature of Baroque poetry stands out as sharply as the extensive use of metaphor; and it was this feature, above all others, that incurred the disfavor of later ages.

Although common to all forms of Baroque poetry, metaphor was most handsomely displayed in amatory and "official" poetry (e.g. state odes, such as those written in Spain by Herrera, in France by Malherbe, and in Russia by Lomonosov); perhaps because of the very nature of the subject matter as well as the circumstances in which most of this poetry came into being, the poet's inventiveness was presented with its greatest challenge. The metaphor could be short or extend through an entire poem, as in the following examples:

> Ses yeux, le paradis des âmes . . .
> [His eyes, the paradise of hearts]

> Vincent Voiture, "Sur sa maitresse recontrée en habit
> de garçon, un soir de carnaval" ("On His Mistress
> Encountered in Boy's Clothing One Carnival Evening")

En crespa tempestad del oro undoso
nada golfos de luz ardiente y pura
mi corazón, sediento de hermosura,
si el cabello deslazas generoso.

[In tempest curled of undulating gold,
my heart, parched in its thirst for pulchritude,
swims gulfs and gulfs of pure and burning light,
if you let down your wond'rous mane of hair]

Francisco de Quevedo, "Afectos varios de su corazón,
fluctuando en las ondas de los cabellos de Lisi"
("The Various Motions of His Heart, Floating on the
Waves of Lisi's Hair")

Ein Feuer sonder Feuer, ein lebendiger Tod,
Ein Zorn, doch ohne Gall, ein angenehme Not,
Ein Klagen ausser Angst, ein überwundner Sieg,
Ein unbehertzer Mut, ein freudenvoller Krieg;
Ein federleichtes Joch, ein nimmerkrankes Leid,
Ein zweifelhafter Trost und süsse Bitterkeit,
Ein unverhofftes Gift und kluge Narretei,
Ja, kürzlich: Lieben ist nur blosse Phantasei.

[A fire without a fire, a living death,
A wrath, yet lacking gall, a pleasant pain,
A plaint born not of fear, lost victory,
A courage faint of heart, a joyful war;
A feath'ry yoke, a never-ailing ill,
A doubtful comfort and sweet bitterness,
An unexpected bane, wise foolery,
Yes, briefly said: Love is but fantasy.]

Ernst Christoph Homburg, "Was ist die Liebe"
("What Is Love?")

A good illustration of metaphor in a meditative poem is Andreas
Gryphius' "Menschliches Elende" ("Human Misery"):

Was sind wir Menschen doch! ein Wohnhaus grimmer
        Schmerzen,
Ein Ball des falschen Glücks, ein Irrlicht dieser Zeit,
Ein Schauplatz herber Angst, besetzt mit scharffem Leid,
Ein bald verschmelzter Schnee und abgebrannte Kerzen . . .

[What are we men indeed? Grim torment's habitation,
A toy of fickle luck, wisp in time's wilderness,

A scene of bitter fear and filled with keen distress,
And tapers burned to stubs, snow's quick evaporation]

The Baroque poetic style was highly rhetorical (its inspiration far more indebted to Aristotle's *Rhetoric* than to his *Poetics*) and employed a wide variety of rhetorical devices in addition to metaphor. In view of the Baroque feeling for paradox and the seemingly contradictory, the frequent use by poets of such rhetorical devices as *oxymoron* (the juxtaposition of words of opposing meanings) and *antithesis* (the balancing of parallel word groups conveying opposing ideas) is understandable. A few examples:

oxymoron:

con que *alegre pena* . . .

[with what pleasing pain]

Juan de Jáuregui, "Afecto amoroso communicado al silencio"
("A Loving Fancy Addressed to Silence")

. . . die Zeit-befreite Zeit.

[the time-less time]

Catharina Regina von Greiffenberg, "Verlangen nach der
herrlichen Ewigkeit" (Longing for Splendid Eternity")

. . . du dunkel-helles Licht.

[You dark-bright light]

Ibid., " Über das unaussprechliche heilige Geistes-Eingeben!"
("The Inexpressible Holy Infusion of the Spirit")

antithesis:

No where but here did ever meete
Sweetnesse so sadd, sadnesse so sweete.

Richard Crashaw, "The Weeper"

Welcome, all *wonders* in one sight!
Eternitie shut in a span,
Summer in winter, day in night,
Heaven in Earth, and God in man . . .

Ibid., "An Hymne of the Nativity, sung as
by the Shepheards"

Nacht, mehr denn lichte Nacht! Nacht, lichter
    als der Tag!

[Night, more than brilliant night! More light
    than day!]

Andreas Gryphius, " Über die Geburt Jesu "
    ("On the Birth of Jesus ")

Tą kto żyje, ma dosyć, choć nie ma niczego,
A bez tej kto umiera, już nic ze wszystkiego.

[Who lives without virtue has enough, though naught,
Who dies without it—naught, though he have all]

Daniel Naborowski, "Cnota grunt wszytkiemu "
    ("Honor the Basis of All ")

Often, the entire poem, or the greater part of it, is woven out of
antithesis, as in the following examples:

Coitado! que em um tempo choro e rio;
    Espero e temo, quero e aborreço;
    Juntamente me alegro e entristeço;
    De uma cousa confio e desconfio.
Avôo sem asas; estou cego e guio;
    E no que valho mais menos mereço
    Calo e dou vozes, falo e emudeço,
    Nada me contradiz, e eu aporfio.
Qu'ria, se ser pudesse, o impossível;
    Qu'ria poder mudar-me, e estar quêdo;
    Usar de liberdade, e ser cativo;
Queria que visto fôsse, e invisível;
    Qu'ria desenredar-me, e mais me enredo:
    Tais os extremos em que triste vivo!

[Poor wretch am I! I weep and laugh at once;
    I hope and fear, I love and yet abhor;
    Conjointly am I happy and unhappy;
    My trust I grant and hasten to retract;
Wingless I fly, and without sight I guide;
    The things I value most I merit least;
    I hold my tongue, orate; speak, mute become;
    Uncontradicted, all I overrule.

Impossibilities I would have done;
    I would be changed and yet remain at rest;
    Both relish liberty and captive be;
I would be seen and yet invisible;
    I would myself unsnarl then more ensnarl;
    Such the extremes in which I sadly live!]

Luís de Camões, "Coitado! que em um tempo choro e rio"

Nic mię nie boli, a płaczę, rzewliwy,
    Nikt mnie nie więzi, a przecię, tęskliwy,
Łańcuch na szyjej noszę, poimany,
    I w srogich pętach chodzę, okowany.
W płomieniu tonę, pałam pośród wody,
Boże się pożal nieszczesnej przygody . . .

[Nothing hurts me and yet I, doleful, weep,
    No one imprisons me and yet, downcast,
I wear a chain upon my neck, ensnared,
    And, fettered, in grim shackles make my way.
In flame I drown, in midst of water burn,
    God, pity have on such a wretched state]

Hieronym (Jarosz) Morsztyn, "Lament niewolnika"
("A Prisoner's Lament")

Both for rhetorical impact and to achieve the oft-desired cumulative effect, poets made abundant use of various devices of repetition. Probably the most widely employed, so much so that it enjoys a particular identification with Baroque literary style, was *anaphora* (the repetition of the same word to introduce two or more clauses or lines). In the following examples, the repetitive passages are easily recognizable in the original and accompanying translations have been omitted:

O spijse die ons uyt den hemel is gegeven!
O dranck die eens gesmaeckt den smaeck vermeeren doet!
O spijse die ons tot int ander leven voedt!
O dranck die crachtelijck de doden geeft het leven!
O spijse die ons niet laet aende aerde cleven . . .

Jacobus Revius, "Avond-Mael"

Hier hastu, Marnia, hier hastu meinen Sinn.
Hier hastu meinen Geist, den lieben, den noch warmen.
Hier hastu meinen Mut. Hier hastu Pein und Harmen.
Hier hastu mich, dein Ganz, du Himmels Bürgerin . . .

> David Schirmer, "Als sie gestorben"

L'amour l'a de l'Olympe ici-bas fait descendre:
L'amour l'a fait de l'homme endosser la péché:
L'amour lui a déjà tout son sang fait épandre:
L'amour l'a fait souffrir qu'on ait sur lui craché:

L'amour a ces halliers à son chef attaché:
L'amour fait que sa Mère à ce bois le voit pendre:
L'amour a dans ces mains ces rudes clous fiché:
L'amour le va tantôt dans le sépulcre étendre . . .

> Jean de La Ceppède, from *Théorèmes Spirituels*

Baci le trombe son, baci l'offese,
baci son le contese . . .

> Giambattista Marino, "La canzone dei baci"

Mudam-se os tempos, mudam-se as vontades,
Muda-se o ser, muda-se a confiança . . .

> Luís de Camões, "Mudam-se os tempos . . ."

Nic to, choć ty masz pałac kosztem wystawiony;
Nic to, że stoł zastawiasz hojnie półmiskami;
Nic to, żec złoto, srebro leży gromadami;
Nic to, że gładka żona i domu zacnego;
Nic to, że mnóstwo wnuków liczysz z boku swego;
Nic to, że masz wsi gęste i wielkie osady . . .

> Daniel Naborowski, "Cnota grunt wszytkiemu"

Ja im mjesec bjeh od noći,
ja im sunce bjeh od dana,
ja božanstvo višńe moći,
ja hvalena, ja spievana—
ja za prikor neba i svita
mom sramotom ponosita . . .

> Ignjat Djordjić, *Uzdasi Mandalijene pokornice*

Another device frequently used by Baroque poets, and very often in conjunction with iteration is *parallelism*. A fine illustration of the effect possible through a fairly elaborate use of the iterative-parallel structure is the following excerpt from the Italian Marinist poet Giovan Leone Sempronio's "*Quid est homo?*":

> È strale, che da l'arco esce e sen passa;
> è nebbia, che dal suol sorge e sparisce;
> è spuma, che dal mar s'erge e s'abbassa.
>
> È fior, che nell'april nasce e languisce;
> è balen, che nell'aria arde e trapassa;
> è fumo, che nel ciel s'alza e svanisce.

Also related to repetition and especially useful in achieving the cumulative effect is *enumeration*. (This device was the basis of the French genre of *blason*, a type of poetic catalogue established in the thirteenth century by Geoffrey of Vinsauf and widely used after Clément Marot's *Blason du Beau Tetin* [1536].) In the following examples, note the combination of enumeration and repetition, the appearance of enumeration with or without ellipsis (the use of the conjunctive *and*) and the preference for groupings of threes and fours:

> O tempo acaba o ano, o mês e a hora,
> A fôrça, a arte, a manha, a fortaleza . . .
>
> [Time marks an end of years, of months, of hours,
> of might, of art, of wit, of manly strength]
>
> Luís de Camões, "O tempo acaba o ano, o mês e a hora"

> Tout s'enfle contre moi,—tout m'assaut, tout me tente,
> Et le monde, et la chair, et l'ange révolté,
> Dont l'onde, dont l'effort, dont le charme inventé
> Et m'abime, Seigneur, et m'ébranle, et m'énchante.
>
> Quelle nef, quel appui, quelle oreille dormante
> Sans péril, sans tomber, et sans etre enchanté,
> Me donras-tu?
>
> [Against me all swells up, assaults me, tempts me,
> The world, the flesh, the angel in revolt,
> Whose wave, whose onslaught, whose deceitful charm
> Engulfs me, Lord, drains me of strength, enchants.

What vessel, what support, what sleeping ear
To ward off peril, falling, and enchantment
Wilst Thou grant me?]

> Jean de Sponde, from *Sonnets de la mort*
> ("Sonnets on Death")

> . . . con sommessi accenti
> interrotti lamenti,
> lascivetti desiri,
> languidetti sospiri . . .

> [midst humble tones,
> broken moans,
> lascivious little desires,
> and languid sighs]

> Giambattista Marino, "La canzone dei baci"
> ("The Song of the Kisses")

goza cuello, cabello, labio y frente,
antes que lo que fué en tu edad dorada
oro, lilio, clavel, cristal luciente,

no sólo en plata o víola troncada
se vuelva, mas tú y ello juntamente
en tierra, en humo, en polvo, en sombra, en nada.

[take pleasure in your forehead, neck, hair, lip,
before what had been in your golden age
carnation, lucent crystal, lily, gold,

not only silver or plucked violet
become, but you and it together turn
into earth, smoke, dust, shadow, nothingness]

Luis de Góngora, "Mientras por competir con tu cabello"

> Auf Nacht, Dunst, Schlacht,
> Frost, Wind, See, Hitz, Süd, Ost, West,
> Nord, Sonn', Feuer, und Plagen
> Folgt Tag, Glanz, Blut, Schnee . . .

> [On night, fog, fight,
> Frost, wind, sea, heat, south, east, west,
> North, sun, fire, ill deed,
> Come day, shine, blood, snow]

> Quirinus Kuhlmann, "Der Wechsel menschlicher Sachen"
> ("The Change of Human Things")

Z czasem wszytko przemija, z czasem bieżą lata,
Z czasem państw koniec idzie, z czasem tego świata.
Z czasem stawa dowcip i rozum niszczeje,
Z czasem gładkość, uroda, udatność wiotszeje . . .

[With time all things do pass, with time years race,
With time end governments, with time this world.
With time wit ceases, reason falls to naught,
With time charm, beauty, grace all wither 'way]

Daniel Naborowski, "Do Anny"("To Anna")

Metaphor, various forms of repetition, particularly anaphora, enumeration, and syntactic parallelism combine in a number of works to produce a poetic structure highly typical of the Baroque. Here the cumulative technique is employed to build to a crescendo that is "relieved" only at the end of the poem. Not only does a structure of this type equip the poet with a stage on which to exhibit his talent for concetti, but by withholding the full sense of the poem until the end, the poet is also able to gratify the Baroque delight in mystery and suspense. There are so many examples of such structuring in Baroque poetry that I shall limit myself here to three short works, in English, German, and Polish:

Like to the falling of a Starre;
Or as the flights of Eagles are;
Or like the fresh springs gawdy hew;
Or silver drops of morning dew;
Or like a wind that chafes the flood;
Or bubbles which on water stood;
Even such is man, whose borrow'd light
Is streight call'd in, and paid to night.

The Wind blowes out; the Bubble dies;
The Spring entomb'd in Autumn lies;
The Dew dries up; the Starre is shot;
The Flight is past; and Man forgot.

Henry King, "*Sic Vita*"

Ein Feuer sonder Feuer, ein lebendiger Tod,
Ein Zorn, doch ohne Gall, ein angenehme Not,
Ein Klagen ausser Angst, ein überwundner Sieg,

Ein unbehertzer Mut, ein freudenvoller Krieg;
Ein federleichtes Joch, ein nimmerkrankes Leid,
Ein zweifelhafter Trost und süsse Bitterkeit,
Ein unverhofftes Gift und kluge Narretei,
Ja, kürzlich: Lieben ist nur blosse Phantasei.

[A fire without a fire, a living death,
A wrath, yet lacking gall, a pleasant pain,
A plaint born not of fear, lost victory,
A courage faint of heart, a joyful war;
A feath'ry yoke, a never-ailing ill,
A doubtful comfort and sweet bitterness,
An unexpected bane, wise foolery,
Yes, briefly said: Love is but fantasy.]

Ernst Christoph Homburg, "Was ist die Liebe?"
("What Is Love?")

Twarde z wielkiem żelazo topione kłopotem,
Twardy dyjament żadnym nie pożyty młotem,
Twardy dąb wiekiem starym skamieniały,
Twarde skały, na morskie nie dbające wały:
Twardsza-ś ty, panno, której łzy me nie złamały,
Nad żelazo, dyjament, twardy dąb i skały.

[Hard the iron smelted with great care;
Hard the diamond hammer never touched;
Hard the oak tree petrified by age;
Hard the cliffs aloof from ocean's waves;
Harder you, whom tears have failed to break,
Than iron, diamond, oak, and cliffs]

Jan Andrzej Morsztyn, "Do panny" ("To a Young Lady")

Fond of elaborate, grandiose, and pompous structures or techniques to startle readers with the wonders (or, to use the frequently encountered Italian term *meraviglie*, "marvels") their inventiveness was capable of producing, Baroque poets also showed a natural inclination for hyperbole. The device became, consequently, one of the most often used—and abused. Here are a few specimens:

La terre brillante de fleurs
Fait éclater mille couleurs
D'aujourd'hui seulement connues . . .

[The earth a-gleam with flowers
Bursts forth a thousand colors
Never beheld before this day]

> Vincent Voiture, "Pour Madame d'Aiguillon"
> ("For Madame d'Aiguillon")

Marcello, or, s'avess'io
mill'alme e mille cori,
sarei nido capace a tanti amori?

[Marcello, now if I possessed
a thousand souls and thousand hearts,
would I be large enough a nest for loves so many?]

> Giambattista Marino, "L'Amore incostante"
> ("Inconstant Love")

La pelegrina voz y el claro acento
por la dulce garganta despedido,
con el suave efecto del oído
bien pueden suspender cualquier tormento.

[The voice of rare delight and lucid tone
dispatched from out that dulcet-throated source,
with their effect of softness on the ear
can well relieve torment of any sort]

> Juan de Tasis, "A una señora que cantaba"
> ("To a Lady Who Was Singing")

So lang' ein Tier sich wird mit seines gleichen paaren;
So lang' ein Schiffer wird die Wellen überfahren;
So lange Sonn' und Mond noch haben ihren Schein
So lang' O Daphnis sollst du mein Herzliebster sein.

[As long as animals mate with their like;
As long as seamen travel over waves;
As long as sun and moon still have their fire,
So long, O Daphnis, will I you desire.]

> Johann Rist, "Sie rühmet ihre Beständigkeit"
> ("She Boasts of Her Constancy")

And lastly, this famous example in seventeenth-century English
poetry, from Andrew Marvell's "To his Coy Mistress":

Had we but World enough, and Time,
This coyness Lady were no crime,
We would sit down, and think which way
To walk, and pass our long Loves Day.
Thou by the *Indian Ganges* side
Should'st Rubies find: I by the Tide
Of *Humber* would complain. I would
Love you ten years before the Flood:
And you should if you please refuse
Till the Conversion of the *Jews.*
My vegetable Love should grow
Vaster than Empires, and more slow.
An hundred years should go to praise
Thine Eyes, and on thy Forehead Gaze.
Two hundred to adore each Breast:
But thirty thousand to the rest.
An Age at least to every part,
And the last Age should show your Heart.

We have seen that Baroque poetry is rich not only rhetorically, but also imagistically. Certain distinguishing features of Baroque imagery merit a closer look at this juncture. In speaking of "distinguishing features," however, I stress again that the devices and techniques examined are in no way "inherently" Baroque, nor can a case be made that any one of them—singly—enjoyed the special favor of Baroque writers. It is rather the use of certain devices and techniques *in concert* that enables us to associate them, as a complex, with the Baroque.

Apart from metaphor and the conceit itself, which are central in the Baroque poetic system, Baroque poets showed a decided preference in their imagery for: (*a*) the concrete and specific, i.e. the particular over the general (in contrast, for the most part, to Renaissance practice), often combining with the naturalistic; (*b*) military images, used extensively in religious, meditative, and amatory poetry and reflecting, I believe, the strife-torn character of the age; (*c*) multiple-sense imagery, expressing the sensuousness of much Baroque art, and related to this sensuousness; (*d*) classical mythology, a legacy of the Renaissance but often used by Baroque poets with levity and in incongruous, nonclassical contexts; (*e*) a rich palette of colors, drawn from the world of nature (e.g. flowers) and from precious stones (rubies, emeralds, pearls, diamonds) and metals (silver, gold); (*f*) the play of light and dark, or *chiaroscuro*; and (*g*) the opposition of hot and cold (e.g. fire: snow).

The sensuousness of Baroque imagery stands out in vivid contrast to the Renaissance. This comes through clearly in Baroque patterns of texture, color, and light. The naturalistically oriented "specificity" and multiple-sense appeal of Baroque art make for a richer textural quality than that of the Renaissance; the colors of Baroque art also appear more varied and intense, more dramatic, than those of the Renaissance. Furthermore, the Renaissance canvas—visual or verbal—was generally if not always bathed in the bright light of day connoting perhaps the anthropocentrism and certitude of the age. Because of such luminosity, the colors of the Renaissance canvas lose their intensity and pale. In the Baroque, however, the light source is seldom bright sun but the warm orange-hued glow of later afternoon or the reddish sky of dawn or sunset; instead of coming from above diffusing all beneath it in a uniform brightness, as in the Renaissance, the light now enters from a side, leaving large areas obscured by darkness or semidarkness. This, complemented by an opposition of light and dark, suggested no longer the clear sense of certitude of Renaissance man but instead the Baroque sense of awe and mystery, the Baroque cognizance of a spiritual realm beyond yet inextricably bound up with the terrestrial, and the Baroque fondness for the dramatic. Now let us see these various aspects of Baroque imagery at work in representative poems:

a) specificity:

> I heard the merry grasshopper then sing,
> The black clad Cricket, bear a second part,
> They kept one tune, and plaid on the same string,
> Seeming to glory in their little art . . .

> Anne Bradstreet, from *Contemplations*

> The raisins now in clusters dryed be,
> The orange, Lemon dangle on the trees:
> The Pomegranate, the Fig are ripe also,
> And Apples now their yellow sides do show.
> Of Almonds, Quinces, Wardens, and of Peach,
> The season's now at hand of all and each . . .

> Anne Bradstreet, "Autumn," *The Four Seasons of the Year*

Gelijck als in een colck een steentgen
valt te gronde
Het water werpt terstont een ringsken in het
ronde,
En van het eene comt een ander schieten uyt . . .

[As when a pebble falls into a pool,
At once the water casts a circle 'round
And after this another follows forth]

Jacobus Revius, "Gods Besluyt" ("God's Virtues")

Der frechen Völker Schar, die rasende Posaun,
Das vom Blut fette Schwert, die donnernde Kartaun
Hat aller Schweiss und Fleiss und Vorrat aufgezehret . . .

[The band of brazen states, the blaring horn,
The sword all smeared with blood, the cannon's roar
Have everyone's sweat, toil and stocks consumed.]

Andreas Gryphius, "Tränen des Vaterlandes"
("My Country's Tears")

O Croix . . .
Ce nectar, par qui seul le monde est rachetable,
T'arrosant, a changé ton absinthe en moly,
Et ton bois raboteux si doucement poli
Qu'il est or' des élus le séjour délectable . . .

[O Cross . . .
That nectar (i.e. the blood of Christ) which alone redeems the
world
In wat'ring you, your wormwood changed to moly,
And did so smoothly polish your rough wood,
That now 'tis the elect's delightful home]

Jean de La Ceppède, from *Théorèmes spirituels*
("Spiritual Theorems")

b) military imagery:

Una bocca omicida,
dolce d'Amor guerrera,
cui natura di gemme arma ed inostra,
dolcemente mi sfida . . .
entran scherzando in giostra
le lingue innamorate . . .

[A murderous mouth,
sweet warrior of Love,
whom nature arms and adorns with jewels,
sweetly challenges me . . .
The enamored tongues
enter the lists playfully]

Giambattista Marino, "La canzone dei baci"
("The Song of the Kisses")

e nel campo d'amor fattasi audace
prova nel guerreggiar diletto e pace.

[and now, made bold on the field of love,
she tastes the delight and peace of battle]

Giambattista Marino, "La pastorella" ("The Shepherdess")

As 'twixt two equall Armies, Fate
Suspends uncertaine victorie,
Our soules, (which to advance their state,
Were gone out), hung 'twixt her, and mee

John Donne, "The Extasie"

Courage my Soul, now learn to wield
The weight of thine immortal Shield.
Close on thy Head thy Helmet bright.
Balance thy Sword against the Fight.
See where an Army, strong as fair,
With silken Banners spreads the air.
Now, if thou bee'st that thing Divine,
In this day's Combat let it shine:
And shew that Nature wants an Art
To conquer one resolved Heart . . .

Andrew Marvell, "A Dialogue between the Resolved Soul
and Created Pleasure"

Luzifer, wann deine Waffen rasseln
In dem blankgeharnschten Heer,
Wann die heisern Kälberfelle prasseln,
Dann erstaunt Land und Meer,
Wenn die lautbar-hellen Feldtrompeten
Uns verjagen Todesnöten . . .

[Lucifer, when all your weapons clank
In the shining-armored band,
When hoarse skins roar 'gainst the drummer's flank,
Then stand gaping sea and land,
When the bugle's bright and piercing bray
Drives our fears of death away]

> Johann Klaj, " Die Soldaten Luzifers singen"
> ("The Soldiers of Lucifer Sing")

Pokój—szczęśliwość, ale bojowanie
Byt nasz podniebny. On srogi ciemności
Hetman i świata łakome marności
O nasze pilno czynią zepsowanie . . .

[Peace would make happy: under the heavens though
We fight our life. He who commands the night
Wages cruel war; and vanities delight
In quickening our corruption with their show]

Mikołaj Sęp Szarzyński, "O wojnie naszej, którą wiedziemy
z szatanem, światem i ciałem" ("On the War We Wage
Against Satan, the World and the Body")

> Masz też mocniejsze na obronę
> Cekauzy swe i armaty,
> Rzucając z oczu w każdą stronę
> Kule ogniste, granaty.

> A tym masz nad nieprzyjaciele,
> Że się mu złoży żelazem
> I chybia też, a ty zaś śmiele
> W serca trafiasz każdym razem . . .

[Besides, for your defense, you train
   A bright artillery.
Grenades explode and bullets rain
   Where'er you cast an eye.

Then, too, your aim is surer than
   Iron's ever is.
You hit the heart of every man,
   Unlike our enemies]

> Jan Andrzej Morsztyn, "Pieśń" ("Song")

c) multiple-sense imagery:

> Un corbeau devant moi croasse,
> Une ombre offusque mes regards;
> Deux belettes et deux renards
> Traversent l'endroit où je passe;
> Les pieds faillent à mon cheval,
> Mon laquais tombe du haut mal;
> J'entends craqueter le tonnerre . . .
>
> [In front of me a raven caws,
> A shadow comes before my eyes,
> Two weasels and two foxes pass
> The place where I am passing by.
> Beneath my horse the feet give way,
> My servant falls to disarray;
> I hear the lightning crackling in the sky]

>> Théophile de Viau, "Ode"

> The aire was all in spice
>   And every bush
> A garland wore; Thus fed my Eyes
>   But all the Eare lay hush.
>
> Only a little Fountain lent
>   Some use for Eares,
> And on the dumb shades language spent
>   The Musicke of her teares . . .

> > Henry Vaughan, "Regeneration"

> D'una sonora cetra a' dolci imperi
> move Lilla le piante agili e snelle . . .
>
> [Upon the sweet command of sonorous lyre,
> my Lilla moves her swift and agile feet]

> > Giovan Leone Sempronio, "La bella ballerina"
> >   ("The Lovely Dancer")

> que yo, más cuerda en la fortuna mía,
> tengo en entrambas manos ambos ojos
> y solamente lo que toco veo . . .

[I, wiser in my fortune now,
have both my eyes in my two hands
and only see that which I touch]

Sor Juana Inés de la Cruz, "A la esperanza" ("To Hope")

d) *classical mythological imagery:*

Give me a storme; if it be love,
Like Danae in that golden showre
I swimme in pleasure . . .

Thomas Carew, "Mediocritie in love rejected"

Die ewig-helle Schar wil nun ihr Licht verschliessen;
Diane steht erblasst . . .

[The ever-brilliant host its light will now conceal;
Diana pallid stands]

Andreas Gryphius, "Morgen Sonnet" ("Morning Sonnet")

Le grand astre va lentement
Vers les saphirs de l'onde amère,
Et Venus, dans l'autre hémisphère,
Donne ordre à leur appartement . . .

[The great star slowly makes its way toward
The sapphires of the waves of bitt'ry salt,
And Venus, in the other hemisphere,
Makes orderly their private dwelling place]

Jules Pilet de La Mesnardière, "Le Soleil couchant"
("The Setting Sun").

Leandro en mar de fuego proceloso
su amor ostenta, su vivir apura;
Icaro en senda de oro mal segura
arde sus alas por morir glorioso . . .

[Leander in a sea of stormy fire
displays his love and drains life to the last;
Icarus on an unsure path of gold
to meet death gloriously burns his wings]

Francisco de Quevedo, "Afectos varios de su corazón,

fluctuando en las ondas de los cabellos de Lisi"
("The Various Motions of His Heart, Floating on the
Waves of Lisi's Hair")

Fossi Alcide novel, che i miei trofei
dove mai non giungesse uman desio,
traspiantandovi in braccio erger vorrei;
  O stringer, qual Sanson, vi pottess'io . . .

[If only I were a new Alcides,
then, pulling you up in my arms, I'd raise
my trophies where ne'er reached human desire;
Or if, like Samson, I could stifle you]

Giambattista Marino, "Durante il bagno"
("During the Bath")

Esta foi a celeste formosura
  Da minha Circe, e o mágico veneno
  Que pôde transformar meu pensamento.

[This was the heavenly enchantment of
My Circe, and the magic potable
That can transform my each and every thought.]

Luís de Camões, "Um mover de alhos, brando e piedoso"

e) color (e.g. *precious stones, metals*):

Eyes, that displaces
The Neighbour Diamond, and out faces
That Sunshine by their owne sweet Graces.

Tresses, that weare
Jewells, but to declare
How much themselves more pretious are.

Whose native Ray,
Can tame the wanton Day
Of Gems, that in their bright shades play.

Each Ruby there,
Or Pearle that dare appeare
Bee its owne blush, bee its own Teare.

Richard Crashaw, "Wishes to his (supposed) Mistresse"

Dieux! la merveilleuse clarté!
Alceste, admirez la nuance
De ce jaune clair qui s'avance
Sous cet incarnat velouté.

L'oeillet d'Inde serait ainsi
Dans sa douce et sombre dorure,
Si sur les pans de sa bordure
La rose tranchait le souci.

Mais voilà cet éclat changé
En un mélange plus modeste.
Voyez ce rocher bleu-céleste
Ou déborde un pâle orangé.

Voyez ces rayons gracieux
Qui, là-bas, forçant le passage,
De fils d'or percent le nuage,
Aussi loin que portent nos yeux.

[O gods! What splendid luminance!
Alceste, admire the subtle shade
Of that advancing yellow light
Appearing 'neath that velvet pink.

The Eastern violet would be
Like this in its soft darksome gilt
If there upon its petals' edge
The rose cleaved through the marigold.

But see that lustrousness has changed
Into a blend more modest now.
Behold that sky-blue jutting rock
Where pallid orange overflows.

Behold, beyond, those graceful beams
Which, forcing their own passageway,
With threads of gold the cloud transpierce
As far as our eyes us convey]

Jules Pilet de La Mesnardière, "Le Soleil couchant"
("The Setting Sun")

Este matiz que al cielo desafía,
iris listado de oro, nieve y grana . . .

[That blend of hues that challenges the sky,

a rainbow striped with scarlet, snow, and gold]

Pedro Calderón de la Barca,
"Estas que fueron pompa y alegría"

A su mejilla el nácar, nácar bebe
adonde en llamas de coral, difunta
fuera la rosa, mas su incendio junta
a la azucena de templada nieve . . .

[Mother-of-pearl upon her cheek imbibes
mother-of-pearl, where might have died a rose
in flames of coral, but its burning fire
joins the white lily flower of tempered snow]

Gabriel Bocángel y Unzueta,
"Grandes los ojos son, la vista breve"

De quantas graças tinha, a Natureza
  Fêz um belo e riquíssimo tesouro,
  E com rubis o rosas, neve e ouro,
  Formou sublime e angélica beleza . . .

[Of all the many graces she possessed,
A beautiful rare treasure Nature made,
And with snow and gold, rubies and roses,
A lofty and angelic beauty shaped]

Luís de Camões, "De quantas graças tinha, a Natureza"

Sovra basi d'argento in conca d'oro
io vidi due colonne alabastrine
dentro linfe odorate e cristalline
franger di perle un candido tesoro . . .

[In shell of gold upon a silver base
two alabaster columns I beheld
'midst crystalline and sweetly scented lymphs
crushing a pure white treasure hoard of pearls]

Giambattista Marino, "Durante il bagno"
("During the Bath")

Is't purper ook zo schoon der rozen die hier bloeien
—Bedauwd met paarlen, als de morgenzon haar groet—,
Hoe moet het purpur van uw Majesteit dan gloeien!

[So lovely is the scarlet of the roses here below,
Glistening with pearls as the morning sun doth greet them,
How must the scarlet of thy majesty then glow!]

Jan Luyken, "De Ziel betracht den Schepper uit
de Schepselen" ("The Soul Contemplates the Creator
in the Creation")

Zwo Brüste, wo Rubin durch Alabaster bricht,
Ein Hals, der Schwänen-Schnee weit weit zurücke sticht . . .

[Two breasts where ruby breaks through alabaster's white,
A throat which snow of swans has put to distant flight]

Christian Hofmann von Hofmannswaldau, "Beschreibung
vollkomener Schönheit" ("Description of Perfect Beauty")

Prid tvo'em zlatom zlato krije
i sobom se zlato srami,
tvoj plam zlatnoj u tebi je
ko u prstenu dragi kami . . .

[Before the gold of you gold hides
and of itself gives rise to shame;
like precious stones upon a hand
upon you seems your golden flame]

Ignjat Djordjić, "Zgoda ljuvena" ("Love's Harmony")

f) the play of light and dark (chiaroscuro):

Dayes, that in spight
Of Darkenesse, by the Light
Of a cleare mind are Day all Night.

Richard Crashaw, "Wishes to his (supposed) Mistresse"

Allbereit hab ich erblicket,
Wie das gülden Aug der Welt
Tausend Strahlen auf das Feld
Über das Gebirg herschicket
Und vertreibet ganz und gar
Was zu Nacht stockfinster war.

[I already did descry
How a thousand beams were sent
Cross the mountains, earthward bent,

From creation's golden eye:
These have driven all away
What pitch-black in darkness lay.]

Johann Matthias Schneuber, "Morgengesang" ("Morning Song")

Mes yeux, ne lancez plus votre pointe éblouie
Sur les brillants rayons de la flammeuse vie;
Sillez-vous, couvrez-vous de ténèbres, mes yeux:
Non pas pour étouffer vos vigueurs coutumières,
Car je vous ferai voir de plus vives lumières,
Mais sortant de la nuit vous ne verrez que mieux . . .

[My eyes, no longer cast your dazzled gaze
Upon the sparkling beams of fiery life;
Envelop, cloak yourselves in darkness, eyes:
Your customary keenness not to dim,
For I shall make you see yet brighter lights,
But leaving night you shall see all the brighter]

Jean de Sponde, from *Stances de la mort*
("Stanzas on Death")

Oh come bella a la solinga grotta,
pastorella romita, entro ti stai!
Oh come chiara, ove più quivi annotta,
l'ombra rallumi co' celesti rai!

[How beautifully, my lonely shepherdess,
in that deserted grotto you abide!
How brightly, where the dark holds greatest sway,
you light the shadows with celestial rays]

Giambattista Marino, "La Maddalena di Tiziano"
("Titian's Magdalen")

Yo vi del rojo sol la luz serena
turbarse, y que en un punto desparece
su alegre faz, y en torno se oscurece
el cielo con tiniebla de horror llena . . .
mas luego vi romperse el negro velo
deshecho en agua, y a su luz primera
restituirse alegre el claro día . . .

[The tranquil light of the red sun I saw
grow agitated, and its cheerful face

fade 'way in moment's time, and then the sky
obscured become with darkness full of dread . . .
but afterward I saw the black veil break,
dissolving into water, and bright day,
restored to its first brightness happily]

> Juan de Arguijo, "La tempestad y la calma"
> ("Storm and Calm")

Już brudnym cieniem okryły się nieba
I zgasły słońca zachodnie podwoje . . .

[A dusky shade already cloaks the sky
And the sun's western orbs extinguished lie]

> Jan Andrzej Morsztyn, "Serenata"

g) *the opposition of hot and cold:*

> Grief melts away
> Like snow in May,
> As if there were no such cold thing . . .
> What frost to that? what pole is not the zone,
> Where all things burn,
> When thou dost turn,
> And the least frown of thine is shown?

> George Herbert, "The Flower"

Hast thou couragious fire to thaw the ice
Of frozen North discoveries?

> John Donne, "Satyre: Of Religion"

Give me more love, or more disdaine;
The Torrid, or the frozen Zone,
Bring equall ease unto my paine . . .

> Thomas Carew, "Mediocritie in love rejected"

And other Confines there behold
Of Light and Darkness, Heat and Cold . . .

> Thomas Traherne, "Shadows in the Water"

Es ruffte Sylvius: wie zierlich sind die Waden
Mit warmen Schnee bedeckt, mit Helffenbein beladen!

[Then Sylvius exclaimed: how lovely are these thighs,
Where warming snow is piled and where sweet ivory lies]

Christian Hofmann von Hofmannswaldau, "Er schauet der Lesbie
durch ein Loch zu" ("He Observes Lesbia Through a Hole")

Sie zünden übers Meer entfernte Seelen an
Und Herzen, denen sich kein Eis vergleichen kann.

[They kindled distant spirits 'cross the seas,
And hearts, with which no ice can be compared.]

Daniel Caspar von Lohenstein, "Die Augen" ("Eyes")

L'Amour, tout dieu qu'il est, avec toute sa flamme,
Ne dissoudra jamais les glaçons de son âme,
Et cette souche enfin n'aimera jamais rien . . .

[Love, though he be divine, with all his fire
Will never melt the ice floe of her heart,
And nothing will that block, alas, e'er love]

Georges de Scudéry, "Aimez ou n'aimez pas . . ."

Pues la por quien helar y arder me siento,
mientras en ti se mira, Amor retrata
de su rostro la nieve y la escarlata
en tu tranquilo y blando movimiento . . .

[Since Cupid on your smooth and quiet stream,
as she looks into it, portrays the snow
and scarlet of her face, for whom I seem
at times to freeze, at other times to glow]

Luis de Góngora, "Oh claro honor del líquido elemento . . ."

Solco di nieve che sfavilla ardori . . .

[A furrow of snow that sparkles with flame]

Giambattista Marino, *Il tempio* ("The Temple")

Voi, che già fuste a lunga schiera amante
ministri sol di fiamme e di faville,
voi, voi, disciolto in tepid'onda il gelo
bagnaste in terra (oh meraviglia!) il cielo . . .

[You, who were once to a long lovers' line
the ministers of naught but flames and sparks,
you, you, now ice dissolved in tepid waves
bathed on the earth (oh, wondrous thing!) the sky]

Giambattista Marino, "La Maddalena di Tiziano"
("Titian's Magdalen")

Ty jak lód, a jam w piekielnej śrzeżodze . . .

[You are like ice, while I burn in the fires of hell]

Jan Andrzej Morsztyn, "Do trupa" ("To a Corpse")

Kak mala iskra v vechnom lde . . .

[A small spark in eternal ice]

Mikhail V. Lomonosov, "Vechernee razmyshlenie o bozhiem
velichestve pri sluchae velikogo severnogo siyaniya"
("Evening Meditation on the Majesty of God
on the Occasion of the Great Northern Lights")

V

The Universality of the Baroque Experience:
Travels, Translations, Influence

The similarity of artistic response to events of supranational significance in the Baroque age enhances the acceptability of Baroque as a period designation. The relative universality of what I think ought to be spoken of as the Baroque literary experience can be appreciated still further by consideration of the mobility of writers, their familiarity with the works of writers in other countries, the availability of translations, and the evidence of influences. An exhaustive examination of these matters is not my purpose here; instead, I just want to suggest the value of such an investigation by reviewing several of the more outstanding instances.

Without any doubt the most admired and influential poet of the Baroque was the Italian Giambattista Marino. In his valuable study, *The Poet of the Marvelous*, James V. Mirollo examines in some detail the impact of Marino on poets in his native Italy and then proceeds to a survey of his influence elsewhere in Italy.

In France, where Marino lived between 1615 and 1623, and where he published *La sampogna* (1620) and *L'Adone* (1623), his influence embraced such important poets as Antoine-Girard de Saint-Amant (cf. the "Advertissement au lecteur" to the 1629 edition of his works), Théophile de Viau, a friend of Saint-Amant, Tristan L'Hermite, who in 1641 gave the title *La Lyre* to a group of poems in memory of Marino's collection *La lira*, Georges de Scudéry, Claude de Malleville, Vincent de Voiture, and Pierre Le Moyne, whose *Peintures morales* (1640–43) clearly is indebted to Marino's *La galería*. Mirollo also mentions a number of French translations of Marino's works.

Although he never visited England, Marino had the opportunity in Paris to meet the English poets Edward Herbert (Lord

Herbert of Cherbury), the English ambassador to France from 1619 to 1624, and Thomas Carew, both of whom translated and adapted several of his works. His influence on Marvell ("Eyes and Tears," "The Garden," "The Fair Singer," among others) and on Crashaw (whose *Sospetto d'Herode*, 1637, is based on the first book of Marino's *La strage degli innocenti*) has been well documented. Among Marino's translators in contemporary England were Samuel Daniel (1562–1610); Drummond of Hawthornden (1585–1649), who wrote a panegyric for James I ("Forth Feasting") that recalls Marino's panegyric to Pope Leo XI, "Il tebro festante"; Edward Sherburne (1618–1720); Thomas Stanley (1625–78); and Philip Ayres (1638–1712). Besides translating and popularizing Marino in England, Stanley also helped disseminate contemporary French poetry through his translations of Saint-Amant, Tristan L'Hermite, Voiture, and others.

Among German Baroque poets, Marino's most fervent admirers were Christian Hofmann von Hofmannswaldau, who knew Italian well enough to translate Guarini's *Pastor fido*, and Barthold Heinrich Brockes (1680–1747), who translated Marino's "La canzone dei baci," the whole of *La strage* and parts of *L'Adone*.

Elsewhere in Europe, Mirollo mentions in passing that Marino influenced the Hungarian poet Miklós Zrínyi and that there were Croatian translations of Marino's sonnets and *La strage*.

Primarily an epic poet, Zrínyi was indeed familiar with Marino's *La strage* and drew from it in his epic *Szigetvár ostroma* ("The Siege of Sziget"). His lyrics, written both before and after "The Siege," are less important. Occasional Marinesque echoes can be discerned in such works as "Fantasia poetica" and "Arianna sírása" ("Lament of Ariadne"), but only rarely are they as verbally dazzling or imagistically rich as Zrínyi's Italian master. How Zrínyi regarded Marino can be gleaned from the title of his major verse collection (which includes "The Siege of Sziget"): *Adriai tengernek Syrénája* ("The Siren of the Adriatic Sea," 1651), which calls to mind the title Marino bestowed upon himself: "Siren of the Tyrrhenian Sea."

Any roster of Slavic poets influenced by Marino would be incomplete without the names of at least two Croatians, Dživo Bunić-Vucić (Ivan Bunić-Vučićević) and Ignjat Djordjić, and that of the important Polish Baroque poet Jan Andrzej Morsztyn. Italian influence generally abounds in the literature of the

Croatian poets of the Ragusan Republic during the Renaissance and Baroque, and with good reason. The long historical association with Venice brought this small island in a sea of Turkish domination firmly within the orbit of Italian (particularly Venetian) culture. Most of the poets knew Italian, a number were bilingual, and often published their works in Italy. Thus, Ivan Gundulić's Croatian versions of the Psalms were published in Rome in 1621; Stijepo Djordjić's collection of seven Psalm translations in Padua in 1686; Andrija Vitaljić's complete collection of Psalm translations in Venice in 1703; and Ignjat Djordjić's *Uzdasi Mandalijene pokornice* in that city in 1728. Marinesque influence on the Hungarian poet Zrínyi has already been discussed. I might add parenthetically that Zrínyi's brother, a Croatian official whose Slavicized name was Petar Zrinski (1621–71), translated his brother's works from Hungarian into Croatian.

The Polish poet Jan Andrzej Morsztyn is rightly regarded as the leading exponent of Marinism in Baroque Poland. A prominent figure in contemporary Polish and French court, diplomatic, and aristocratic circles, and a well-traveled European gentleman, Morsztyn enjoyed wide literary associations. His translation of Corneille's *Le Cid* was one of the literary successes of his day. To the excellent translation of *Gerusalemme liberata* by Piotr Kochanowski he added his own version of the *Aminta* and was so great a devotee of the poetry of Marino (whom he could have met in Paris) that he not only translated a number of Marino's lyrics but also modeled many of his own poems on those of the Italian. Morsztyn's second collection of lyrics bears the title *Lutnia* ("The Lute," 1661), which of course recalls Marino's *La lira*.

Among Iberian poets, Marino was imitated by Juan de Tasis (1582–1622), who knew Marino in Italy, Luis de Carrillo y Sotomayor, a resident of Naples, and Quevedo, who traveled in Italy and performed official functions there on behalf of the Spanish government. Lope de Vega also expressed high praise for Marino in a letter prefaced to his comedy *Virtud, pobreza y mujer* ("Virtue, Poverty and Woman," 1625), which in fact was dedicated to the Italian poet.[1] In the case of Spain and Portugal, the influences really worked both ways. Scholars have already amply demonstrated Marino's own indebtedness to Montemayor, Lope, and Camões.

[1] Mirollo, *The Poet of the Marvelous* (New York, 1963), p. 265 and below.

Paralleling Marino's influence in his own country was Góngora's great influence among poets in Spain and the Americas. The controversy in Spain surrounding Góngora's poetic innovations, which involved especially Quevedo, was echoed on the other side of the Atlantic. Góngora was probably the most admired and most imitated Spanish poet in the New World. When his writings were attacked by the Portuguese theologian Manuel Faria e Souza (1590–1649), the Peruvian poet-priest Juan Espinosa Medrano (1632–88) sprang to the defense with his *Apologética en favor de don Luis de Góngora, príncipe de los poetas líricos de España* (1662).

The rivalry and hostility that marked English and Spanish relations in the later sixteenth and seventeenth centuries did not keep English writers from familiarizing themselves with Spanish literature. For obvious reasons, the interest in Spanish culture was greatest among Catholic writers, notably Crashaw who had a good command of both Spanish and Italian. He translated part of Marino's *La strage* and took a particular interest in the writings of the Spanish mystic St. Teresa de Jesús whom he made the subject of his "The Flaming Heart" and "Hymne to the Name and Honour of the Admirable Saint Teresa." The translation in 1655 of the *Lusíadas* by Sir Richard Fanshawe, the English ambassador to Portugal and Spain at the time, made the great Portuguese epic of Camões accessible to English readers a half century after the famous translation of the *Gerusalemme liberata* by Edward Fairfax.

Among French poets known and admired in the English-speaking world during the Baroque age the most important by all evidence was the Protestant Guillaume de Salluste du Bartas, the author of *La Semaine, ou Création du Monde* (1578). (The *Seconde Semaine, ou Enfance du Monde* appeared in 1584.) His Protestantism and the subject of his Christian epic won du Bartas, in the well-known Joshua Sylvester translation of the first *Semaine,* a wide following among English readers. Apart from such an illustrious admirer as John Milton, the Sylvester translation of du Bartas also left its mark on *Christ's Victory and Triumph, in Heaven, in Earth, over and after Death* (1610) by Giles Fletcher the Younger (c. 1588–1623) and on the poetry of one of the most prominent Colonial American poets, Anne Bradstreet.

Because of the Puritan domination of Colonial American culture, it would be inaccurate to equate the role of English literature in the development of the Colonial American with that of Spain in relation to Spanish America (e.g. Mexico). But it is safe to say that with due consideration of the contribution of Puritanism and the realities of the new life in America, seventeenth-century American literature still owed much to England. Major Colonial poets such as Anne Bradstreet, Michael Wigglesworth, and Edward Taylor were well versed in the writings of their British contemporaries and reflect the influence of these writings in various ways. Moreover, the Americans were often published in England and thus could feel themselves to be a part of the English literary community. Bradstreet's *The Tenth Muse Lately Sprung up in America* was first published in London in 1650, and Wigglesworth's *Day of Doom* (1662) was reissued in both England and America shortly after its first American edition.

English literature also had its admirers and imitators on the Continent. The Dutch poet Constantijn Huygens visited the English court of James I in 1619, which provided an occasion to meet Ben Jonson and possibly also John Donne. After his return to London in 1621 to assume the position of secretary to his country's embassy, he had a better opportunity to meet Donne, whose works he admired greatly and which he could appreciate in their original language. The German poet Hofmannswaldau also visited London and Oxford in 1639. He learned English well enough to translate Joseph Hall's (1574–1656) satirical work *Characters of Virtues and Vices* (1608) and seems to have read Spenser, Drayton, Jonson, Quarles, and Donne.

Apart from imitations of the Marinist style (notably, for example, in the case of Hofmannswaldau) and occasional contacts with English poetry of the period, as with Hofmannswaldau in the first half of the century and Barthold Brockes (1680–1747) and others somewhat later, it was Holland primarily from which German Baroque poets sought to learn. This was particularly true of the Silesian Lutherans who had no university in their native Silesia and found themselves drawn, like students elsewhere in the Germanic-speaking world, to the important center of learning at Leyden (Leiden). Considering the brilliant flowering of culture then taking place in Holland, the attractions of the Netherlands were obvious.

Influenced above all by a Dutch poetic miscellany, *Den Bloehm-*

hof van de Nederlandshe Jeught (1608 and 1610), the leading poet of the German Baroque, Martin Opitz, visited Holland in 1618 and sought out the poet who attracted him most, Daniel Heinsius, a professor at Leyden and an accomplished poet in both Dutch and Latin. Besides translating a number of Heinsius' poems, whose importance particularly for his own *Trost Gedichte* have long been appreciated, Opitz, under the influence of Dutch prosody, formulated important and far-reaching metric reforms for German that were embodied in his *Buch von der deutschen Poeterey* (written 1624). Opitz's interest in Heinsius was shared also by the poet and philologist Justus Georgius Schottel, who came to Leyden to study law.

Andreas Gryphius, too, was attracted to contemporary Dutch literature. After the Thirty Years' War he became a tutor-companion in Leyden and remained there until 1644. The foremost dramatic writer of Baroque Germany, Gryphius was naturally drawn to the works of the great Dutch dramatist of the time, Vondel. Gryphius' knowledge of the Dutch language and interest in Vondel can be judged from the fact that he translated Vondel's tragedy *De Gebroeders* (1640).

Members of the respected Königsberg literary society, Die Kürbis-Hütte—Simon Dach, Robert Roberthin, and Heinrich Albert—shared the interest in Dutch literature of Opitz, Gryphius, and others, concentrating chiefly on the poetry of Dirck Camphuysen with whom they felt affinities and whom they translated and imitated.

Other important German Baroque poets drawn to seventeenth-century Netherlands culture were Paul Fleming, who studied at Leyden and took his medical degree there in 1640, and Philipp Zesen, who studied at Leyden and later resided in Holland for a number of years (1655–67), becoming fluent enough in Dutch to compose poems in that language as well as in his native German.

In the case of German-Dutch literary relations in the Baroque age, the movement would appear to have gone one way. But at least one major German writer and thinker had his Dutch admirers. That was Jakob Böhme. The German mystic's most prominent Dutch admirer undoubtedly was the Amsterdam Anabaptist and mystic Jan Luyken (major work: *Jesus en de Ziel*, 1618), the author of principally amatory verse before falling under Böhme's influence.

On the basis of the great significance of Silesia for the development of German Baroque literature (Opitz, Gryphius, Hofmannswaldau, Kuhlmann, Logau, Lohenstein, Benjamin Neukirch), the wide influence of the Silesian mystics (Abraham von Franckenberg, Daniel von Czepko, Angelus Silesius), and the clustering of a few poets—Franckenberg, Opitz, Gryphius—in the culturally dynamic port city of Danzig (Gdańsk, in Polish) during the Thirty Years' War, there would seem to be a circumstantial case for extensive German-Polish literary interaction in the Baroque period. Until research produces evidence to the contrary, however, one is compelled to take the position that such interaction did not occur on any significant level. Slavic names and places and occasional stock characters crop up from time to time in German Baroque literature (e.g. the "Russian" and "Baltic" poems of Paul Fleming), but there is virtually nothing else to give the case substance. Even the works of Opitz, who in 1636 became the court historian and secretary to the Polish king Władysław IV with his permanent residence in Danzig, reflect little awareness of contemporary, or earlier, Polish vernacular (as opposed to Polish Latin) culture. Conversely, with respect to German, the same was true of the Polish Protestant writer Zbigniew Morsztyn who knew German well and most of whose *Emblemata* were written after he had emigrated to Prussia in 1660. Moreover, there was no Polish mystic development in the seventeenth century paralleling that of the Silesian Germans, so the possibility of interaction in this very important sphere of thought and writing must be discounted. Contacts between German and Polish Protestant groups certainly existed, but no noticeable literary impact seems to have been recorded on either side.

With Poland's own impressive indigenous Renaissance culture in both the vernacular language and Latin and the overall Italian orientation of Polish culture in the sixteenth and seventeenth centuries, Polish writers in the period of the Baroque doubtless felt there was little cause to search out literary models in a contemporary Germany with whom there had been no outstanding cultural associations previously. Furthermore, the principal foreign influence on Polish culture from the time of Humanism down to the second half of the eighteenth century was Italy. Italian Humanists (notably Buonacorsi ["Callimachus"]) had spent some time in Poland; the Polish king Sigismund I was married to a member of the Bona Sforza family, which opened Poland to a host of Italian influences during the Renaissance; for much of the sixteenth century Polish students preferred to study in Italy (Padua, particularly) when they went abroad and upon return to Poland maintained a lively interest in things Italian; there is ample evidence that Italian *commedia dell'arte* troupes regularly visited Polish cities on tour. Until Jan Andrzej Morsztyn's translation of Corneille's *Le Cid* (1662), Polish interest even in French literature was minimal save perhaps for the Renaissance poet Kochanowski's knowledge of and interest in the work of the Pléiade. Everything considered, the most influential non-Polish literary personalities in Baroque Poland were Marino (principally because of Morsztyn) and Tasso whose *Gerusalemme liberata* found a wide readership and several imitators for reasons already indicated.

German Baroque literature fared better elsewhere in the Slavic world than it did in Poland. The Jesuit von Spee's highly regarded *Güldenes Tugendbuch* and *Trutz Nachtigall* were ably translated into Czech by the Jesuit Felix Kadlinský and widely circulated under the titles *Zlatá ctnosti kniha . . .* (1662) and *Zdoroslavíček v kratochvilném háječku postaveny* (1665), respectively. Then, much later, when as a result of Peter the Great's vast program to Europeanize and "modernize" Muscovy, Russian students were for the first time permitted to travel and study in the West, Russia's first important native poet and one of the outstanding figures in eighteenth-century Russian literature and science, Mikhail Vasilevich Lomonosov (1711–65) journeyed first to Marburg then to Freiburg to enroll in the famous universities there. One result of his stay in Germany, his closer familiarity with German poetry, had a considerable influence on the course of later Russian poetic development. His recognition of the suitability of German syllabo-tonic (or syllabo-accentual) versification for Russian resulted in the abandonment of the Polish-derived syllabic metric system, which was basically unsuited to Russian, and set Russian prosody on the course it has followed with only minor changes to the present. Lomonosov's views on poetry and prosody were embodied in a letter he sent the President of the Russian Academy of Sciences from Germany in 1739 along with his first important poetic work, the "Oda na vzyatie Khotina" ("Ode on the Capture of Khotin"), which was intended as a demonstration of the validity and advantages of his poetic theories. The impact of German poetic practice on Lomonosov was very much like that of the Dutch on Opitz, and in the evolution of the modern prosodic systems of their respective languages both men played a strikingly similar role.

The influence on Lomonosov's odic writing of the "official poetry" of the late German Baroque poet Johann Christian Günther (1695–1723) (there are, for example, direct borrowings in Lomonosov's ode on Khotin from Günther's ode to Prince Eugene celebrating the Peace of Passarowitz with the Turks: "Eugen ist fort, ihr Musen, nach!" 1718) left its stamp on most Russian odic verse down to the early nineteenth century, largely because it followed the path established for this genre by Lomonosov (cf., for example, the heroic odes celebrating Russian victories over the French in northern Italy in the 1790s by Russia's greatest eighteenth-century poet, Gavrila Romanovich Derzhavin, 1743–1816).

Among Slavic literatures in the Baroque age the Polish is the only one with anything resembling a legitimate claim to an international character of sorts. The Romanian poet Miron Kostyn (1633–91 or 1692) chose Polish as the language in which to write a lengthy verse *Description of the Moldavian and Multanian Lands* (*Opisanie ziemi mołdawskiej i multanskiej*, 1684), which he offered to the Polish king Jan III Sobieski. The Polish metric system (the syllabic) and Polish Renaissance and early Baroque literature exerted strong influence on Belorussian and Ukrainian vernacular and Church Slavonic writing in the second half of the seventeenth and in the early eighteenth centuries, and on Russian (Muscovite) literature in the first three decades of the eighteenth century, principally through the agency of Belorussian and Ukrainian clerics and Schoolmen who were invited into Muscovite service from the distinguished center of Orthodox learning at the Kiev Academy after a large part of the eastern Ukraine passed from Polish to Muscovite domination in the second half of the seventeenth century.

The knowledge of Polish Baroque literature did not move only in an eastern direction, however. The best-known and most-admired Polish writer of the Baroque was the Jesuit professor of poetics at the Jesuit academies of Wilno and Polotsk, Maciej Kazimierz Sarbiewski (1595–1640) who wrote exclusively in

Latin. His text on poetics, *De Perfecta Poesi* (written 1619–26?, first published 1954), served as an exemplar for similar manuals in the Ukraine and Muscovy in the later seventeenth and early eighteenth centuries; his books of lyrics went through sixty editions in various European countries where Sarbiewski enjoyed prestige and emulation under the Latinized name of Sarbievius. Vernacular translations were also made; in 1646, for example, a number of his poems were rendered into English by a certain G. Hils and apparently attracted some attention. Among contemporaries, Grotius greatly admired Sarbiewski's poems, and there is reason to believe that Henry Vaughan's treatment of hermetic motifs was influenced by them. Later, in England, Coleridge warmly recalled the poetry of the "divine Casimire" and planned, but never executed, modern translations of Sarbiewski's lyrics.

The above survey of travels, translations, and influences, although no more than a sketch, should shed some light on the relative "smallness" of the world of Baroque literature. Despite the breakdown of the cohesion of the universal cultural system of Latin and the fragmentation brought on by the rise of the vernacular literatures, largely in the sixteenth and seventeenth centuries, Europe in the Baroque age was still very much a family of nations bound together by a variety of mutual concerns. That this was indeed true of European political and religious life at the time has been, I think, amply chronicled; the demonstration that this was true also of European literary experience in the same period is one of the aims of this book.

Supplementary Bibliography

Adrianova-Perets, V. P. (ed). *Russkaya sillabicheskaya poeziya XVII–XVIII v.v.*, Leningrad, 1970.

Alewyn, Richard (ed.). *Deutsche Barockforschung*. Dokumentation einer Epoche. Köln-Berlin, 1965.

Allem [Allemand], Maurice (ed.). *Anthologie poétique française XVIIᵉ siècle.* 2 vols. Paris, 1965.

Alonso, Damaso. *Evolución de la sintaxis de Góngora*. Madrid, 1928.

———. *La lengua poetica de Góngora*. 2d ed. Madrid, 1950.

———. *Estudios y ensayos gongorinos*. Madrid, 1955.

———. *Góngora y el Polifemo*. 2 vols. Madrid, 1961.

Artigas, M. *Don Luis de Góngora y Argote*. Madrid, 1925.

Bitnar, Vilém. *Postavy a problémy českého baroku literárního*. Prague, 1938.

Blecua, José Manuel (ed.). *Floresta lirica española*. Madrid, 1957.

Blunt, Sir Anthony. *Artistic Theory in Italy 1450–1600*. Oxford, 1966. First pub. Oxford, 1940.

Bogišić, Rafo (ed.). *Zbornik stihova XVII. stoljeća*. Zagreb, 1967.

———. *Leut i trublja. Antologija starije hrvatske poezije*. Zagreb, 1971.

Brereton, Geoffrey (ed.). *The Penguin Book of French Verse*. Vol. 2. Baltimore, Md., 1958.

Bunić-Vučićević, Ivan. *Gedichte*, ed. Renate Lachmann-Schmohl. München, 1965.

Bush, Douglas. *English Literature in the Earlier Seventeenth Century*. Oxford, 1945.

Camões, Luís de. *Rimas*, ed. Álvaro J. Da Costa Pimpão. Coimbra, 1953.

Cave, Terence C. *Devotional Poetry in France c. 1570–1613*. Cambridge, 1969.

Cohen, J. M. (ed.). *The Penguin Book of Spanish Verse*. Baltimore, Md. 1956.

Cioranescu, Alexandre. *El barroco, o el descubrimiento del drama*. La Laguna, 1957.

Croce, Benedetto. *Saggi sulla letteratura italiana del Seicento*. Bari, 1911.

Cysarz, Herbert. *Deutsches Barock in der Lyrik*. Leipzig, 1936.

Dalgish, Jack (ed.). *Eight Metaphysical Poets*. New York, 1961.

Dürr-Durski, Jan. "Od manieryzmu do baroku, *Przegląd Humanistyczny*, XV, 1 (1971), 1–17.

Duviard, Ferdinand (ed.). *Anthologie des poètes français* (XVIIᵉ siècle). Paris, 1947.

Ermatinger, E. *Barock und Rokoko in der deutschen Dichtung.* Berlin-Leipzig, 1926.

Espinás, José M. (ed.). *Antología de la poesía amorosa española.* Barcelona, 1953.

Fischerówna, Róża. *Samuel Twardowski jako poeta barokowy.* Cracow, 1931.

Forster, Leonard (ed.). *The Penguin Book of German Verse.* Baltimore, Md. 1957.

Frank, Horst-Joachim. *Catharina Regina von Greiffenberg.* Göttingen, 1967.

Friedlander, Walter. *Mannerism and Anti-Mannerism in Italian Painting.* New York, 1957.

Friedrich, Carl J. *The Age of the Baroque, 1610–1660.* New York, 1952.

———, and Blitzer, Charles. *The Age of Power.* Ithaca, 1957.

Gates, Eunice Joiner. *Documentos gongorinos.* Mexico, 1960.

Gillespie, Gerald. *German Baroque Poetry. New York,* 1971.

Góngora, Luis de. *Poesías: Polifemo, Soledades and Other Poems,* ed. J. W. Barker. Cambridge, 1942.

Green, Otis H. *Spain and the Western Tradition.* Vol. IV. Madison, Milwaukee, and London, 1966.

Guillen, Jorge. *Language and Poetry.* Cambridge, Mass., 1961.

Haller, Rudolf. *Geschichte der deutschen Lyrik vom Ausgang des Mittelalters bis zu Goethes Tod.* Bern, München, 1967.

Hart, Henry H. *Luis de Camoëns and the Epic of the Lusiads.* Norman, Okla., 1962.

Holmes, Elizabeth. *Henry Vaughan and the Hermetic Philosophy.* Oxford, 1932.

Hrabák, Josef. *Starší česká literatura.* Prague, 1964.

Inglis, Fred (ed.). *English Poetry 1550–1660.* London, 1965.

Jones, D. Mervyn. *Five Hungarian Writers.* Oxford, 1966.

Jones, R. O. (ed.). *Poems of Góngora.* Cambridge, 1966.

Kalista, Zdeněk. *Z legend českého baroka.* Olomouc, 1934.

Kane, Elisha K. *Gongorism and the Golden Age.* Chapel Hill, N.C., 1928.

Knuvelder, Gerard. *Handboek Tot De Geschiedenis Der Nederlandse Letterkunde. Der Tweede Deel.* (Tweede, herziene Druk.) Hertogenbosch, 1958.

Leonard, Irving A. *Baroque Times in Old Mexico.* 2nd printing. Ann Arbor, Mich., 1966.

Lind, L. R. (ed.). *Lyric Poetry of the Italian Renaissance.* New Haven and London, 1954.

———, and Bergin, Thomas G. (eds.). *Lyric Poetry of the Italian Renaissance: An Anthology with Verse Translations.* New Haven and London, 1954.

"Literarny Barok" issue, *Litteraria, XIII* (1971).

Maulnier, Thierry, and Aury, Dominique. *Poètes précieux et baroques.* Anger, 1941.

Mišianik, Ján *et al. Dejiny staršej slovenskej literatury.* Bratislava, 1958.
———— (ed.). *Antológia staršej slovenskej literatury.* Bratislava, 1964.
Moret, André (ed.). *Anthologie du lyrisme baroque en Allemagne.* Paris, 1957.
Morsztyn, Jan Andrzej. *Wybór poezji,* ed. Maria Bokszczanin. Warsaw, 1963.
Morsztyn, Zbigniew. *Muza domowa,* ed. Jan Dürr-Durski. 2 vols. Warsaw, 1954.
Nowak-Długewski, Juliusz. "Barok w Polsce," *Polonistyka,* XX, 6 (1967), 1–11.
Panowsky, Erwin. *Studies in Iconology.* New York, 1939.
Pascal, Roy. *German Literature in the 16th and 17th Centuries.* London, 1968.
Petersson, Robert T. *The Art of Ecstasy: Teresa, Bernini, and Crashaw.* New York, 1970.
Plancarte, Alfonso Méndez (ed.). *Poetas Novohispanos: Segundo Siglo (1621–1721).* Parte Primera. Mexico, 1944.
Praz, Mario. *Secentismo e marinismo in Inghilterra.* Firenze, 1925.
————. *Studi sul concettismo.* Firenze, 1946.
Robb, Nesca A. *Neoplatonism of the Italian Renaissance.* London, 1935.
Rotermund, Erwin. *Christian Hofmann von Hofmannswaldau.* Stuttgart, 1963.
Rousset, Jean (ed.). *Anthologie de la poésie baroque française.* 2 vols. Paris, 1961.
Salinas, Pedro. *Reality and the Poet in Spanish Poetry.* Baltimore, Md., 1966.
Schaller, H. *Die Welt des Barock.* München, 1936.
Schmidt, Albert-Marie (ed.). *Poètes du XVIᵉ Siècle.* Paris, 1953.
Spoljar, Krsto (ed.). *Ljubav Pjesnika: Mala antologija hrvatske ljubavne poezije.* Zagreb, 1956.
Swardson, H. R. *Poetry and the Fountain of Light.* Columbia, Mo., 1962.
Szyrocki, Marian. *Andreas Gryphius.* Tübingen, 1964.
Tapie, Victor. *Baroque et classicisme.* Paris, 1957.
Torbarina, J. *Italian Influences on Poets of the Ragusan Republic.* London, 1931.
Trogrančić, Franjo. *Storia della letteratura croata dall'umanesimo alla rinascita nazionale (secolo XV–XIX).* Rome, 1953.
Tschizewskij [Čiževskij], Dmitrij. *Slavische Barockliteratur I.* München, 1970.
Tuve, Rosemond. *Elizabethan and Metaphysical Imagery.* Chicago, 1947.
Unger, Leonard. *Donne's Poetry and Modern Criticism.* Chicago, 1950.
Van Ingen, Ferdinand. *Vanitas und Memento Mori in der deutschen Barocklyrik.* Groningen, 1966.
Vašica, Josef. *České literární baroko.* Prague, 1938.
Viëtor, Karl. *Probleme der deutschen Barockliteratur.* Leipzig, 1928.
Von Faber du Faur, Curt. *German Baroque Literature.* New Haven and London, 1958.
Wedgwood, C. V. *The Thirty Years' War.* London, 1938.

Weevers, Theodor. *Poetry of the Netherlands in Its European Context 1170–1930*. London, 1960.

Wehrli, Max (ed.). *Deutsche Barocklyrik*. Basel-Stuttgart, 1967.

Weinberg, Bernard (ed.). *French Poetry of the Renaissance*. Carbondale and Edwardsville, Ill., 1964.

Weintraub, Wiktor. "O niektórych problemach polskiego baroku," *Przegląd Humanistyczny*, IV, 5 (1960), 1–21.

Wilson, D. B. *Descriptive Poetry in France from Blason to Baroque*. Manchester, 1967.

Winegarten, Renée. *French Lyric Poetry in the Age of Malherbe*. Manchester, 1954.

Yates, Frances. A. *Giordano Bruno and the Hermetic Tradition*. London, 1964.

PART TWO

Texts

I

The World of the Spirit

RELIGIOUS AND MYSTIC POETRY

§ *English*

FROM *HOLY SONNETS*

1.

Thou hast made me, And shall thy worke decay?
Repaire me now, for now mine end doth haste,
I runne to death, and death meets me as fast,
And all my pleasures are like yesterday;
I dare not move my dimme eyes any way,
Despaire behind, and death before doth cast
Such terrour, and my feeble flesh doth waste
By sinne in it, which it t'wards hell doth weigh;
Onely thou art above, and when towards thee
By thy leave I can looke, I rise againe;
But our old subtle foe so tempteth me,
That not one houre my selfe I can sustaine;
Thy Grace may wing me to prevent his art,
And thou like Adamant draw mine iron heart.

4.

Oh my blacke Soule! now thou art summoned
By sicknesse, deaths herald, and champion;
Thou art like a pilgrim, which abroad hath done
Treason, and durst not turne to whence hee is fled,

Or like a thiefe, which till deaths doome be read,
Wisheth himselfe delivered from prison;
But damn'd and hal'd to execution,
Wisheth that still he might be imprisoned.
Yet grace, if thou repent, thou canst not lacke;
But who shall give thee that grace to beginne?
Oh make thy selfe with holy mourning blacke,
And red with blushing, as thou art with sinne;
Or wash thee in Christs blood, which hath this might
That being red, it dyes red soules to white.

14.
Batter my heart, three person'd God; for, you
As yet but knocke, breathe, shine, and seeke to mend;
That I may rise, and stand, o'erthrow mee, 'and bend
Your force, to breake, blowe, burn and make me new.
I, like an usurpt towne, to'another due,
Labour to'admit you, but Oh, to no end,
Reason your viceroy in mee, mee should defend,
But is captiv'd, and proves weake or untrue.
Yet dearely'I love you, 'and would be loved faine,
But am betroth'd unto your enemie:
Divorce mee, 'untie, or breake that knot againe,
Take mee to you, imprison mee, for I
Except you'enthrall mee, never shall be free,
Nor ever chast, except you ravish mee.

                                 John Donne (1572–1631)

This Crosse-Tree here
Doth JESUS   beare,
Who   sweet'ned   first,
The   Death accurs't.

Here all things ready are, make hast, make hast away;
For, long this work wil be, & very short this Day.
Why then, go on to act: Here's wonders to be done,
Before the last least sand of Thy ninth houre be run;
Or e're dark Clouds do dull, or dead the Mid-dayes Sun.

Act when Thou wilt,
Bloud will   be spilt;
Pure Balm, that shall
Bring Health to All.
Why   then,   Begin
To powre   first in
Some Drops of Wine,
In   stead   of   Brine,
To search the Wound,
So   long   unsound:
And,   when that's
done, Let Oyle, next,
run, To cure the Sore
Sinne   made before.
And O! Deare Christ,
E'en as Thou di'st,
Look down, and see
Us weepe for Thee.
And tho (Love knows)
Thy dreadfull Woes
Wee   cannot   ease;
Yet doe Thou please,
Who   Mercie   art,
T'accept each Heart,
That   gladly would
Helpe,   if   it could.
Meane while, let mee,
Beneath   this   Tree,
This Honour have,
To make my grave.

Robert Herrick (1591–1674)

CLASPING OF HANDS

Lord, thou art mine, and I am thine,
If mine I am: and thine much more
Then I or ought, or can be mine.
Yet to be thine, doth me restore;
So that again I now am mine,
And with advantage mine the more,
Since this being mine, brings with it thine,
And thou with me dost thee restore.
   If I without thee would be mine,
   I neither should be mine nor thine.

Lord, I am thine, and thou art mine:
So mine thou art, that something more
I may presume thee mine, then thine.
For thou didst suffer to restore
Not thee, but me, and to be mine,
And with advantage mine the more,
Since thou in death wast none of thine,
Yet then as mine didst me restore.
   O be mine still! still make me thine!
   Or rather make no Thine and Mine!

George Herbert (1593–1633)

THE ALTAR

A broken A L T A R, Lord, thy servant reares,
Made of a heart, and cemented with teares:
   Whose parts are as thy hand did frame;
   No workmans tool hath touch'd the same.
        A HEART alone
        Is such a stone,
        As nothing but
        Thy pow'r doth cut.
        Wherefore each part
        Of my hard heart
        Meets in this frame,
        To praise thy Name:
That, if I chance to hold my peace,
These stones to praise thee may not cease.

O let thy blessed S A C R I F I C E be mine,
And sanctifie this A L T A R to be thine.

George Herbert

E A S T E R - W I N G S

Lord, who createdst man in wealth and store,
  Though foolishly he lost the same,
    Decaying more and more,
      Till he became
        Most poore:
        With thee
        O let me rise
      As larks, harmoniously,
  And sing this day thy victories;
Then shall the fall further the flight in me.

My tender age in sorrow did beginne:
  And still with sicknesses and shame
    Thou didst so punish sinne,
      That I became,
        Most thinne.
        With thee
      Let me combine
    And feel this day thy victorie:
  For, if I imp my wing on thine,
Affliction shall advance the flight in me.

George Herbert

C O L O S S. 3:3—
O U R   L I F E   I S   H I D   W I T H   C H R I S T   I N   G O D

My words & thoughts do both express this notion,
That *Life* hath with the sun a double motion.
The first *Is* straight and our diurnall friend,
The other   *Hid* and doth obliquely bend.
Our life is wrapt *In* flesh, and tends to earth:
The other winds towards *Him*, whose happie birth

Taught me to live here so, *That* still one eye
Should aim and shoot at that which *Is* on high:
Quitting   with   daily labour   all   *My* pleasure,
To gain   at   harvest   an eternall   *Treasure.*

George Herbert

PARADISE

I blesse thee, Lord, because I G R O W
Among thy trees, which in a R O W
To thee both fruit and order O W.

What open force, or hidden C H A R M
Can blast my fruit, or bring me H A R M,
While the inclosure is thine A R M ?

Inclose me still for fear I S T A R T.
But to me rather sharp and T A R T,
Then let me want thy hand & A R T.

When thou dost greater judgements S P A R E,
And with thy knife but prune and P A R E,
Ev'n fruitfull trees more fruitfull A R E.

Such sharpnes shows the sweetest F R E N D:
Such cuttings rather heal then R E N D:
And such beginnings touch their E N D.

George Herbert

LOVE-JOY

As on a window late I cast mine eye,
I saw a vine drop grapes with *J* and *C*
Anneal'd on every bunch. One standing by
Ask'd what it meant. I, who am never loth
To spend my judgement, said, It seem'd to me
To be the bodie and the letters both
Of *Joy* and *Charitie.* Sir, you have not miss'd,
The man reply'd; It figures *Jesus Christ.*

George Herbert

BITTER-SWEET

Ah my deare angrie Lord,
Since thou dost love, yet strike;
Cast down, yet help afford;
Sure I will do the like.

I will complain, yet praise;
I will bewail, approve:
And all my sowre-sweet dayes
I will lament, and love.

George Herbert

ANA-$\left\{\begin{array}{c}\text{MARY}\\\\\text{ARMY}\end{array}\right\}$-GRAM

How well her name an *Army* doth present,
In whom the *Lord of Hosts* did pitch his tent!

George Herbert

§ *Dutch*

HY DROECH ONSE SMERTEN

T'en zijn de Joden niet, Heer Jesu, die u cruysten,
Noch die verradelijck u togen voort gericht,
Noch die versmadelijck u spogen int gesicht,
Noch die u knevelden, en stieten u vol puysten,
T'en sijn de crijchs-luy niet die met haer felle vuysten
Den rietstock hebben of den hamer opgelicht,
Of het vervloecte hout op Golgotha gesticht,
Of over uwen rock tsaem dubbelden en tuyschten:
Ick bent, ô Heer, ick bent die u dit heb gedaen,
Ick ben den swaren boom die u had overlaen,
Ick ben de taeye streng daermee ghy ginct gebonden,
De nagel, en de speer, de geessel die u sloech,
De bloet-bedropen croon die uwen schedel droech:
Want dit is al geschiet, eylaes! om mijne sonden.

HE BORE OUR GRIEFS

No, it was not the Jews who crucified,
Nor who betrayed you in the judgment place,
Nor who, Lord Jesus, spat into your face,
Nor who with buffets struck you as you died.
No, it was not the soldiers fisted bold
Who lifted up the hammer and the nail,
Or raised the cursed cross on Calvary's hill,
Or, gambling, tossed the dice to win your robe.
I am the one, O Lord, who brought you there,
I am the heavy cross you had to bear,
I am the rope that bound you to the tree,
The whip, the nail, the hammer, and the spear,
The blood-stained crown of thorns you had to wear:
It was my sin, alas, it was for me.

> Jacobus Revius (1586–1658)
> Trans. by Henrietta Ten Harmsel

UITVAERT VAN MARIA VAN DEN VONDEL

Wanneer dit tijtlijk leven endt,
Begint het endelooze leven,
By Godt en engelen bekent,
En zaligen alleen gegeven.

Daer zit de Godtheit op den troon,
In 't middenpunt van alle ronden,
Dat overal, en eenigh schoon,
Noit zijnen omvang heeft gevonden.

Dit trekt alle oogen naer zich toe,
Als d'eerste zon van alle zonnen,
De bron van 't licht, noit straelens moê,
Van geene schaduwen verwonnen.

Wat goet zich in 't geschapen spreit
By sprengkelen, is hier volkomen
In schoonheit, maght, en heerlijkheit,
Een zee, de springaêr aller stroomen.

Wat herquam van het enkel Een
Doolt, als in ballingschap verschoven,

Vint geene rustplaets hier beneên,
En zoekt het vaderlant daer boven.

Zoo waelt de lely van 't kompas,
Die met den zeilsteen wert bestreeken,
Rondom, en zoekt de starlichte as,
Haer wit, waer van zy was versteeken.

Maria steegh met haer gemoedt,
Van werreltsche ydelheên gescheiden
En los, naer dit volkomen goet,
Waertoe d'elenden 't hart bereiden.

Twee vleugels, ootmoet en gedult,
Verhieven haer uit aertsche dampen,
Daer 't eeuwigh Een 't gebrek vervult,
En vleesch en geest niet langer kampen.

Haer leste stem en aêm was Godt,
De troost der aengevochte harten,
Het beste deel, en hooghste lot,
Zoo voerze heene uit alle smarten.

Wat kroontge, op dat uw liefde blijk',
Met parle, zilver, en gesteente,
En palm, en roosmarijn, het lijk?
O Speelnoots, dit 's een dor gebeente.

Zy leefde tien paer jaeren lang,
Maer nu van 's werrelts last ontbonden,
Verwachtze om hoogh geen' ondergang.
Het hemelsche uurwerk telt geen stonden.

Een rey van englen kroon' de ziel
Met lauwerier in 's hemels hoven,
Nu 't kleet des lichaems haer ontviel.
Zy noode ons met gebeên daer boven.

ON THE DEATH OF MARIA VAN DEN VONDEL

When mortal life ends under sod
Begins the unending life in heaven,
Known unto angels and to God,
And only to the blessèd given.

There sits the Godhead on the throne,
The centre of concentric rounds,
 The omnipresent Good, the One,
Not circumscribed by any bounds.

This draws all eyes, the Sun of suns,
Light's well-spring by no light surpassed,
 Of never-waning radiance,
And by no shadows overcast.

What good there in creation be
Sprinkled in drops is here alive
 In perfect beauty and majesty,
An ocean whence all streams derive.

Man, who descends from that one Best,
Is like an exile who must roam
 Without a place where he can rest,
And seeks above his Father's home.

Thus wanders on the compass bowl
The needle that the loadstone served,
 And searches for the star-bright goal
From which it for an instant swerved.

Maria's soul did, purged of love
For worldly vanities, depart
 Unto that perfect Good above
For which life's woes prepare the heart.

Humility and patience wing
Her on beyond the mists of life,
 Where One supplies the missing thing
And flesh and spirit cease their strife.

"God" was the word she whispered last,
The solace of the afflicted soul,
 The Best on which our lot is cast.
Thus ended she her earthly role.

Why should ye decorate with gold
And palm and rosemary and stones,
 In token of love, her mortal mould?
Oh girls, these are but barren bones.

Her years did number but a score.
But now that she has dropped the load

Of life, her light will set no more.
Time counts no hours in God's abode.

The soul divested of its veil
Of flesh be crowned by angels' care
  With laurel in the heavenly dale,
And call us thither with her prayer.

Joost van den Vondel (1587–1679)
Trans. by Adriaan J. Barnouw

OP MIJNEN GEBOORT-DAGH

Noch eens September, en noch eens die vierde dagh
  Die mij verschijnen sagh!
Hoe veel Septembers, Heer, en hoe veel' vierde dagen
  Wilt ghij mij noch verdragen?
Ick bidd om geen verlang: 'tkan redelyck bestaen,
  Het ghen' ick heb gegaen:
En van mijn' wiegh tot hier zijn soo veel dusend schreden
  Die ick heb doorgetreden
(Met vallen, lieve God, en opstaen, soo ghij weett,)
  Dat die all 't selve leed
En all' de selve vreughd naer mij hadd door te reisen,
  Sich drijmael sou bepeisen
Wat besten oorber waer, gelaten of gedaen.
  Mij, Heere, laet vrij gaen;
Mijn' roll is afgespeelt, en all wat kan gebeuren
  Van lacchen en van treuren
Is mij te beurt geweest, en all wat beuren sal
  Sal 'tselve niet met all,
En d'oude schaduw zijn van dingen die wat schijnen
  En komende verdwijnen.
Wat wacht ick meer op aerd, waerom en scheid' ick niet?
  'K wacht, Heer, dat ghij 'tgebiedt.
Maer, magh ick noch een' gunst by d'andere begeeren,
  Laet mij soo scheiden leeren,
Dat yeder een die 't siet mijn scheiden en het sijn
  Wensch' eenerhand te zijn.

ON MY BIRTHDAY

September is back again and that fourth morn
    Whose sunrise saw me born.
How many a September and fourth day
    Lord, wilt Thou let me stay?
I ask no respite; I have further gone
    Than man may count upon,
And from my cradle on so many steps, dear God,
    My weary feet have trod
(With many a fall and rise, as Thou must know,)
    That he who had to go
Through all my joy and sorrow after me
    Would be in a quandary
Which he had better do: go forth or stay.
    Lord, speed me on my way.
My part is played, and all that happens here,
    The laughter and the tear,
Happened to me, and all that shall befall
    Won't be the same at all,
A shadow only of things that seem to exist
    And vanish into mist.
Why stay on earth? Why don't I take my leave?
    I wait, Lord, Thy reprieve.
But if one other favor Thou wilt give,
    Then teach me so to leave
That everyone who sees me die will pray
    That he may die my way.

Constantijn Huygens (1596–1687)
Trans. by Adriaan J. Barnouw

SONDAGH

Is 't Sabbath dagh, mijn ziel, of Sondagh? geen van tween.
De Sabbath is voorby met syne dienstbaerheden:
En de sonn die ick sie scheen gisteren als heden.
Maer die ick niet en sie en schijnt niet soo se scheen.

Son, die ick niet en sie als door mijn' sonden heen,
Soon Gods, die desen dagh het aerdrijck weer betreeden,
Fier als een Bruydegom ter loop-baen ingereden,
'Ksie Sondagh sonder end door dijne Wonden heen.

'Tzy dan oock Sondagh nu, men magh't Gods Soon-dagh noemen,
Ja, en Gods Soen-dagh toe. Maer laet ick ons verdoemen,
Waer ick van drijen gae ick vind ons inde Schuld.
God Son, God Soon, God Soen, hoe langh duert dijn geduld?

Hoe langhe lydt ghij, Heer, dijn' Soondagh, Soendagh, Sondagh,
Ondanckbaerlick verspilt, verspeelt, verspelt in Sond-dagh?

SUNDAY

Is it Sabbath, my soul, or Sunday? Neither one.
The Sabbath of the old law is no more:
The sun I see today did shine before;
The sun I see not shines not as it shone.

Sun that I do not see but through my sin,
God's son who once again dost walk the earth,
Bright as a bridegroom in Thy shining worth,
Thy wounds I see Sunday undying in.

Sunday it is, but should be Son-day named,
God's Sum-day too, which shows we should be damned
In justice; each of three shows our disgrace.
God's Sun, God's Son, God's Sum, how great Thy grace?

How long allow'st Thou, Lord, thy Sum-day, Son-day, Sunday,
Ungrateful man to spoil and spill and spell as Sin-day?

Constantijn Huygens
Trans. by Frank J. Warnke

CHRISTUS STERVENDE

Die alles troost en laaft, verzucht, bezwymt, ontverft!
Die alles ondersteunt geraakt, o my! aan 't wyken.
Een doodsche donkerheit komt voor zyne oogen stryken,
Die quynen, als een roos die dauw en warmte derft.

Ach werelt, die nu al van zyne volheit erft;
Gestarnten, Engelen, met uwe Hemelryken;
Bewoonderen der Aarde, ey! toeft gy te bezwyken,
Nu Jesus vast bezwykt, nu uwe Koning sterft?

Daar hy het leven derft, wil ik het ook gaan derven:
Maar hoe hy meerder sterft, en ik meer wil gaan sterven,
   Hoe my een voller stroom van leven overvloeit.

O hooge wonderen! wat geest is zoo bedreven,
   Die vat hoe zoo veel sterkte uit zoo veel zwakheid groeit,
En hoe het leven sterft om dooden te doen leven?

CHRIST DYING

   The comforter of all, expiring, wan,
The world's support, condemn'd to death and anguish;
A fatal darkness dims those eyes which languish
   Like roses faint, depriv'd of dew and sun.

   O world, O heir of this abundant prize,
O angels, starry powers in your spheres,
Inhabitants of earth, have ye no tears,
   While Jesus sinks his head, while your king dies?

Since he departs from life, I long for death:
But even as I wish an end to breath,
   A brimming stream of life o'erflows my soul.

O highest wonder! How can it be said
   That strength can come from feebleness so whole,
That life can die to save from death the dead?

Heiman Dullaert (1636–84)
Trans. by Frank J. Warnke

AEN MYNE UITBRANDENDE KAERSE

   O haast gebluschte vlam van myne kaers! nu dat
Gy mynen voortgang stut in 't naerstig onderzoeken
Van nutte wetenschap, in wysheidvolle boeken,
   Voor een leergierig oog zoo rykelyk bevat,
   Verstrekt gy my een boek, waar uit te leeren staat
Het haast verloopen uur van myn verganklyk leven;
Een grondles, die een wys en deuchtzaam hart kan geven;
   Aan een aandachtig man, wien zy ter harte gaat.
   Maar levend zinnebeeld van 't leven dat verdwynt,
Gy smoort in duisternis nu gy uw licht gaat missen;

En ik ga door de dood uit myne duisternissen
Naar 't onuitbluschlyk licht, dat in den Hemel schynt.

ON MY CANDLE BURNING OUT

O rapidly extinguished candle flame,
Since thou dost fail me in my busy search
For useful knowledge hid in volumes rich
    For the eye which lust of knowing still doth claim.
Supply me with a book wherein to learn
My life's too brief and quickly running hour:
A lesson which the virtuous heart may pour
    Into the heart of him who can discern.
Emblem which doth our transient life define,
Thou chok'st in darkness as thy light doth die,
But I through death from out my darkness fly
    To the unquench'd light which doth in Heaven shine.

Heiman Dullaert
Trans. by Frank J. Warnke

DE ZIELE BETRACHT DE NABYHEYT GODTS

Ick meende oock de Godtheyt woonde verre,
In eenen troon, hoogh boven maen en sterre,
    En heften menighmael myn oogh,
    Met diep versuchten naer om hoogh;
Maer toen ghy u beliefden t'openbaren,
Toen sagh ick niets van boven nedervaren;
    Maer in den grondt van myn gemoet,
    Daer wiert het lieflyck ende soet
Daer quamt ghy uyt der diepten uytwaerts dringen.
En, als een bron, myn dorstigh hart bespringen,
    Soo dat ick u, ô Godt! bevondt,
    Te zyn den grondt van mynen grondt.
Dies ben ick bly dat ghy myn hoogh beminden,
My nader zyt dan al myn naeste vrinden.
    Was nu alle ongelyckheyt voort,
    En 't herte reyn gelyck het hoort,
Geen hooghte, noch geen diepte sou ons scheyden,
Ick smolt in Godt, myn lief; wy wierden beyde

Een geest, een hemels vlees en bloedt,
De wesentheyt van Godts gemoedt,
Dat moet geschien. Och help getrouwe Heere,
Dat wy ons gantsch in uwen wille keeren.

THE SOUL CONSIDERS ITS NEARNESS TO GOD

I thought that Godhead made its home afar,
Enthroned beyond the moon and every star,
    And often lifted up my eyes
    Thither with deep and heartfelt sighs;
But when it pleased thee to illuminate me,
I saw no heavenly light descend to greet me;
    But at my spirit's deepest root
    All was lovely, all was sweet.
For thou cam'st from the depths and outwards spread,
And like a well my thirsty heart was fed;
    So was it, God, that thee I found
    To be the ground beneath my ground.
Then I rejoiced that thou, my highest dearest,
Wert closer to me than my earthly nearest!
    All disproportion fled from me,
    My heart was pure, as it should be.
No heights, no depths shall separate us twain;
I melt in God, my Love; we shall remain
    One soul, one heavenly flesh and blood,
    The being and the mind of God.
It must occur; O help, eternal Lord,
To turn us to thy will and to thy word.

Jan Luyken (1649–1712)
Trans. by Frank J. Warnke

§ *German*

SPIELE WOHL!
DAS LEBEN EIN SCHAUSPIEL

Was ist dein Lebenslauf und Tun, o Mensch? Ein Spiel.
Den Inhalt sage mir? Kinds, Weibs und Tods Beschwerde.

Was ist es vor ein Platz, darauf wir spieln? Die Erde.
Wer schlägt und singt dazu? Die Wollust ohne Ziel.
Wer heisst auf das Gerüst uns treten? Selbst die Zeit.
Wer zeigt die Schauer mir? Mensch, das sind bloss die Weisen.
Was ist vor Stellung hier? Stehn, schlafen, wachen, reisen.
Wer teilt Gesichter aus? Allein die Eitelkeit.

Wer macht den Schauplatz auf? Der wunderbare Gott.
Was vor ein Vorhang deckts? Das ewige Versehen.
Wie wird es abgeteilt? Durch Leben, Sterben, Flehen.
Wer führt uns ab, wer zeucht uns Kleider aus? Der Tod.

Wo wird der Schluss erwart't des Spieles? In der Gruft.
Wer spielt am besten mit? Der wohl sein Amt kann führen.
Ist das Spiel vor sich gut? Das Ende muss es zieren.
Wenn ist es aus? O Mensch, wenn dir dein Jesus ruft.

ACT WELL!
LIFE IS A PLAY

What is your course of life, your deed, oh man? A play.
Will you the plot recount? Child's, woman's, dying's care.
The place on which we play? Earth does us actors bear.
Who drums and sings for it? Base pleasure's endless sway.

Who bids us tread the boards? Time does this office own.
Who are the spectators? That task but wise men keep.
What then is here performed? Stay, journey, wake, and sleep.
Who passes out the masks? But vanity alone.

Who opens up the house? God is His majesty.
What curtain hides the stage? Eternal accident.
What does its scenes divide? Life, death, and argument.
Who leads us off and takes our costumes? Death is he.

Where will the play's end come? Within the funeral hall.
Who plays it best? The man who well his task has borne.
Is it good of itself? The end must it adorn.
When is it done? Oh man, when Jesus you does call.

Daniel von Reigersfeld Czepko (1605–60)
Trans. by George C. Schoolfield

ANDACHT

Ich lebe; doch nicht ich. Derselbe lebt in mir.
Der mir durch seinem Tod das Leben bringt herfür.
Mein Leben war sein Tod, sein Tod war mir mein Leben,
Nur geb ich wieder ihm, was er mir hat gegeben.
Er lebt durch meinen Tod. Mir sterb ich täglich ab.
Der Leib, mein irdnes Teil, der ist der Seelen Grab.
Er lebt nur auf den Schein. Wer ewig nicht will sterben,
Der muss hier in der Zeit verwesen und verderben,
Weil er noch sterben kann. Der Tod, der geistlich heisst,
Der ist alsdann zu spat, wann uns sein Freund hinreisst,
Der unsern Leib bringt um. Herr, gib mir die Genade,
Dass dieses Leibes Brauch nicht meiner Seelen schade.
Mein Alles und mein Nichts, mein Leben, meinen Tod,
Das hab ich bei mir selbst. Hilfst du, so hats nicht Not.
Ich will, ich mag, ich soll, ich kann mir selbst nicht raten;
Dich will ichs lassen tun; du hast bei dir die Taten.
Die Wünsche tu ich nur. Ich lasse mich ganz dir.
Ich will nicht meine sein. Nimm mich nur, gib dich mir!

DEVOTION

I live; yet 'tis not I. He lives in me,
Who through his death my life did fast decree.
My life to him was death, his death my life,
Now give I him again what once he gave.
Through the death of me he lives. I die each day,
The grave of my body shuts my soul away;
It only seems to live. Who will not die
Must here in time decay and waste and sigh,
While yet he can, die. The spirit's death
Comes then too late, when his friend has robb'd our breath
And laid our body low, Lord, give me grace,
That my body's use may not my soul disgrace.
My Everything, my Nought, my Death, my Life
I have in me. If thou help'st I am safe.
Nor will, nor may, nor can I judge my needs;
That leave I thee, for thou alone hast deeds;
But wishes I. To thee then give I me.
I will not be mine. Only take me; give me thee.

Paul Fleming (1609–40)
Trans. by Frank J. Warnke

ÜBER DIE GEBURT JESU

Nacht, mehr denn lichte Nacht! Nacht, lichter als der Tag!
Nacht, heller als die Sonn, in der das Licht geboren,
Das Gott, der Licht in Licht wohnhaftig, ihm erkoren!
O Nacht, die alle Nacht und Tage trotzen mag!

O freudenreiche Nacht, in welcher Ach und Klag
Und Finsternis und was sich auf die Welt verschworen,
Und Furcht und Höllenangst und Schrecken war verloren!
Der Himmel bricht; doch fällt nunmehr kein Donnerschlag.

Der Zeit und Nächte schuf, ist diese Nacht ankommen
Und hat das Recht der Zeit und Fleisch an sich genommen
Und unser Fleisch und Zeit der Ewigkeit vermacht.

Die jammertrübe Nacht, die schwarze Nacht der Sünden,
Des Grabes Dunkelheit muss durch die Nacht verschwinden.
Nacht, lichter als der Tag! Nacht, mehr denn lichte Nacht!

ON THE BIRTH OF JESUS

Night more than any light! Night more than any day!
Night brighter than the sun where light is born;
Which God, who dwells in light, chose as his own!
O Night which days and nights all comfort may!

O Night of joy where all lament and pain
And darkness grim and all to earth betray'd
And fear of Hell and horror are allay'd!
Though Heaven opes, no thunder falls amain.

Who made all days and nights this night is come,
And taken weights of time and flesh to him,
And render'd flesh and time forever bright.

The wretched night, the dark night of our sins,
The darkness of the grave, to nought returns.
Night more than any day! Night more than any light!

Andreas Gryphius (1616–64)
Trans. by Frank J. Warnke

AN DEN HEILIGEN GEIST

Ich schmacht, o Lebenslust! Erquicke mein Gemüt!
Ich brenn o süsser Tau! Befeuchte meine Glieder!

Ich zag, o höchste Freud! Komm du mit Trost hernieder!
Ich gleite, treue Stärk! Befeste meinen Schritt!

Man hasst mich, bleib mein Freund! O unverfälschte Güt!
Ich schlummer, lichte Flamm! Strahl auf mein Augenlider!
Bleib du mein Gast und Wirt! Mir ist die Welt zuwider.
Ich seufz, erhöre mich, und gib mir, was ich bitt!

Ich irre, führe mich, Verstand, auf rechte Wege!
Ich zweifel, Wahrheit! Steh mit deiner Weisheit bei!
Ich diene, Freiheit! Reiss die harten Band entzwei!

Ich zitter, Schutz! Halt auf des Himmels Donnerschläge!
Ich schwind, o Ewigkeit! Erhalte für und für!
O Leben aller Ding! Ich sterbe, leb in mir!

ON THE HOLY GHOST

I languish, love of life! Refresh my heart!
I burn, O sweetish dew! Make moist my limbs!
I quake, O highest joy! Send solace down!
I slip, devoted strength! Make fast my pace!

I'm hated, stay my friend! O unfalse good!
I slumber, radiant flame! My eyelids glint!
Remain my guest and host! Hostile the world!
I sigh, hear me and grant me what I ask!

I err, show me, O reason, the right way!
I doubt, truth! Keep your wisdom by my side!
I serve, O freedom! Rip the bonds apart!

I tremble, refuge! Stay sky's thunderclaps!
I wilt, eternity! Keep me e'ermore!
Life of all things! I die, do live in me.

Andreas Gryphius

FROM THE *CHERUBINISCHE WANDERSMANN*

1. Mit Schweigen wirds gesprochen
    Mensch, so du willt das Sein der Ewigkeit aussprechen,
    So musstu dich zuvor des Redens ganz entbrechen.

2. Gott nichts und alles

   Gott ist ein Geist, ein Feuer, ein Wesen und ein Licht
   Und ist doch wiederumb auch dieses alles nicht.

3. Ein Abgrund ruft dem Andern

   Der Abgrund meines Geistes ruft immer mit Geschrei
   Den Abgrund Gottes an: Sag, welcher tiefer sei?

4. Es ist kein Tod

   Ich glaube keinen Tod; sterb ich gleich alle Stunden,
   So hab ich jedesmal ein besser Leben funden.

5. Du musst zum Kinde werden

   Mensch, wirstu nicht ein Kind, so gehstu nimmer ein,
   Wo Gottes Kinder seind: die Tür ist gar zu klein.

6. Der Himmel ist in dir

   Halt an, wo laufstu hin, der Himmel ist in dir;
   Suchstu Gott anderswo, du fehlst ihn für und für.

7. Der Mensch ist Ewigkeit

   Ich selbst bin Ewigkeit, wann ich die Zeit verlasse
   Und mich in Gott und Gott in mich zusammenfasse.

8. Du selbst musst Sonne sein

   Ich selbst muss Sonne sein, ich muss mit meinem Strahlen
   Das farbenlose Meer der ganzen Gottheit malen.

9. Alles in einem

   In einem Senfkörnlein, so dus verstehen willt,
   Ist aller oberen und untrern Dinge bild.

10. Die geheimbe Himmelfahrt

    Wann du dich über dich erhebst und lässt Gott walten,
    So wird in deinem Geist die Himmelfahrt gehalten.

11. Zufall und Wesen

    Mensch, werde wesentlich; denn wann die Welt vergeht,
    So fällt der Zufall weg, das Wesen, das besteht.

12. Die Rose

    Die Rose, welche hier dein äussres Auge sieht,
    Die hat von Ewigkeit in Gott also geblüht.

13. Das göttliche Sehen

> Wer in dem Nächsten nichts als Gott und Christum sieht,
> Der siehet mit dem Licht, das aus der Gottheit blüht.

14. Die Zeit ist Ewigkeit

> Zeit ist wie Ewigkeit und Ewigkeit wie Zeit,
> So du nur selber nicht machst einen Unterscheid.

FROM THE *ANGELIC WANDERER*

1. With silence shall it be spoken

> If you wish to express eternal verity,
> So must you from all speech first gain your liberty.

2. God nothing and everything

> God is a spirit, fire, an essence, and a light,
> Yet being all these things indeed unlike them quite.

3. One abyss calls to the other

> My soul's abyss cries out e'er with an anguished plea
> To God's abyss and asks: Pray, which the deeper be?

4. There is no death

> No death for me exists; I perish every hour
> For with each I have found a better life can flower.

5. You must become a child

> Man, till you be a child, you never can go fore
> Where all God's children are; too narrow is the door.

6. Heaven is in you

> Hold on, where do you hasten, heaven is in you;
> Seek God elsewhere, He's lost for ever more to you.

7. Man is eternity

> I am eternity, when I time's lure decline,
> And God within myself and me in God combine.

8. You must be sun yourself

> I must be sun myself, must paint with all my rays
> The color-empty sea of all Divinity.

9. All in one

> In just a single grain of mustard, you shall know,
> The image lies of everything both high and low.

10. The inner Ascension
     When you above yourself raise up and God's rule not restrain,
     So in your soul at last will the Ascension reign.

11. Chance and essence
     Man, essence must you be, for when the world decays
     Chance drops away while essence ever steadfast stays.

12. The rose
     The rose which here you see before your outer eye,
     Indeed in God has bloomed from all eternity.

13. The godly seeing
     Who in the world beyond but Christ and God beholds,
     He sees them with the light which from the Godhead flows.

14. Time is eternity
     Time's like eternity, eternity like time,
     So long as you among them no distinction find.

Angelus Silesius (Johann Scheffler) (1624–77)

ÜBER DAS UNAUSSPRECHLICHE HEILIGE
GEISTES-EINGEBEN

Du ungesehner Blitz, du dunkel helles Licht
Du herzerfüllte Kraft, doch unbegreiflichs Wesen!
Es ist was Göttliches in meinem Geist gewesen,
Das mich bewegt und regt; ich spür ein seltnes Licht.

Die Seel ist von sich selbst nicht also löblich licht.
Es ist ein Wunder-Wind, ein Geist, ein webend Wesen,
Die ewig Atemkraft, das Erz-Sein selbst gewesen,
Das ihm in mir entzünd dies himmelflammend Licht.

Du Farben-Spiegel-Blick, du wunderbuntes Glänzen!
Du schimmerst hin und her, bist unbegreiflich klar;
Die Geistes Taubenflüg in Wahrheits Sonne glänzen.

Der gottbewegte Teich ist auch getrübet klar!
Er will erst gegen ihn die Geistes Sonn beglänzen
Den Mond; dann dreht er sich, wird Erden ab auch klar.

THE INEXPRESSIBLE HOLY INFUSION
OF THE SPIRIT

You unseen lightning flash, you dark bright light;
You heart-endowèd force, beyond all ken!
A godly thing it was my spirit gripped
That moved and stirred me; rare the light I sensed.

A splendid luminosity the soul.
A wonder wind, a spirit, woven essence,
Eternal power of breath, arch-being itself
Did kindle heaven-glowing light in me.

You mirror glimpse of magic-tinted hues!
You glimmer to and fro, are strangely clear;
The spirit's dove flights gleam in truth's bright sun.

The God-moved pool, yet turbid, is still clear!
First will it through the spirit's sun illume
The moon; then turning, make the earth clear too.

Catharina Regina von Greiffenberg (1633–94)

VON DER LETZTEN ZEIT

Was ist ein Tag, ein Jahr, die Zeit von hundert Jahren,
In welcher aus der Welt viel tausend Seelen fahren?
Ein Spiel, das vielen kurz und vielen lang muss sein,
Nach welchen jeder schläft gern oder ungern ein.*

Ein Tag kommt, dessen Macht die Jahre wird verschlingen;
Ein Jahr kommt, dessen Lauf nicht mehr wird Tage bringen.
O wunderbares Jahr! o wunderbarer Tag,
In welchem aufersteht, wer in dem Grabe lag!

Wer soll nicht alle Tag an dieses Jahr gedenken,
Das aller Menschen Stand wird in zwei Teil verschränken,
Wo stete Trauernacht, wo stetes Freudenlicht,
Des Himmels Wollust strahlt, der Höllen Marter sticht?

Darumb, ihr Sterblichen, lasst niemals eure Zeiten
Von engen Stegen euch auf breite Wege leiten!
Die Zeiten bleiben stets vor Gottes Augen stehn,
Der keiner Zeiten Werk lässt unbelohnt hingehn.

* A variant of this line found in some editions reads:
O Mensch, nimm alle Zeit genau in Augenschein!

Wollt ihr nicht mit der Zeit und nach der Zeit verderben,
So legt die Zeit wohl an im Leben und im sterben!
Erwägt ohn Unterlass die allerletzte Zeit,
Wenn uns ein Augenblick setzt in die Ewigkeit!

CONCERNING THE FINAL TIME

What is a day, a year, the time of hundred years,
In which a myriad of spirits disappears?
A game, where some must long, some brief must seek the prize—
And after which, like it or not, each shuts his eyes.*

A day will come, whose might will make the years its feed,
A year will come, whose course no further days will breed.
Oh supernatural year! Oh supernatural day!
When all will rise who long beneath the gravestones lay.

Who shall not every day that year then contemplate
Which will in double part divide all time's estate.
Where constant funeral-dark, where constant joyful light
Will shine with Heaven's bliss and with Hell's torment smite.

Oh let each day, you folk all vile and impudent,
At both your eardrums beat the final day's lament:
The whole world must before its judge stand presently,
Who lets no time of sin pass with impunity.

Would you, oh mortal man, not be with time undone,
See that your time does well in life and dying run.
He's wise, who pious turns, nor does that time forget,
When into timelessness he's by an instant set.

Martin Hanke (1633–1709)
Trans. by George C. Schoolfield

§ *French*

FROM *THÉORÈMES SPIRITUELS*

Aux monarques vainqueurs la rouge cotte d'armes
Appartient justement. Ce roi victorieux

* A translation of the variant reading of the line:
Oh, man, you must all time most closely scrutinize!

Est justement vêtu par ces moqueurs gens d'armes
D'un manteau qui le marque et prince et glorieux.

O pourpre, emplis mon têt de ton jus précieux
Et lui fais distiller mille pourprines larmes,
A tant que méditant ton sens mystérieux,
Du sang trait de mes yeux j'ensanglante ces carmes.

Ta sanglante couleur figure nos péchés
Au dos de cet Agneau par le Père attachés:
Et ce Christ t'endossant se charge de nos crimes.

O Christ, ô saint Agneau, daigne-toi de cacher
Tous mes rouges péchés, brindelles des abîmes,
Dans les sanglants replis du manteau de ta chair.

FROM *SPIRITUAL THEOREMS*

To conquering monarchs there belongs by right
The crimson surcoat. The victorious king*
Is justly garbed by mocking men-at-arms
In robes which mark him prince and glorious.

O purple,** pour your precious liquid in my head,
Make it a myriad crimson tears distill,
Till, contemplating your mysterious sense,
I stain these songs with blood milked from my eyes.

Your bloodred color represents our sins
Which God the Father bound to this Lamb's back,
And, donning you, this Christ assumes our crimes.

O Christ, O holy Lamb, deign to conceal
All my red sins, the kindling twigs of hell,
Within your flesh's mantle's bleeding folds.

Jean de La Ceppède (1550?–1622)

FROM *THÉORÈMES SPIRITUELS*

Voici L'Homme, ô mes yeux, quel objet déplorable!
La honte, le veiller, la faute d'aliment,

* Christ.
** Royal purple.

Les douleurs, et le sang perdu si largement
L'ont bien tant déformé qu'il n'est plus désirable.

Ces cheveux, l'ornement de son chef vénérable,
Sanglantés, hérissés, par ce couronnement,
Embrouillés dans ces joncs, servent indignement
A son têt ulcéré d'une haie exécrable.

Ces yeux, tantôt si beaux, rebattus, renfoncés,
Ressalis, sont hélas! deux soleils éclipsés,
Le corail de sa bouche est ores jaune pâle.

Les roses et les lys de son teint sont flétris:
La reste de son corps est de couleur d'opale,
Tant de la tête aux pieds ses membres sont meurtris.

FROM *SPIRITUAL THEOREMS*

Behold the Man, my eyes—what woeful sight!—
Whom shame, night vigilance and lack of food,
Torments and blood lost so abundantly
Have so deformed his beauty is no more.

His hair, pride of his venerable head,
All drenched in blood and bristled by this crown,
A tangled mess in thorns, indignantly
His festered visage serves as loathsome fence.

These eyes are sunken which were once so fair;
They are, alas, but two suns in eclipse.
The coral of his mouth is now a sickly pale;

The roses and the lilies have expired:
His body everywhere is opal-hued,
His limbs from head to foot battered and bruised.

Jean de La Ceppède

SUR LA GUERRE

Fureur, pillage, sang, campagnes désolées;
Deuil, solitude, effroi, plaintes, larmes, douleurs;
Villages embrasés, villes démantelées;
Faites de mon tableau les traits et les couleurs.

Inviolables lois, lâchement violées,
Par votre indigne sort exprimez nos malheurs;
Et vous, douces vertus, tristement exilées,
Écrivez nos combats de l'encre de vos pleurs.

Dans nos maux, juste Dieu, tu montres ta justice:
De nos propres desseins tu fais notre supplice;
Et par nos propres mains, tu te venges de nous.

Nos péchés, contre nous, ont armé ta puissance:
Mais que, sur une croix, ton Fils percé de coups,
Éteigne, par son sang, le feu de ta vengeance.

ON WAR

Fields desolated, frenzy, pillage, blood;
Bereavement, solitude, fears, plaints, griefs, tears;
Towns set afire and cities laid to waste;
From you my canvas takes its forms and shades.

Laws sacred, desecrated cowardly,
Express our woes by your unworthy fate;
And you, sweet virtues, sadly exiled hence,
For ink to write our struggles use your tears.

Just God, You show Your justice in our plagues.
You mould our anguish from our own designs,
And take revenge on us by our own hands.

Our sins against ourselves have armed Your strength,
But on a cross Your Son, pierced through with wounds,
Your fiery vengeance waters with His blood.

Laurent Drelincourt (1626–81)

SUR LES PIERRES PRÉCIEUSES

Quoi, sort-il tant de feux, de rayons, de lumières,
D'un si froid, si grossier et si noir élément?
Et tant d'Astres, naissant dans ces sombres carrières,
Font-ils donc de la Terre un second Firmament?

Minéraux éclatants, terrestres Luminaires,
Dont la tête des Rois brille superbement,

Je ne puis vous compter que pour des biens vulgaires,
Et pour moi votre éclat n'est qu'un faible ornement.

Invisible Soleil, qui donna l'être au Monde,
Viens former dans mon coeur, par ta vertu féconde,
Pour célestes Joyaux, l'Espérance et la Foi.

Mais que, cessant un jour d'espérer et de croire,
J'obtienne dans ton Ciel, et possède avec Toi,
La Couronne sans prix des rayons de ta Gloire.

ON PRECIOUS STONES

What's this? So many fires, and rays, and light
From such a cold, rude, darksome element?
And such Stars in these somber quarries born
To make of Earth a second Firmament?

Exploding minerals, terrestrial Lamps,
Magnificently shining on kings' heads,
I can regard you naught but vulgar things,
Your flashing for me tins'lly ornaments.

Invisible Sun, the Earth's creator,
Descend into my heart and by your power
Bring forth the heav'nly gems of Hope and Faith.

But one day, ceasing to believe and hope,
May I receive and share with you in Heaven
The priceless Crown of rays your Glory beams.

                                        Laurent Drelincourt

§ *Italian*

DEL MONDO E SUE PARTI

Il mondo è un animal grande e perfetto,
statua di Dio, che Dio lauda e simiglia:
noi siam vermi imperfetti e vil famiglia,
ch'intra il suo ventre abbiam vita e ricetto.
   Se ignoriamo il suo amor e 'l suo intelletto,
né il verme del mio ventre s'assottiglia

a saper me, ma a farmi mal s'appiglia:
dunque bisogna andar con gran rispetto.
    Siam poi alla terra, ch'è un grande animale
dentro al massimo, noi come pidocchi
al corpo nostro, e però ci fan male.
    Superba gente, meco alzate gli occhi,
e misurate quanato ogn'ente vale:
quinci imparate che parte a voi tocchi.

THE WORLD AND ITS PARTS

    A great and perfect animal is the world,
God's statue, which doth ever give him praise:
Vile worms are we, in our imperfect ways,
and make our life within this body curl'd.
    We know nought of his love or intellect,
no more than doth the worm within my frame
concern himself to know me, but to harm;
therefore we ought to live in great respect.
    Thus are we in this earth, great animal
within the greatest; we are like to lice
on our own bodies, ignorant and foul.
    Proud race of man, I bid you raise your eyes,
and measure what you're worth against the all:
Then learn your true position and be wise.

Tommaso Campanella (1568–1639)
Trans. by Frank J. Warnke

IL BUON LADRONE—A PIETRO VALERI

    Qui sagace l'ingegno e 'l saldo amore
e di Cristo e del ladro oggi si mira;
questo del primo ardir perde il vigore,
quei del giusto rigor depone or l'ira.
    Questi l'empio furor cangia in fervore
a quei fervor ne l'altrui petto inspira;
quei vuol, quei dona, e in quello e in questo core
l'industria, o Pietro, e la pietà s'ammira.
    Cristo, ai martir giunto di morte in atto,
dà glorie a quello e con pietoso zelo
ne la sua povertà prodigo è fatto.

Rapace è l'altro, e dal corporeo velo
pria che l'anima uscisse, egli ad un tratto
ruba a costui con un sospiro il cielo.

THE GOOD THIEF—TO PIETRO VALERI

Behold this day the wisdom and the love
of Christ and of this thief who here expire;
the one his former boldness doth remove,
the other doth cast off his righteous ire.
The one his impious rage doth change to fervor,
the other doth that gracious flame inspire;
one steals, one gives, and in both hearts the savour
of wit and pity let us both admire.
Christ in the very moment of his dying
gives glory to this man, with pitying zeal
in poverty his gracious gifts displaying.
Rapacious is the thief, before his soul
can leave its fleshly veil, he turns and, sighing,
doth all at once the heavens from him steal.

Giuseppe Artale (1628–79)
Trans. by Frank J. Warnke

§ *Mexican*

LEVÁNTAME, SEÑOR, QUE ESTOY CAÍDO

Levántame, Señor, que estoy caído,
sin amor, sin temor, sin fe, sin miedo;
quiérome levantar, y estoyme quedo;
yo propio lo deseo y yo lo impido.

Estoy, siendo uno solo, dividido;
a un tiempo muero y vivo, triste y ledo;
lo que puedo hacer, eso no puedo;
huyo del mal y estoy en él metido.

Tan obstinado estoy en mi porfía,
que el temor de perderme y de perderte
jamás de mi mal uso me desvía.

Tu poder y tu bondad truequen mi suerte
que en otros veo enmienda cada día,
y en mí nuevos deseos de ofenderte.

RAISE ME UP, LORD, WHO AM FALLEN DOWN

Raise me up, Lord, who am fallen down,
bereft of love, of dread, of faith, of fear;
I long to raise myself and stay in place;
I do desire it and myself impede.

I am, who am one only, cleft in twain;*
I live and die, make merry and complain;
what I can do cannot by me be done;*
I flee from evil and am trapped in it.

So obstinate am I in my self-will,
that even fear of losing Thee and me
deters me never from my evil ways.

I pray Thy might and mercy turn my fate,
for every day I see in others change
and in myself new wish Thee to offend.

Miguel de Guevara (1585–1646)

PONER AL HIJO EN CRUZ, ABIERTO EL SENO

Poner al Hijo en cruz, abierto el seno,
sacrificarlo porque yo no muera,
prueba es, mi Dios, de amor muy verdadera,
mostraros para mí de amor tan lleno.

Que—a ser yo Dios, y Vos hombre terreno—
os diera el sér de Dios que yo tuviera
y en el que tengo de hombre me pusiera
a trueque de gozar de un Dios tan bueno.

* For the translation of the asterisked lines I am indebted to Samuel Beckett's translation in *An Anthology of Mexican Poetry*, ed. Octavio Paz (Bloomington, Ind., 1965), p. 62.

Y aun no era vuestro amor recompensado,
pues a mí en excelencia me habéis hecho
Dios, y a Dios al sér de hombre habéis bajado.

Deudor quedaré siempre por derecho
de la dueda que en cruz por mí ha pagado
el Hijo por dejaros satisfecho.

TO CRUCIFY THE SON, AND PIERCE THE HEART

To crucify the Son, and pierce the heart,
to sacrifice Him that I might not die,
is truest proof of love, oh Lord my God,
to show Thyself so full of love for me.

That—were I God and Thou a mortal man—
the godliness I had I'd give to Thee,
and lay me down in my mortality
that of so good a God I might have joy.

And yet Thy love received no recompense,
when godhead's excellency Thou gav'st me,
while Thee to lowly manhood didst descend.

A debtor I shall always be by right
of the debt paid for me upon the cross,
that Thou mightst be requited, by the Son.

Miguel de Guevara

NO ME MUEVE, MI DIOS, PARA QUERERTE*

No me mueve, mi Dios, para quererte,
el cielo que me tienes prometido;
ni me mueve el infierno tan temido
para dejar por eso de ofenderte.

Tú me mueves, Señor; muéveme el verte
clavado en una cruz y escarnecido;
muéveme el ver tu cuerpo tan herido;
muévenme tus afrentas y tu muerte.

* This poem is generally attributed to Guevara, although some scholars
dispute his authorship and classify it as anonymous.

Muéveme, en fin, tu amor, en tal manera
que aunque no hubiera cielo yo te amara
y aunque no hubiera infierno te temiera.

No tienes que me dar porque te quiera;
porque aunque cuanto espero no esperara,
lo mismo que te quiero te quisiera.

I AM NOT MOVED TO LOVE THEE, OH MY LORD

I am not moved to love Thee, oh my Lord,
by promises of heaven Thou didst make;
nor am I moved by hell which all men fear
to cease in further giving Thee offense.

Thou mov'st me, Lord; moves me the sight of Thee
nailed on the cross and made a mockery;
moves me Thy body rent by bloody wounds;
move me Thy degradation and Thy death.

And, last, Thy love moves me in such a way,
that without heaven I should still love Thee,
and without hell I should still dread of Thee.

Thou need'st no gift make me that I love Thee,
for though my hopes were doomed to hopelessness
as now I love I should love Thee no less.

Miguel de Guevara

§ *Polish*

NA ONE SŁOWA JOPOWE: HOMO NATUS DE MULIERE, BREVI VIVENS TEMPORE etc.

Z wstydem poczęty człowiek, urodzony
Z boleścią, krótko tu na świecie żywie,
I to odmiennie, nędznie, bojaźliwie;
Ginie, od Słońca jak cień opuszczony.

I od takiego, Boże nieskończony,
W sobie chwalebnie i w sobie szczęśliwie

Sam przez się żyjąc, żądasz jakmiarz chciwie
Być milowany i chcesz być chwalony.

Dziwne są twego miłosierdzia sprawy:
Tym sie Cherubim, przepaść zrozumności,
Dziwi zdumiały, i stąd pała prawy
Płomień, Seraphim, w szczęśliwej miłości.

O Święty Panie, daj, niech i my mamy
To, co mieć każesz, i w tobie oddamy!

ON THESE WORDS OF JOB:
HOMO NATUS DE MULIERE,
BREVI VIVENS TEMPORE etc.

Man, birthed in shame, lives very painfully,
Briefly in change, his state on earth, and knows
He, like a shadow, fearful as he grows,
Will perish abandoned by the sun, and die.

And yet, O God, within yourself most high,
At one with what you are, whose glory flows
Endless and happy—you, for praise, impose
Your greed on us, nor human love deny.

Your charity is strange: the Cherubim,
A chasm of understanding, wonders: and
To Seraphim the righteous flame shines dim
Although they burn by it, love's brightest brand.

Most holy Lord, let us possess no more
Than you would give us and we can restore.

Mikołaj Sęp Szarzyński (c. 1550–81)
Trans. by Jerzy Peterkiewicz and Burns Singer

O WOJNIE NASZEJ, KTÓRĄ WIEDZIEMY
Z SZATANEM, ŚWIATEM I CIAŁEM

Pokój—szczęśliwość, ale bojowanie
Byt nasz podniebny. On srogi ciemności
Hetman i świata łakome marności
O nasze pilno czynią zepsowanie.

Nie dosyć na tym, o, nasz możny Panie!
Ten nasz dom—ciało, dla zbiegłych lubości
Niebacznie zajźrząc duchowi zwierzchności,
Upaść na wieki żądać nie przestanie.

Cóż będę czynił w tak straszliwym boju,
Wątły, niebaczny, rozdwojony w sobie?
Królu powszechny, prawdziwy pokoju,
Zbawienia mego jest nadzieja w Tobie!

Ty mnie przy sobie postaw, a przezpiecznie
Będę wojował i wygram statecznie.

ON THE WAR WE WAGE AGAINST SATAN, THE WORLD AND THE BODY

Peace would make happy: under the heavens though
We fight our life. He who commands the night
Wages cruel war; and vanities delight
In quickening our corruption with their show.

And there is more, O Lord, that you must know:
Our home, this body, greedy, fleeting, bright,
Heedlessly envious of the spirit's might,
Continually covets endless woe.

Weak, careless and divided, what can I,
Engaged in all this combat, gain alone?
O universal King, O peace most high,
Your mercy is my hope, or I have none.

Let me come close, Lord, teach me what to do,
Then I shall fight them and, thus saved, win through.

Mikołaj Sęp Szarzyński
Trans. by Jerzy Peterkiewicz and Burns Singer

DO ŚW. JANA BAPTYSTY

Któż by cię nie miał za wielkiego gońca?
    Za zorzę raczej prawdziwego słońca?
Zorza języki ptasze, kiedy wschodzi,
    Do muzyk i chwał niebieskich przywodzi;
Ty, gdy się rodzisz, do boskiego krzyku
    W niemym ojcowskim gwałt czynisz języku;

Zaś kiedy zorza ustępuje słońcu,
  Krwawym szkarłatem rudzi się przy końcu,
Ty, kiedy słońce nowe świat szeroki
  Oświęca, krwie twej wylewasz potoki.

TO ST. JOHN THE BAPTIST

Of course you are the messenger, you who
  Shed the grey brightness which the sun breaks through.
As when the pale dawn provokes the birds to play
  Their music glorifies the shape of day,
So your birth violates your father's tongue
  Till, from his lips, a shriek of praise is wrung.
And as the sun burns red when the last gleam
  Of styptic dawn admits a blood-red stream,
Your blood, too, gushes on the world whose fate
  The sun you herald will illuminate.

Jan Andrzej Morsztyn (1613–93)
Trans. by Jerzy Peterkiewicz and Burns Singer

EMBLEMA 39

Oblubienica szukając w nocy Oblubieńca swego nalazła go
śpiącego na krzyżu.
Napis: Szukałam w nocy na łożu tego, którego lubi dusza moja,
patrzałam, alem go nie nalazła. Kant. 3:1.

Cały dzień biegam i już ledwie dyszę,
  Nadstawiam ucha, jeśli gdzie usłyszę
O mym kochanku, aż mi powiedziano,
  Że go w pokoju na łóżku widziano.
Stąpam na palcach nie chcąc mu smacznego
  Snu przerwać, alić Oblubieńca mego
Nie masz i zimne miejsce, kędy leżał.
  Czyli mi zniknął? Czy kędy wybieżał?
Szukam, poglądam, aż widzę, że leży
  Bez materaców, poduszek, odzieży
Na krzyżu swoim—ból, męka i prace
  To jego pościel, jego materace.
O mój kochanku, takież to pokoje?
  Takie twe wczasy—krzyż i krwawe boje?

Takiż to sen twój, taki odpoczynek
—Z czartem i śmiercią krwawy pojedynek,
Na który się już zawczasu gotujesz,
A mojej grzesznej duszy obiecujesz
Przez twą śmierć srogą, przez twe ucierpienie
Żywot szczęśliwy i wieczno zbawienie.

EMBLEM 39

The Bride came to seek the Bridegroom during the night, and
found him—asleep upon the cross.
Inscription: By night on my bed I sought him whom my soul
loveth: I sought him, but I found him not. Song of Solomon 3:1.

Breathless I run; all day I've searched this place
    Straining my eyes and ears to catch some trace
Of him I love. And then some men reply
    That he was seen asleep at home. So I
Enter our house and tiptoe to his door
    Afraid to waken him whom I adore.
But he is gone, and where he lay feels chill.
    Yes, he has vanished. I search again, until,
Not without hope, at last I see him lie
    Without a sheet or pillow, nakedly
Stretched on the cross. His only bedding is
    Pain, passion, torment, his death agonies.
O, my Beloved, is this then your room
    And your repose? this cross? this blood? this doom?
Is combat sleep? a duel where you meet
    Death and the devil, promising defeat
Since only then can you my sinful soul
    Restore to joy and make my sickness whole
When from your death, eternal my salvation
    Though, for my sins, endless your mortification.

Zbigniew Morsztyn (c. 1628–c. 1689)
Trans. by Jerzy Peterkiewicz and Burns Singer

EMBLEMA 51

Miłość święta okrąg świata obraca, żeby był jeszcze okrąglejszy.
Napis: Będzie okrąg świata okrąglejszy.

Świat jest okrągły i wszytkie w nim sfery,
Choć różnej barzo wielkości i cery,
Słońce i księżyc, gwiazdy, ociążała
Ta ziemia, która morzem się oblała,
Są okrągłymi, a z wiecznej miłości
Mają przymioty swojej okrągłości.
Ta ten nakręca wielki zegar świata,
Ta w nim kieruje księżyce i lata,
A to dla człeka czyni śmiertelnego,
Który jest świata konterfet wielkiego;
Serce do słońca wielką relacyją
Ma, a księżyca mózg influencyją.
Toż w zwierzu, w rybach, w płazie, to się dzieje
W kruszcach, toż w drzewach, ziołach, i co sieje
Ręka; taż miłość wszystkiego jest duszą,
Bez niej i biedne mrówki się nie ruszą.
A zaś te wszytkie rzeczy tylko cienie
Są tamtych, które przez swe odkupienie
Taż święta miłość ludziom obiecuje
I co im w przyszłym żywocie daruje.

EMBLEM 51

The universal sphere is revolved by holy love so that it may become more perfectly spherical.
Inscription: The sphere will be more perfectly a sphere.

Round universe, where only spheres can range
    Though sizes differ and the colors change:
The sun, the moon, the stars, the heavy earth
    That draped itself in oceans at its birth,
Eternal love allows each to possess
    All properties of roundness, nothing less.
And this same love winds up the world, is clock,
    And teaches months and years the way to walk:
And all for man, for mortal man, because
    He is the image of great nature's laws.
Red hearts, red sun, but one vast congruence:
    The moon exerts her silver influence
Upon his brain. The same occurs in metals;
    In beasts, fish, reptiles; inhabits trees and petals,
Makes wildness grow and what is sown by hand.
    In ants it happens, instructing them to stand

And walk and run. Yet shadows all of these
  To what salvation's holy pure decrees
Has promised men by love which will be given
When they live finally through it in heaven.

Zbigniew Morsztyn
Trans. by Jerzy Peterkiewicz and Burns Singer

SONET NA CAŁĄ MĘKĘ PAŃSKĄ

Wielkiej miłości i nieogarnionej
Tryumf, czy piekła łupy, czy mogiły
Zawisnej śmierci, czy niebieskiej siły
Są cudem męki, co zniósł Bóg wcielony?

Moc, myśl, żal, strach, pot, krew, sen zwyciężony,
Zdrada, powrozy, łzy, sądy i niemiły
Twarzy policzek i rózgi, co biły,
Słup, cierń, krzyż, gwóźdź, żółć i bok otworzony

Są to dobroci dary, a nie męki,
Nie dary, ale łaski źrzódła żywe,
Nie źrzódła, ale Boskiej cuda ręki,

Tej ręki, co nam zbawienie szczęśliwe
Z swych ran wylała, za które niech dzięki
Oddaje-ć serce, o dobro prawdziwe!

SONNET ON THE LORD'S PASSION

Of great and unencompassable love
A triumph, or the spoils of hell, or graves
Of envious death, or heaven's wondrous might
The torments which the Lord Incarnate bore?

Might, strength, grief, fear, sweat, blood, defeated dream,
Deceit, ropes, verdicts, tears, unpleasant blows
On face and stinging switches' beatings,
Post, thorns, cross, nails, bile, opened flank—these are

Beneficence's gifts, not punishments.
Not gifts, but living springs of charity.
Not springs, but wonders from the hand of God,

That hand, which poured out from its awful wounds
A glorious salvation unto man,
For which our hearts give thanks, O goodness true!

Stanisław Herakliusz Lubomirski (1642–1702)

§ *Czech*

FROM *CAPELLA REGIA MUSICALIS.*
KAPLE KRÁLOVSKÁ ZPĚVNÍ.

Triumf, triumf, veselme se,
již victoria stala se,
silný s silným jest bojoval,
nad ďáblem zvítězil, vyhrál,
potlouk jej, křesťané, slavný král,
slavný král.

Kristus nahý, satan v zbroji,
že jest se strojil hned k boji,
prv zbodeného již čekal,
však on se nelekal,
s křížem, bez meče Ježíš ďábla flekal,
jej flekal.

Pekelné místo obloupil,
smrti i ďáblu na krk vstoupil,
věčně ukoval, svaté vzal,
plesejte, zpívejte, trubte,
bubnujte, zvítězil slavný král,
slavný král.

Všickni pekelní knížata
tarasovali hned vrata,
mníc, že obstojí v pokoji.
Však on polámal, roztřískal
závory pekelné, mocný král,
mocný král.

Zimu pryč zahnal, jarní čas,
půst pryč, nastal kvas, nastal kvas,
již po trápení jest radost,
ženichům pouští se slavnost,

neb bývá po mračnu zas jasnost,
zas jasnost.

Hody se již začínají,
Beránka všickni jíst mají,
chudí, bohatí, žebráci,
kunstýři, učení žáci,
laikové, kněží i vojáci,
vojáci.

Ptáčkové se proletují,
čápi klektají na stodolách,
čížek, slavíček plesají,
"vít, vít" zpívajíc v pahrbkách
a v lesích, v hájcích, v polích i v horách,
i v horách.

Louky zelené koberce,
stromy rozvíjí praporce,
slunce radostí se směje,
bubnujíc voda se leje,
větříček libý sem tam věje,
tam věje.

Ejhle Beránek, přistupte,
bez stříbra, zlata jej kupte,
pekelné brány polámal,
rozbil, potlouk i roztřískal,
vám se bez obrany podal,
slavný král.

Buď'mež tedy jeho hosti,
když nás zůve k své slavnosti,
tak pojď'me všickni s radostí,
pospíchejme s ochotností,
budem s ním v věčné radosti,
v radosti.

TRIUMPH

Triumph, triumph! Joyfully
come celebrate a victory!
Mighty power has fought with power,
crushed the devil, conquering:

He has triumphed, glorious king,
glorious king.

Christ defenseless stood his ground,
Satan armed to strike Him down,
Yet He flinched not from the blow.
With the cross—no sword He bore—
Jesus beat the devil sore,
beat him sore.

Ransacked hell's infernal town,
bringing death and devil down,
spirited the saints away.
Sound the drums and trumpets, sing!
He hath triumphed, glorious king,
glorious king.

Every prince of hell in haste
rushed to barricade the gates,
thinking to survive the storm.
Down He broke them, splintering
gates of hell, the mighty king,
mighty king.

Spring has come, the winter ceased,
now the time to feast, to feast;
after sorrow radiant joy,
glory of the bridal days,
after darkness shining rays,
shining rays.

Now the festival is come,
time for all to eat the Lamb,
poor and rich and beggar men,
artists, clerks, enlightened men,
laymen, priests, and fighting men,
fighting men.

Across the sky the birds are flying,
from the barns the storks are crying,
nightingale and chaffinch dance.
Up aloft their twittering fills
groves and forests, fields and hills,
fields and hills.

Green the meadows' lush array,
trees unfurl their banners gay,

sunlight beams in glad delight,
as the drumming waters flow
eddying breezes softly blow,
softly blow.

Hail the Lamb! Christians, draw nigh!
Him nor gold nor silver buy—
He that burst the gates of hell,
smashing, cracking, splintering,
now Himself the Offering,
Glorious King.

Come, He bids us to His door
to enjoy His boundless store;
joy and gladness we shall draw
from His love for evermore.
Rejoice with Him for evermore,
evermore!

Václav Karel Holan Rovenský (1644–1718)
Trans. by D. Gosselin and A. French

§ *Russian*

VECHERNEE RAZMYSHLENIE
O BOZHIEM VELICHESTVE PRI SLUCHAE
VELIKOGO SEVERNOGO SIYANIYA*

Litse svoe skryvaet den;
Polya pokryla mrachna noch;
Vzoshla na gory cherna ten;
Luchi ot nas sklonilis proch;
Otkrylas bezdna zvezd polna;
Zvezdam chisla net, bezdne dna.

Peschinka kak v morskikh volnakh,
Kak mala iskra v vechnom lde,
Kak v silnom vikhre tonki prakh,
V svirepom kak pero ogne,
Tak ya, v sey bezdne uglublen,
Teryayus, myslmi utomlen!

* To facilitate printing, Russian texts in this book have been transliterated
from the Cyrillic into the Latin alphabet.

Usta premudrykh nam glasyat:
Tam raznykh mnozhestvo svetov;
Neschetny solntsa tam goryat,
Narody tam i krug vekov:
Dlya obshchey slavy bozhestva
Tam ravna sila estestva.

No gde zh, natura, tvoy zakon?
S polnochnykh stran vstaet zarya!
Ne solntse l stavit tam svoy tron?
Ne ldisty l meshchut ogn morya?
Se khladny plamen nas pokryl!
Se v noch na zemlyu den vstupil!

O vy, kotorykh bystry zrak
Pronzaet v knigu vechnykh prav,
Kotorym maly veshchi znak
Yavlaet estestva ustav,
Vam put izvesten vsekh planet,—
Skazhite, chto nas tak myatet?

Chto zyblet yasny nochyu luch?
Chto tonki plamen v tverd razit?
Kak molniya bez groznykh tuch
Stremitsya ot zemli v zenit?
Kak mozhet byt, chtob merzly par
Sredi zimy rozhdal pozhar?

Tam sporit zhirna mgla s vodoy;
Il solnechny luchi blestyat,
Sklonyas skvoz vozdukh k nam gustoy;
Il tuchnykh gor verkhi goryat;
Il v more dut prestal zefir,
I gladki volny byut v efir.

Somneni polon vash otvet
O tom, chto okrest blizhnikh mest.
Skazhite zh, kol prostranen svet?
I chto maleyshikh dale zvzed?
Nesvedom tvarey vam konets?
Skazhite zh, kol velik tvorets?

EVENING MEDITATION ON THE MAJESTY
OF GOD ON THE OCCASION OF THE
GREAT NORTHERN LIGHTS

The day conceals its countenance,
Dark night has covered over fields;
Black shade has climbed the mountains' heights;
The sun's rays have inclined from us;
A star-filled vault has opened up;
No number is there to the stars,
No bottom is there to the vault.*

A grain of sand in waves of sea,
A small spark in eternal ice,
A light dust in a roaring wind,
A feather in a raging fire
Am I, engulfed in this abyss,
As worn by thought, I lose my way.

The mouths of sages do proclaim
A multitude of worlds are there;
Innumerable suns burn bright;
And people live and die as we;
And to God's glory ever more,
There nature has an equal force.

But where, O Nature, is your law?
The dawn comes up from northern lands!
Does not the sun set there its throne?
Do icy seas not stir the fire?
We have been cloaked by a cold flame!
At night, day came upon the earth!

O You, whose swift gaze penetrates
The volume of eternal laws,
To whom the small sign of a thing
Reveals a principle of life:
To you the planets' course is known.
What is it so disturbs us, tell?

At night, what vibrates lucid rays?
What subtle flame cuts firmament?
And without stormy thunderclouds,
Wherefrom does lightning rush to earth?

* The highly elliptical nature of the last two lines of the original necessitates
an additional line in the translation of the stanza.

How can it be that frozen steam
In midst of winter brings forth fire?

Dense fog and water quarrel there;
Or brightly glitter rays of sun,
Inclining to us through thick air.
Or tops of fertile mountains burn;
Or zephyrs cease to blow the sea,
And tranquil waves the ether beat.

Your answer is replete with doubts
About the places nearest man.
Pray tell us, how vast is the world?
What lies beyond the smallest stars?
Is creatures' end unknown to You?
Pray tell, how great is God Himself?

Mikhail Vasilevich Lomonosov (1711–65)

UTRENNEE RAZMYSHLENIE O
BOZHIEM VELICHESTVE

Uzhe prekrasnoe svetilo
Prosterlo blesk svoy po zemli
I bozhie dela otkrylo:
Moy dukh, s veseliem vnemli;
Chudyasya yasnym tol lucham,
Predstav, kakov zizhditel sam!

Kogda by smertnym tol vysoko
Vozmozhno bylo vozletet,
Chtob k solntsu brenno nashe oko
Moglo, priblizhivshis, vozzret,
Togda b so svekh otkrylsya stran
Goryashchi vechno Okean.

Tam ognenny valy stremyatsya
I ne nakhodyat beregov;
Tam vikhri plamenny krutyatsya,
Boryushchis mnozhestvo vekov;
Tam kamni, kak voda, kipyat,
Goryashchi tam dozhdi shumyat.

Siya uzhasnaya gromada
Kak iskra pred toboy odna.

O kol presvetlaya lampada
Toboyu, bozhe, vozzhena
Dlya nashikh povsednevnykh del,
Chto ty tvorit nam povelel!

Ot mrachnoy nochi svobodilis
Polya, bugry, morya i les
I vzoru nashemu otkrylis,
Ispolnenny tvoikh chudes.
Tam vsyakaya vzyvaet plot:
Velik zizhditel nash gospod!

Svetilo dnevnoe blistaet
Lish tolko na poverkhnost tel;
No vzor tvoy v bezdnu pronitsaet,
Ne znaya nikakikh predel.
Ot svetlosti tvoikh ochey
Lietsya radost tvari vsey.

Tvorets! pokrytomu mne tmoyu
Prostri premudrosti luchi
I chto ugodno pred toboyu
Vsegda tvoriti nauchi,
I na tvoyu vziraya tvar,
Khvalit tebya, bessmertny tsar.

MORNING MEDITATION ON
THE MAJESTY OF GOD

Already the fair luminary
Has spread its brilliance 'cross the earth
And all the deeds of God uncovered.
My soul, perceive it with delight!
And marv'ling at such radiant beams,
Just think how God Himself must be!

If mortals only had the power
To soar so high above the earth,
So that our perishable eye
Could see the sun, once close to it,
On all sides would there be revealed
An ocean burning for all time.

There fiery billows lock in struggle
And, seeking, come upon no shores.

Contending for a host of ages,
There flaming whirlwinds twist and turn;
And rocks, like water, boil and bubble;
The rains roar down in burning streams.

This awesome mass of flame and torrent
Is but a mere spark before You.
Oh, how this brightest of all torches
Was kindled, God, by You alone
For all our day's activities
Which You have ordered us to do!

The fields and hillocks, seas and forests,
Have freed themselves from darkest night
And, filled with all Your divers wonders,
Revealed themselves unto our gaze.
There every creature does proclaim:
Our Lord the Creator is great!

The light of day casts forth its brightness,
But lightens only surfaces.
Your gaze instead much deeper reaches
Not knowing any boundaries.
From out the brilliance of your eyes
Joy flows to all created things.

To me, Creator, steeped in darkness,
Extend the rays of wisdom fair
And pray instruct me to do always
What would find pleasure in Your eyes;
And when beholding all Your works,
To give You praise, immortal King.

Mikhail Vasilevich Lomonosov

MEDITATIVE POETRY

A. MUTABILITY AND BREVITY

§ *Dutch*

EEN COMEDIANT

Hij is een Alle-mann, altijd en allerweghen
Waer 'them den honger maeckt; een Bedlaer met een degen;
Een Papegay om Go'; een laccher van gebreck;
Een Meerkatt in een Mensch; een meesterlicke Geck;
Een Schilderij die spreeckt; een spoock van weinig' uren;
Een levendige *Print* van 's Werelts kort verduren;
Een *hijpocrijt* om 'tjock; een schaduw diemen tast;
Een drolligh Aristipp, dien alle kleeding past.
 Hij is dat ijeder een behoort te konnen wesen:
Verandering van staet verandert maer sijn wesen
Nae't noodich wesen moet: geraeckt hij op een Throon,
Sijn hert ontstijght hem niet nae 'tstijgen vande kroon:
Vervalt hij van soo hoogh tot op het bedel-bidden,
'Tgelaet past op 'tgeluck; 'thert drijft in 'tgulde midden,
En onder 'tmommen-hooft steeckt noch de selve mann
Die op en neder gaet, en niet bewegen, kan.
 De Werelt is 'traduijs daerop de Menschen mommen,
Veel' staen op sprekens roll, veel dienender voor stommen:
Veel' draven, veel' staen still, veel' dalen, veel' gaen op,
Veel sweeten om gewinn, veel scheppen 't mette schopp:
Geluckigh hij alleen, die krijgen kan en houwen
En missen dat hij moet, en matelicken rouwen,
En lacchen matelick in suer of soet gelagh,
En seggen, Is't nu soo, God kent den naesten dagh.

A COMEDIAN

He is an everyman at all times and all places
Where hunger makes him one: a beggerman in laces,
A parrot for God's love, a mocker from distress,
A monkey in a man; a master fool, no less;
A picture endowed with speech, a short-lived apparition,
A live print of the world's brief tenure and transition;
A hypocrite for fun; a shade of solid grit;

A clownish customer whom any clothes will fit.
He is what everyone should know to be on purpose.
The changes of his state are changes on the surface,
As circumstance demands. Should he ascend a throne,
His kingship's in the crown, his heart remains his own.
When from that high estate he turns into a beggar,
The face falls with the fate, the heart will never stagger.
Under the maskèd head the selfsame man is found,
Who is ummutable while he is upped or downed.
This great world is the stage on which men go a-mumming.
Some have a speaker's part, and others go for dumbling.
Some run, some stand, some fall, and others rise on top.
Some sweat to keep alive, others haul in the crop.
Lucky alone is he who knows to get and hold it,
To miss what he must lose and, out of luck, not scold it,
And show a smile when pleased and show a smile when vexed,
Saying, "It's thus today. God knows the day comes next."

Constantijn Huygens
Trans. by Adriaan J. Barnouw

§ German

DER WECHSEL MENSCHLICHER SACHEN

Auf Nacht, Dunst, Schlacht,
  Frost, Wind, See, Hitz, Süd, Ost, West,
  Nord, Sonn, Feuer, und Plagen
Folgt Tag, Glanz, Blut, Schnee,
  Still, Land, Blitz, Wärm, Hitz, Lust,
  Kält, Licht, Brand und Not:
Auf Leid, Pein, Schmach, Angst,
  Krieg, Ach, Kreuz, Streit, Hohn,
  Schmerz, Qual, Tück, Schimpf als Spott
Will Freud, Zier, Ehr, Trost,
  Sieg, Rat, Nutz, Fried, Lohn, Scherz,
  Ruh, Glück, Glimpf stets tagen.

Der Mond, Glunst, Rauch, Gems,
  Fisch, Gold, Perl, Baum, Flamm, Storch,
  Frosch, Lamm, Ochs und Magen
Liebt Schein, Stroh, Dampf,
  Berg, Flut, Glut, Schaum, Frucht, Asch,

Dach, Teich, Feld, Wies und Brot:
Der Schütz, Mensch, Fleiss, Müh, Kunst, Spiel,
 Schiff, Mund, Prinz, Rach,
 Sorg, Geiz, Treu und Gott
Suchts Ziel, Schlaf, Preis, Lob,
 Gunst, Zank, Port, Kuss, Thron, Mord,
 Sarg, Geld, Hold, Danksagen.

Was gut, stark, schwer, recht,
 lang, gross, weiss, eins, ja, Luft, Feuer,
 hoch, weit genennt,
Pflegt bös, schwach, leicht,
 krumm, breit, klein, schwarz, drei, nein,
 Erd, Flut, tief, nah zu meiden.
Auch Mut, Lieb, Klug, Witz,
 Geist, Seel, Freund, Lust, Zier, Ruhm, Fried,
 Scherz, Lob muss scheiden.
Wo Furcht, Hass, Trug, Wein,
 Fleisch, Leib, Feind, Weh, Schmach, Angst,
 Streit, Schmerz, Hohn schon rennt.

Alles wechselt, alles liebet; alles scheinet was zu hassen:
Wer aus diesem nach wird denken, muss der Menschen Weisheit
 fassen.

THE CHANGE OF HUMAN THINGS

On night, fog, fight,
 Frost, wind, sea, heat, south, east, west,
 North, sun, fire, ill deed,
Come day, shine, blood, snow,
 Calm, land, bolt, warmth, heat, joy,
 Cold, light, blaze, and dread.
To wound, rack, shame, fear,
 War, groan, cross, strife, scorn,
 Ache, gripe, trick, mocking prod
Will joy, grace, rank, balm,
 Palm, wit, use, peace, praise, jest,
 Rest, cheer, luck succeed.

Chamois, moon, spark, smoke, fish,
 Gold, pearl, tree, flame, stork,
 Frog, lamb, ox, craw's need
Love peak, light, straw,

Steam, flood, glow, foam, fruit, ash,
Roof, pond, field, pasture, bread:
The shot, man, work, toil, art, game,
Ship, mouth, prince, feud,
Care, faith, miser, God
For mark, sleep, prize, praise,
Aid, brawl, port, kiss, throne, death,
Grave, thanks, coin, love plead.

What good, strong, thick, straight,
Long, great, white, one, yes, air, fire,
High, far is named,
Thinks bad, weak, thin,
Bent, broad, small, black, three, no,
Earth, flood, deep, near to shun.
His heart, love, wit, sense,
Mind, soul, friend, joy, pride, fame, peace,
Jest, praise are done,
Whom fear, hate, fraud, wine,
Flesh, lust, foe, woe, shame, fear,
Strife, pain, scorn have claimed.

All is changing, all is loving; all things seem some things to hate:
He must human wisdom fathom, who this but would contemplate.

Quirinus Kuhlmann (1651–89)
Trans. by George C. Schoolfield

§ *Spanish*

ALEGORÍA DE LA BREVEDAD
DE LAS COSAS HUMANAS

Aprended, Flores, de mí,
lo que va de ayer a hoy,
que ayer maravilla fuí,
y hoy sombra mía aun no soy.

La Aurora ayer me dió cuna,
la noche ataúd me dió;
sin luz muriera si no
me la prestará la luna:

pues de vosotras ninguna
deja de acabar así,

    Aprended, Flores, de mí,
    lo que va de ayer a hoy,
    que ayer maravilla fuí,
    y hoy sombra mía aun no soy.

Consuelo dulce el clavel
es a la breve edad mía,
pues quien me concedió un día,
dos apenas le dio a él:
efímeras del vergel,
yo cárdena, él carmesí.

    Aprended, Flores, de mí,
    lo que va de ayer a hoy,
    que ayer maravilla fuí,
    y hoy sombra mía aun no soy.

Flor es el jazmín, si bella,
no de las más vividoras,
pues dura pocas más horas
que rayos tiene de estrella;
si el ámbar florece, es ella,
la flor que él retiene en si.

    Aprended, Flores, de mí,
    lo que va de ayer a hoy,
    que ayer maravilla fuí,
    y hoy sombra mía aun no soy.

El alhelí, aunque grosero
en fragancia y en color,
más días ve que otra flor,
pues ve los de un mayo entero:
morir maravilla quiero,
y no vivir alhelí.

    Aprended, Flores, de mí,
    lo que va de ayer a hoy,
    que ayer maravilla fuí,
    y hoy sombra mía aun no soy.

A ninguna flor mayores
términos concede el Sol
que al sublime girasol,
Matusalén de las flores:

ojos son aduladores
cuantas en él hojas vi.

Aprended, Flores, de mí,
lo que va de ayer a hoy,
que ayer maravilla fuí,
y hoy sombra mía aun no soy.

ALLEGORY OF THE BREVITY OF THINGS HUMAN

Learn, flowers, from me, what parts we play
from dawn to dusk. Last noon the boast
and marvel of the fields, today
I am not even my own ghost.

The fresh aurora was my cot,
the night my coffin and my shroud;
I perished with no light, save what
the moon could lend me from a cloud.
And thus, all flowers must die—of whom
not one of you can cheat the doom.

Learn, flowers, from me, what parts we play
from dawn to dusk. Last noon the boast
and marvel of the fields, today
I am not even my own ghost.

What most consoles me from my fleetness
is the carnation fresh with dew,
since that which gave me one day's sweetness
to her conceded scarcely two:
Ephemerids in briefness vie
my scarlet and her crimson die.

Learn, flowers, from me, what parts we play
from dawn to dusk. Last noon the boast
and marvel of the fields, today
I am not even my own ghost.

The jasmine, fairest of the flowers,
is least in size as in longevity.
She forms a star, yet lives less hours
than it has rays. Her soul is brevity.
If amber could a flower be grown
it would be she, and she alone!

Learn, flowers, from me, what parts we play
from dawn to dusk. Last noon the boast
and marvel of the fields, today
I am not even my own ghost.

The gillyflower, though plain and coarse,
enjoys on earth a longer stay.
And sees more suns complete their course
—as many as there shine in May.
Yet better far a marvel die
than live a gillyflower, say I!

Learn, flowers, from me, what parts we play
from dawn to dusk. Last noon the boast
and marvel of the fields, today
I am not even my own ghost.

To no flower blooming in our sphere did
the daystar grant a longer pardon
than to the Sunflower, golden-bearded
Methusaleh of every garden.
Eying him through as many days
as he shoots petals forth like rays.

Yet learn from me, what parts we play
from dawn to dusk. Last noon the boast
and marvel of the fields, today
I am not even my own ghost.

Luis de Góngora (1600–81)
Trans. by Roy Campbell

DE LA BREVEDAD ENGAÑOSA DE LA VIDA

Menos solicitó veloz saeta
destinada señal, que mordió aguda;
agonal carro por la arena muda
no coronó con más silencio meta,

que presurosa corre, que secreta
a su fin nuestra edad. A quien lo duda,
fiera que sea de razón desnuda,
cada Sol repetido es una cometa.

¿Confiésalo Cartago, y tú lo ignoras?

Peligro corres, Licio, si porfías
en seguir sombras y abrazar engaños.

Mal te perdonarán a ti las horas;
las horas que limando están los días,
los días que royendo están los años.

ON THE DECEPTIVE BREVITY OF LIFE

The speedy arrow sought less ardently
its destined target, which it sharply bit;
the ancient chariot o'er speechless sand
the winning post crowned no more silently,

than stealthily, precipitately runs
our age to its demise. To him who doubts,
fierce though he be and stripped of reason's gift,
each sun repeated is a comet's sign.

Confesses Carthage, and you know it not?
Licio, danger lurks if you persist
in chasing shadows and embracing dreams.

You hardly will be pardoned by the hours,
the hours that keep on wearing 'way the days,
the days that keep on gnawing 'way the years.

Luis de Góngora

TODO TRAS SÍ LO LLEVA EL AÑO BREVE

Todo tras sí lo lleva el año breve
de la vida mortal, burlando el brío,
al acero valiente, al mármol frío
que contra el Tiempo su dureza atreve.

Antes que sepa andar el pie, se mueve
camino de la muerte, donde envío
mi vida oscura: pobre y turbio río,
que negro mar con altas ondas bebe.

Todo corto momento es paso largo
que doy, a mi pesar, en tal jornada,
pues, parado y durmiendo, siempre aguijo.

Breve suspiro, y último, y amargo,
es la muerte, forzosa y heredada;
mas si es ley y no pena, ¿qué me aflijo?

THE TOO BRIEF YEAR OF MORTAL LIFE TAKES ALL

The too brief year of mortal life takes all
with it, holding to ridicule man's pace,
the valiant steel, the frigid marble stone
which vainly pit their hardness against time.

Before it learns to walk the foot sets out
along the path of death, where I dispatch
my obscure life: a poor and muddy stream
which the black sea consumes with mighty waves.

Each little moment is a lengthy step
which I, to my regret, take on this trip,
since, upright or asleep, I spur ahead.

A brief, an ultimate and bitter breath
is death, both necessary and bequeathed;
if law, not punishment, why do I grieve?

Francisco de Quevedo (1580–1645)

§ *Mexican*

A LA MATERIA PRIMA

Materia que de vida te informaste,
¿en cuántas metamórfosis viviste?
Ampo oloroso en el jazmín te viste,
y en la ceniza pálida duraste.

Después que tanto horror te desnudaste,
rey de las flores púrpura vestiste.
En tantas muertas formas, no moriste:
tu sér junto a la muerte eternizaste.

¿Que discursiva luz nunca despiertes,
y no mueras al ímpetu invisible
de las aladas horas, homicida?

¿Qué, no eres sabia junto a tantas muertes?
¿Qué eres, naturaleza incorruptible
habiendo estado viuda a tanta vida?

TO PRIMAL MATTER

Within how many metamorphoses,
matter informed with life, hast thou had being?
Sweet-smelling snow of jessamine thou wast,
and in the pallid ashes didst endure.

Such horror by thee to thyself laid bare,
king of flowers, the purple thou didst don.
In such throng of dead forms thou didst not die,
thy deathbound being by thee immortalized.

For thou dost never wake to reason's light,
nor ever die before the invisible
murderous onset of the winged hours.

What, with so many deaths art thou not wise?
What art thou, incorruptible nature, thou
who hast been widowed thus of so much life?

Luis de Sandoval y Zapata (17th century; dates unknown)
Trans. by Samuel Beckett

RIESGO GRANDE DE UN GALÁN EN METÁFORA DE MARIPOSA

Vidrio animado, que en la lumbre atinas
con la tiniebla en que tu vida yelas,
y al breve punto de morir anhelas
en la circunferencia que caminas.

En poco mar de luz ve obscuras ruinas,
Nave que desplegaste vivas velas:
la más fúnebre noche que recelas
se enciende entre la luz, que te avecinas.

No retire tu espíritu cobarde
el vuelo de la luz donde te ardías;
abrásate en el fuego que buscabas.

Dichosamente entre sus lumbres arde:
porque al dejar de ser lo que vivías,
te empezaste a volver en lo que amabas.

GRIEVOUS PERIL OF A GALLANT IN MOTH METAPHOR

Animated glass that drawest nigh
unto the light, with thy life-freezing dark,
and from the fluttering circumference
pantest toward the sudden point of death.

In tiny sea of brightness gulfs of gloom
behold, thou ship that spreadest living sail;
the more funereal night of thy dismay
takes fire from the light thou comest to.

Let not thy coward spirit from the light
in which thou burnest turn aside its wings;
in the fire of thy seeking be consumed.

Joyfully amid its flames flagrate:
for ceasing to be that which thou hast lived
thou turnest into that which thou hast loved.

Luis de Sandoval y Zapata
Trans. by Samuel Beckett

§ *Portuguese*

MUDAM-SE OS TEMPOS, MUDAM-SE AS VONTADES

Mudam-se os tempos, mudam-se as vontades,
   Muda-se o ser, muda-se a confiança;
   Todo o mundo é composto de mudança,
   Tomando sempre novas qualidades.
Contìnuamente vemos novidades,
   Diferentes em tudo da esperança;
   Do mal ficam as mágoas na lembrança,
   E do bem, se algum houve, as saudades.
O tempo cobre o chão de verde manto,

Que já coberto foi de neve fria,
E em nim converte em chôro o doce canto.
E, afora êste mudar-se cada dia,
Outra mudança faz de mor espanto,
Que não se muda já como soía.

TIMES EVER CHANGE
AND WITH THEM CHANGE OUR WILLS

Times ever change and with them change our wills.
Each being changes, as does confidence,
For all the world is made of naught but change,
Assuming qualities forever new.
We ever see before us novelties,
At variance in everything from hopes.
Long cling to mind the sorrows of past wounds,
As yearnings for the good there might have been.
Time casts a cloak of green upon the fields
Which erstwhile shivered 'neath the wintry snow,
And my sweet song transforms to bitter plaint;
And, save for that which changes every day,
Another change of greater dread occurs—
That henceforth nothing more will change again.

Luís de Camões (1524–80)

§ *Polish*

ŻYWOT LUDZKI

Pytasz się, co jest żywot na tym świecie człeczy?
Weź sobie dwie przeciwne odpowiedzią rzeczy:
Jeśli patrzysz na ciało, z wiecznością złożony
Moment: jeśli na duszę, jest wiek nieskończony.
Albo tak: żywot ludzki, moment czasu ścisły,
Z którego jednak wieków wieczności zawisły,
Przesmyk z macierzyńskiego żywota do grobu,
Od ześcia ciała z duszą do rozstania obu.
Kędy za każdym krokiem, jeśli padnie, człeka
Albo żywot, albo śmierć nieskończona czeka.

Rzadko zamierzonego kto kresu dobieży,
Przeto na ostrożności wszytka rzecz należy.
Każdą godzinę sobie niechaj kładzie kresem,
Kto z Bogiem żyć, niż wiecznie woli gorzeć z biesem.

MAN'S LIFE

You ask, What is the life of man on earth?
Take two opposing things as your response:
The body, see, is just a moment fused
With the eternal; but the soul, an age
Unfinished, or instead: man's life is but
A moment fixed in time on which depend
Ages' eternities; a narrow path
From womb to grave, from soul and body's link
Till both do part; at each step, should man fall,
'Tis life or death eternal which awaits.
Rare is the man who runs the measured span,
Wherefor all things must ever be on guard.
Who wants to live with God, not burn in hell,
Should think of every single hour his span.

Wacław Potocki (1621–96)

KRÓTKOŚĆ ŻYWOTA

Godzina za godziną niepojęcie chodzi:
Był przodek, byłeś ty sam, potomek się rodzi.
Krótka rozprawa: jutro—coś dziś jest, nie będziesz,
A żeś był, nieboszczyka imienia nabędziesz;
Dźwięk, cień, dym, wiatr, błysk, głos, punkt—żywot ludzki słynie.
Słońce więcej nie wschodzi to, które raz minie,
Kołem niehamowanym lotny czas uchodzi,
Z którego spadł niejeden, co na starość godzi.
Wtenczas, kiedy ty myślisz, jużeś był, nieboże;
Między śmiercią, rodzeniem byt nasz ledwie może
Nazwan być czwartą częścią mgnienia; wielom była
Kolebka grobem, wielom matka ich mogiła.

THE BREVITY OF LIFE

Our comprehension fades with every hour:
A forebear lived, and you, now heirs are born.
In short—today you're here, tomorrow gone.
But that you were, deceased will be your name;
Sound, smoke, clouds, wind, flash, voice—man's life resounds.
The sun does not ascend what once it passed.
Elusive time elapses unrestrained,
And often fells those looking to old age;
You think ahead, and then no longer are.
Between our birth and death our earthly life
Seems but an instant's time; the cradle was
A grave to many, and the womb a tomb.

Daniel Naborowski (1573–1640)

NA TOŻ

Dzień jeden drugi goni i potem zostawa
Tam, skąd wiek wszytkokrotny odwrotu nie dawa.
Żaden dzień i godzina bez szkody nie bywa
Człowieku, który ze dniem zarówno upływa.
Karmia byt nasz godziny, która leci snadnie;
Więcej się ten nie wraca, kto z regestru spadnie;
Już w nocy wiekuistej sen przydzie spać twardy.
Na to masz zawsze pomnieć, o człowiecze hardy:
Dwakroć żyje, kto żyjąc umrzeć się gotuje;
Umiera dwakroć, kto się śmiertelnym nie czuje.

ON THE SAME

One day pursues the next and then remains
There whence eternal time grants no return.
No day and hour pass without harm to man,
Who passes likewise with the fleeting day.
Our earthly life sustains time in its course;
Who leaves the register comes back no more.
In the eternal night the sleep is deep;
You always must remember this, proud man.
Who while alive prepares for death lives twice,
Who thinks himself immortal meets death twice.

Daniel Naborowski

B. TRANSITORINESS

§ *English*

VERTUE

Sweet day, so cool, so calm, so bright,
The bridall of the earth and skie:
The dew shall weep thy fall to night;
 For thou must die.

Sweet rose, whose hue angrie and brave
Bids the rash gazer wipe his eye:
Thy root is ever in its grave,
 And thou must die.

Sweet spring, full of sweet dayes and roses,
A box where sweets* compacted lie;
My musick shows ye have your closes,**
 And all must die.

Onely a sweet and vertuous soul,
Like season'd timber, never gives;
But though the whole world turn to coal,
 Then chiefly lives.

         George Herbert

SIC   VITA

Like to the falling of a Starre;
Or as the flights of Eagles are;
Or like the fresh springs gawdy hew;
Or silver drops of morning dew;
Or like a wind that chafes the flood;
Or bubbles which on water stood;
Even such is man, whose borrow'd light
Is streight call'd in, and paid to night.
 The Wind blowes out; the Bubble dies;
 The Spring entomb'd in Autumn lies;
 The Dew dries up; the Starre is shot;
 The Flight is past; and Man forgot.

      Henry King (1592–1669)

* Perfumes.
** Cadences.

NOX NOCTI INDICAT SCIENTIAM. David

When I survay the bright
   Coelestiall spheare:
So rich with jewels hung, that night
Doth like an Aethiop bride appeare,

My soule her wings doth spread
   And heaven-ward flies,
Th'Almighty's Mysteries to read
In the large volumes of the skies.

For the bright firmament
   Shootes forth no flame
So silent, but is eloquent
In speaking the Creators name.

No unregarded star
   Contracts its light
Into so small a Charactar,
Remov'd far from our humane sight:
But if we stedfast looke,
We shall discerne
In it as in some holy booke,
How man may heavenly knowledge learne.

It tells the Conqueror,
   That farre-stretcht powre
Which his proud dangers traffique for,
Is but the triumph of an houre.
That from the farthest North;
   Some nation may
Yet undiscovered issue forth,
And ore his new got conquest sway.

Some Nation yet shut in
   With hills of ice
May be let out to scourge his sinne
'Till they shall equall him in vice.

And then they likewise shall
   Their ruine have,
For as your selves your Empires fall,
And every Kingdome hath a grave.

Thus those Coelestiall fires,
   Though seeming mute,

The fallacie of our desires
And all the pride of life confute.

For they have watcht since first
    The World hath birth:
And found sinne in it selfe accurst
And nothing permanent on earth.

William Habington (1605–54)

§ *American*

A SONG OF EMPTINESS TO FILL UP THE EMPTY PAGES FOLLOWING VANITY OF VANITIES

Vain, frail, short liv'd, and miserable Man,
Learn what thou art when thine estate is best:
A restless Wave o'th' troubled Ocean,
A Dream, a lifeless Picture finely drest:

A Wind, a Flower, a Vapour, and a Bubble,
A Wheel that stands not still, a trembling Reed,
A rolling Stone, dry Dust, light Chaff, and Stubble,
A Shadow of Something, but nought indeed.

Learn what deceitful Toyes, and empty things,
This World, and all its best Enjoyments bee:
Out of the Earth no true Contentment springs,
But all things here are vexing Vanitee.

For what is *Beauty*, but a fading Flower?
Or what is *Pleasure*, but the Devils bait,
Whereby he catcheth whom he would devour,
And multitudes of Souls doth ruinate?

And what are *Friends* but mortal men, as we?
Whom Death from us may quickly separate;
Or else their hearts may quite estranged be,
And all their love be turned into hate.

And what are *Riches* to be doted on?
Uncertain, fickle, and ensnaring things;
They draw Mens Souls into Perdition,
And when most needed, take them to their wings.

Ah foolish Man! that sets his heart upon
Such empty Shadows, such wild Fowl as these,
That being gotten will be quickly gone,
And whilst they stay increase but his disease.

As in a Dropsie, drinking draught begets,
The more he drinks, the more he still requires:
So in this world whoso affection sets,
His Wealths encrease encreaseth his desires.

O happy Man, whose portion is above,
Where Floods, where Flames, where Foes cannot bereave him,
Most wretched man, that fixed hath his love
Upon this World, that surely will deceive him!

For, what is *Honour*! What is *Sov'raignty*,
Whereto mens hearts so restlessly aspire?
Whom have they Crowned with Felicity?
When did they ever satisfie desire?

The Ear of Man with hearing is not fill'd:
To see new sights still coveteth the Eye:
The craving Stomack though it may be still'd,
Yet craves again without a new supply.

All Earthly things, man's Cravings answer not,
Whose little heart would all the World contain,
(If all the Worlds should fall to one man's Lot)
And notwithstanding empty still remain,

The *Eastern Conqueror* was said to weep,
When he the *Indian* Ocean did view,
To see his Conquest bounded by the Deep,
And no more Worlds remaining to subdue.

Who would that man in his Enjoyments bless,
Or envy him, or covet his estate,
Whose gettings do augment his greediness,
And make his wishes more intemperate?

Such is the wonted and the common guise
Of those on Earth that bear the greatest Sway:
If with a few the case be otherwise
They seek a Kingdom that abides for ay.

Moreover they, of all the Sons of men,
That Rule, and are in Highest Places set,

Are most inclin'd to scorn their Bretheren
And God himself (without great grace) forget.

For as the Sun doth blind the gazer's eyes,
That for a time they nought discern aright:
So Honour doth befool and blind the Wise,
And their own Lustre 'reaves them of their sight.

Great are the Dangers, manifold their Cares;
Thro' which, whilst others Sleep, they scarcely Nap:
And yet are oft surprised unawares,
And fall unweeting into Envies Trap!

The mean Mechanick finds his kindly rest,
All void of fear Sleepeth the Country-Clown,
When greatest Princes often are distrest,
And cannot Sleep upon their Beds of Down.

Could *Strength* or *Valour* men Immortalize,
Could *Wealth* or *Honour* keep them from decay,
There were some cause the same to Idolize,
And give the lye to that which I do say.

But neither can such things themselves endure
Without the hazard of a Change one hour,
Nor such as trust in them can they secure
From dismal dayes, or Deaths prevailing pow'r.

If *Beauty* could the beautiful defend
From Death's dominion than fair *Absalom*
Had not been brought to such a shameful end:
But fair and foul unto the Grave must come.

If *Wealth* or *Scepters* could Immortal make,
Then wealthy *Croesus*, wherefore art thou dead?
If *Warlike-force*, which makes the World to quake,
Then why is *Julius Caesar* perished?

Where are the *Scipio's* Thunder-bolts of War?
Renowned *Pompey*, *Caesars* Enemie?
Stout *Hannibal*, *Romes* Terror known so far?
Great *Alexander*, what's become of thee?

If *Gifts* and *Bribes* Death's favour might but win,
If *Power*, if force, or *Threatnings* might it fray,
All these, and more, had still surviving been:
But all are gone, for Death will have no Nay.

Such is this World with all her Pomp and Glory,
Such are the men whom worldly eyes admire:
Cut down by Time, and now become a Story,
That we might after better things aspire.

Go boast thy self of what thy heart enjoyes,
Vain Man! triumph in all thy worldly Bliss:
Thy best enjoyments are but Trash and Toyes:
Delight thy self in that which worthless is.

> Omnia praetereunt praeter amare Deum.

> Michael Wigglesworth (1631–1705)

§ *German*

ACH LIEBSTE, LASS UNS EILEN

Ach Liebste, lass uns eilen,
    Wir haben Zeit:
Es schadet das Verweilen
    Uns beiderseit.

Der edlen Schönheit Gaben
    Fliehn Fuss für Fuss,
Dass alles, was wir haben,
    Verschwinden muss.

Der Wangen Zier verbleichet,
    Das Haar wird greis,
Der Augen Feuer weichet,
    Die Brunst wird Eis.

Das Mündlein von Korallen
    Wird ungestalt,
Die Händ als Schnee verfallen
    Und du wirst alt.

Drumb lass uns jetz geniessen
    Der Jugend Frucht,
Eh als wir folgen müssen
    Der Jahre Flucht.

Wo du dich selber liebest,
    So liebe mich,

Gib mir, dass, wann du gibest,
    Verlier auch ich.

AH DEAREST, LET US HASTE US

Ah Dearest, let us haste us,
    While we have time;
Delaying doth but waste us
    And lose our prime.

The gifts that beauty nourish
    Fly with the year,
And everything we cherish
    Must disappear.

The cheeks so fair turn pallid,
    And grey the hair,
The flashing eyes turn gelid,
    And ice, desire.

From coral lips must flee then
    The outline bold;
The snowy hands decay then,
    And thou art old.

So therefore let us swallow
    Youth's precious fruit,
E'er we are forc'd to follow
    The years in flight.

As thou thyself then lovest,
    Love also me;
Give me, that when thou givest
    I lose to thee.

                              Martin Opitz (1597–1639)
                              Trans. by Frank J. Warnke

MENSCHLICHES ELENDE

Was sind wir Menschen doch? Ein Wohnhaus grimmer
    Schmerzen,
Ein Ball des falschen Glücks, ein Irrlicht dieser Zeit,
Ein Schauplatz herber Angst, besetzt mit scharfem Leid,
Ein bald verschmelzter Schnee und abgebrannte Kerzen.

Dies Leben fleucht davon wie ein Geschwätz und Scherzen.
Die vor uns abgelebt des schwachen Leibes Kleid
Und in das Totenbuch der grossen Sterblichkeit
Längst eingeschrieben sind, sind uns aus Sinn und Herzen.

Gleich wie ein eitel Traum leicht aus der Acht hinfällt
Und wie ein Strom verscheusst, den keine Macht aufhält,
So muss auch unser Nam, Lob, Ehr und Ruhm verschwinden.

Was itzund Atem holt, muss mit der Luft entfliehn,
Was nach uns kommen wird, wird uns ins grab nachziehn.
Was sag ich? Wir vergehn, wie Rauch von starken Winden.

HUMAN MISERY

What are we men indeed? Grim torment's habitation,
A toy of fickle luck, wisp in time's wilderness,
A scene of bitter fear and filled with keen distress,
And tapers burned to stubs, snow's quick evaporation.

This life does flee away like jest or conversation;
Those who before us laid aside the body's dress
And in the domesday-book of monster mortalness
Old entry found, have left our mind's and heart's sensation.

Just as an empty dream from notice lightly flees,
And as a stream is lost whose course no might may cease,
So must our honor, fame, our praise and name be ended.

What presently draws breath, must perish with the air,
What after us will come, someday our grave will share.
What do I say? We pass as smoke on strong winds wended.

Andreas Gryphius
Trans. by George C. Schoolfield

VERGÄNGLICHKEIT DER SCHÖNHEIT

Es wird der bleiche Tod mit seiner kalten Hand
Dir endlich* mit der Zeit um deine Brüste streichen,
Der liebliche Korall der Lippen wird verbleichen;
Der Schultern warmer Schnee wird werden kalter Sand.

Der Augen süsser Blitz, die Kräfte deiner Hand,
Für welchen solches fällt, die werden zeitlich weichen.

* A variant reading has "Lesbie" (Lesbia) here in place of "endlich."

Das Haar, das itzund kann des Goldes Glanz erreichen,
Tilgt endlich Tag und Jahr als ein gemeines Band.

Der wohlgesetzte Fuss, die lieblichen Gebärden,
Die werden teils zu Staub, teils nicht und nichtig werden,
Denn opfert keiner mehr der Gottheit deiner Pracht.

Dies und noch mehr als dies muss endlich untergehen.
Dein Herze kann allein zu aller Zeit bestehen,
Dieweil es die Natur aus Diamant gemacht.

BEAUTY'S TRANSITORINESS

Then pallid death at last will with his icy hand,
Where time hides in the palm, your lovely breasts contain;
The coral of your lips will from its beauty wane,
Your shoulders' warmth of snow will change to icy sand.

Sweet lightning of your eyes, the powers of your hand,
That do such conquests make, will but brief hours remain.
Your locks, which presently the glance of gold attain,
The day and year at last will ruin in common band.

Your well-placed foot will then, your movements in their grace,
To naught and nothing part, and part to dust give place.
Before your splendor's god no offering more is laid.

This and still more than this at last must pass away.
Your heart alone has strength its constant self to stay,
Since nature this same heart of diamond has made.

Christian Hofmann von Hofmannswaldau (1617–79)
Trans. by George C. Schoolfield

§ *Italian*

CHE NON È STABILITÀ IN COSA MORTALE

Non sia speme tra noi se non celeste,
ch'ogn'altro verde a breve andar s 'imbianca;
volano le giornate a fuggir preste
e col tempo fugace il vivir manca.
  Pungono gli ostri le velate teste
più d'ogni spina; ed ogni man si stanca

che impugni scettro; e chiude una terrestre
tomba ogni impero, ogni virtù più franca.
    Non basti a prolungar solo un momento,
forsennato mortale, il viver breve,
e pensi all'avvenir cent'anni e cento.
    Tornerà il maggio, e tornerà la neve;
ma non tornerà più quando sia spento
l'uman calore e dileguar sì lieve.

THE IMPERMANENCE OF MORTAL THINGS

For man no hope but heaven can exist,
the others all too soon from green turn white.
Our days on earth fly by in haste to flee
and with the flight of time life fades away.
    The royal purple pricks the veiled heads
more sharply than the thorn; and every hand
which holds the scepter tires; an earthly tomb
each empire seals, each firmer property.
    'Tis not enough to lengthen life's brief span
a single moment's time, O mortal fool,
and think thereby to gain a hundred years.
    May will return, and winter will return,
but human warmth, once spent, will ne'er return
to vanish slowly in a second life.

Francesco Bracciolini (1566–1645)

QUID EST HOMO?

Oh Dio, che cosa è l'uom? L'uom è pittura
di fugaci colori ornata e cinta,
che in poca tela e in fragil lin dipinta
tosto si rompe, e tosto fassi oscura.
    O Dio, che cosa è l'uom? L'uom è figura
dal tempo e de l'età corrotta e vinta,
che in debil vetro effigiata e finta,
a un lieve colpo altrui cade e non dura.
    È strale, che da l'arco esce e san passa;
è nebbia, che dal suol sorge e sparisce;
è spuma, che dal mar s'erge e s'abbassa.

È fior, che nell'april nasce e languisce;
è balen, che nell'aria arde e trapassa;
è fumo, che nel ciel s'alza e svanisce.

QUID EST HOMO?

O Lord, what thing is man? A painting he
of fleeting colors girded and bedecked,
which painted on small canvas and frail flax,
is quick to break and quick to grow obscure.
    O Lord, what thing is man? A picture he,
by time and age decayed and overcome,
which drawn and simulated on weak glass,
succumbs to each light blow and does not last—
    a shaft, which flees the bow and pierces chest;
a mist, which springs from earth and vanishes;
a foam, which rises from the sea and falls;
    a bloom, which April brings to life and wilts;
a lightning bolt, which burns and cuts the air;
the smoke, which rises in the sky and fades.

Giovan Leone Sempronio (1603–46)

IL TEMPO CON UNO SPECCHIO IN MANO. PER L'INSTABILITÀ DEL MONDO.

Quegl'io che 'n giro volgo i mesi e l'anno,
divido i giorni ed in minuti l'ore,
della bellezza e dell'età tiranno
fo gioir Morte ed attristare Amore.
    Del volo mio non conosciuto il danno
rendo a un bel volto inaridito il fiore,
che mentre parto apporto e morte e affanno
all vita adombrandola d'orrore.
    All'invisibil mio continuo assalto,
benché sembri all'aspetto infermo e vecchio,
l'altezze abbasso e la bassezza esalto.
    Contempli il mondo stolto in questo specchio
com'ei si cangi, ed io di salto in salto
nuove forme e sembianze or t'apparecchio.

TIME WITH A MIRROR IN HAND.
ON THE INSTABILITY OF THE WORLD.

'Tis I who make revolve the months and years,
divides in minutes all the days and hours;
the mortal foe of beauty and of youth
I bring Death happiness and Love remorse.

Unknown the harm my flight precipitates;
a face once fair I make a withered bloom,
and parting I bring death and woe to life,
a pall of horror casting over it.

In my assault, unseen, continuous,
although I seem in aspect sick and old,
I tear the lofty down and raise the low.

This glass I hold reflects the foolish world
in all its changes, and from leap to leap
I now prepare new forms and semblances.

Giovanni Canale (16??-??)

§ *Spanish*

MIENTRAS POR COMPETIR CON TU CABELLO

Mientras por competir con tu cabello
oro bruñido el Sol relumbra en vano,
mientras con menosprecio en medio el llano
mira tu blanca frente el lilio bello;

mientras a cada labio, por cogello,
siguen más ojos que al clavel temprano,
y mientras triunfa con desdén lozano,
de el luciente cristal tu gentil cuello;

goza cuello, cabello, labio y frente,
antes que lo que fué en tu edad dorada
oro, lilio, clavel, cristal luciente

no sólo en plata o víola troncada
se vuelva, mas tú y ello juntamente
en tierra, en humo, en polvo, en sombra, en nada.

WHILE IN A COMPETITION WITH YOUR HAIR

While in a competition with your hair
the sun, like burnished gold, must gleam in vain,
while your white forehead contemplates with scorn
the lovely lily growing 'midst the plain;

while more eyes follow each lip, in pursuit,
than early-blossoming carnations seek,
and while with proud disdain your gentle neck
o'er lucent crystal triumphs easily,

take pleasure in your forehead, neck, hair, lip
before what had been in your golden age
carnation, lucent crystal, lily, gold,

not only silver or plucked violet
become, but you and it together turn
into earth, smoke, dust, shadow, nothingness.

Luis de Góngora

LETRILLA LÍRICA

Rosal, menos presunción,
donde están las clavellinas,
pues serán mañana espinas
las que agora rosas son.

¿De qué sirve presumir,
rosal, de buen parecer,
si aún no acabas de nacer
cuando empiezas a morir?
Hace llorar y reír
vivo y muerto tu arrebol,
en un día o en un sol;
desde el oriente al ocaso
va tu hermosura en un paso,
y en menos tu perfección.

Rosal, menos presunción,
donde están las clavellinas,
pues serán mañana espinas
las que agora rosas son.

No es muy grande la ventaja
que tu calidad mejora:
si es tu mantilla la aurora,
es la noche tu mortaja:
no hay florecilla tan baja
que no te alcance de días,
y de tus caballerías,
por descendiente del alba,
se está riyendo la malva,
caballera de un terrón.

Rosal, menos presunción,
donde están las clavellinas,
pues serán mañana espinas
las que agora rosas son.

LYRICAL SONG

Less presumption, rosebush, please,
where the little pinks are,
for tomorrow will be thorns
what today are roses.

What use is it, rosebush, tell,
to presume on beauty,
for no sooner are you born
than you start in dying.
Your red both alive and dead
causes tears and laughter,
in a day or in a sun;
from ascent to sunset
in a step your beauty fades,
and in less—perfection.

Less presumption, rosebush, please,
where the little pinks are,
for tomorrow will be thorns
what today are roses.

The advantage is not great
brought in by your merits;
if the dawn serves as your shawl
then the night your shroud is.
There's no little flower so low

in days it's no equal,
and as to your noble past,
from the dawn descended;
even mallows laugh at it,
riding on their hummocks.

Less presumption, rosebush, please,
where the little pinks are,
for tomorrow will be thorns
what today are roses.

                                        Francisco de Quevedo

¡CÓMO DE ENTRE MIS MANOS TE RESBALAS!

¡Cómo de entre mis manos te resbalas!
¡Oh cómo te deslizas, edad mía!
¡Qué mudos pasos traes, oh muerte fría,
pues con callado pie todo lo igualas!

Feroz, de tierra el débil muro escalas,
en quien lozana juventud se fía;
mas ya mi corazón del postrer día,
atiende al vuelo sin mirar las alas.

¡Oh condición mortal! ¡Oh dura suerte!
¡Que no puedo querer vivir mañana
sin la pensión de procurar mi muerte!

Cualquier instante de la vida humana
es nueva ejecución, con que me advierte
cuán fragil es, cuán mísera, cuán vana.

HOW EASILY YOU SLIP BETWEEN MY HANDS!

How easily you slip between my hands!
Oh how you slide away, years of my life!
What silent steps you take, oh frigid death,
when with hush'd tread you equalize all things.

Fiercely you scale the weak wall of the earth
in which our vigorous youthhood puts its trust;

my heart already waits the final day,
when you appear in flight with wings unseen.

Oh mortal state! Oh man's unyielding fate!
To live tomorrow I can have no hope
without the cost of buying my own death!

Each single instant of man's life on earth
is a new summons warning me to heed
how fragile, miserable, and vain it is.

Francisco de Quevedo

§ *Mexican*

A SU RETRATO

Este que ves, engaño colorido,
que del arte ostentando los primores,
con falsos silogismos de colores
es cauteloso engaño del sentido;

este, en quien la lisonja ha pretendido
excusar de los años los horrores,
y venciendo del tiempo los rigores
triunfar de la vejez y del olvido,

es un vano artificio del cuidado,
es una flor al viento delicada,
es un resguardo inútil para el hado,

es una necia diligencia errada,
es un afán caduco y, bien mirado,
es cadáver, es polvo, es sombra, es nada.

TO HER PORTRAIT

This coloured counterfeit that thou beholdest,
vainglorious with the excellencies of art,
is, in fallacious syllogisms of colour,
nought but a cunning dupery of sense;

this in which flattery has undertaken
to extenuate the hideousness of years,

and, vanquishing the outrages of time,
to triumph o'er oblivion and old age,

   is an empty artifice of care,
is a fragile flower in the wind,
is a paltry sanctuary from fate,

   is a foolish sorry labour lost,
is conquest doomed to perish and, well taken,
is corpse and dust, shadow and nothingness.

Sor Juana Inés de la Cruz (1648–95)
Trans. by Samuel Beckett

§ *Polish*

O NIETRWAŁEJ MIŁOŚCI
RZECZY ŚWIATA TEGO

I niemiłować ciężko, i miłować
Nędzna pociecha, gdy żądzą zwiedzione
Myśli cukrują nazbyt rzeczy one,
Które i mienić i muszą sie psować.

Komu tak będzie dostatkiem smakować
Złoto, sceptr, sława, rozkosz i stworzone
Piękne oblicze, by tym nasycone
I mógł mieć serce i trwóg się warować?

Miłość jest własny bieg bycia naszego:
Ale z żywiołów utworzone ciało,
To chwaląc, co zna początku równego,
Zawodzi duszę, której wszystko mało,

Gdy ciebie, wiecznej i prawej piękności
Samej nie widzi, celu swej miłości.

ON THE IMPERMANENT LOVE OF
THE THINGS OF THIS WORLD

No easy thing to love not, and to love
Is but vain comfort when, misled by lust,
Thoughts sugarcoat excessively those things
Which must in time change form and then decay.

Where is the man who'll ever have his fill
Of gold, the scepter, fame, all worldly joys
And lovely countenances and, sufficed,
Take heart and make light of anxieties?

Love is the proper course of life on earth.
The body, though, of elements created,
By praising that which in like way began,
Deceives the soul, which ne'er can be content,

If You, true and eternal beauty,
It does not see, the object of its love.

Mikołaj Sęp Szarzyński

CNOTA GRUNT WSZYTKIEMU

Fraszka wszytko na świecie, fraszka z każdej strony!
Nic to, choć ty masz pałac kosztem wystawiony;
Nic to, że stół zastawiasz hojnie półmiskami;
Nic to, żeć złoto, srebro leży gromadami;
Nic to, że gładka żona i domu zacnego;
Nic to, że mnóstwo wnuków liczysz z boku swego;
Nic to, że masz wsi gęste i wielkie osady;
Nic to, że sług za tobą niemałe gromady;
Nic to, że równia nie znasz dowcipowi swemu;
Nic to, że się ty światu podobasz wszytkiemu;
Nic to, żeć szczęście płynie nieodmiennym torem;
Nic to, choćbyś opatem abo był pryjorem;
Nic to, choć masz papieskie i carskie korony;
Nic to, że cię wyniosło Szczęście nad Tryjony;
Nic to, byś miał tysiąc lat szczęsne panowanie,
Bo iż to wszytko mija, za nic wszytko stanie,
Sama cnota i sława, która z cnoty płynie,
Nade wszytko ta wiecznie trwa i wiecznie słynie.
Tą kto żyje, ma dosyć, choć nie ma niczego,
A bez tej kto umiera, już nic ze wszytkiego.

HONOR THE BASIS OF ALL

All things on earth are trifles, nothing more!
'Tis naught, you've raised a palace at great cost;
'Tis naught, your dining table is renowned;

'Tis naught, you've gold and silver piled in heaps;
'Tis naught, your wife is fair and of good stock;
'Tis naught, grandchildren crowd you on all sides;
'Tis naught, your lands are rich and holdings vast;
'Tis naught, you've servants by the droves on call;
'Tis naught, your wit is keen and without peer;
'Tis naught, you're liked by everyone you meet;
'Tis naught, your fortune keeps a steady course;
'Tis naught, an abbot, prior you become;
'Tis naught, you wear the crown of king or pope;
'Tis naught, Good Fortune raised you over Troy;
'Tis naught, you rule a thousand years in peace;
For all things pass, all finally is naught.
'Tis honor and the glory that it brings
Which live forever, have eternal fame.
Who lives with honor has enough, though naught,
Who dies without it—naught, though he have all.

Daniel Naborowski

§ *Modern Latin* (*Polish*)

LYRICORUM LIB. II. ODE V
E REBUS HUMANIS EXCESSUS

Humana linquo: tollite praepetem
Nubesque ventique. Ut mihi devii
    Montes resedêre! ut volanti
        Regna procul populosque vastus

Subegit aër! Jam radiantia
Delubra Divûm, jam mihi regiae
    Turres recessêre, & relictae in
        Exiguum tenuantur urbes:

Totasque, quà se cumque ferunt vagae,
Despecto gentes. O lacrymabilis
    Incerta fortunae! o fluentûm
        Principia interitusque rerum!

Hîc ducta primis oppida moenibus
Minantur in coelum: hîc veteres ruunt
    Muriqué turresque: hîc supinas
        Paene cinis sepelivit arces.

Hîc mite coelum; sed rapidae ruunt
In bella gentes: hîc placidâ sedent
  In pace; sed latè quietos
    Dira lues populatur agros.

Hîc paene tellus tota micantibus
Ardet sub armis: stant acies adhuc
  Pendente Fatorum sub ictu,
    Et dubio Furor haesitavit.

In bella passu. Parte aliâ recens
Jam mixta Mavors agmina mutuam
  Collisit in mortem, & cadentûm
    Caede virûm cumulisque latos

Insternit agros. Hîc Mareoticae
Secura merces aequora navigant,
  Portusque certatim frequentes
    Centum operis populisque fervent.

Nec una Marti causa, nec unius
Sunt arma moris. Bellat adulterae
  Ridentis e vultu voluptas,
    Inque Helenâ procus ardet Orbis.

Hîc verba bellis vindicat: hic canis,
Heu vile furtum! se mala comparant:
  Rarum sub exemplo superbit,
    Nec sceleris scelus instar omne est.

Eous illinc belligerâ latet
Sub classe pontus: jam Thetis aeneâ
  Mugire flammarum procellâ, &
    Attonitae trepidare cautes,

Et ipsa circùm litora percuti
Majore fluctu. Sistite, barbari;
  Ferroque neu simplex, & igni, &
    Naufragio geminate Fatum.

Parùmne Tellus in miseras patet
Immensa mortes? hinc miserabili
  Quassata terrarum tumultu
    Stare pavent titubantque regna,

Unâque tandem funditus obruunt
Cives ruinâ. State tacitus cinis,

Cui serus inscribat viator
CUM POPULO JACET HIC ET IPSO

CUM REGE REGNUM. Quid memorem super-
infusa totis aequora portubus
    Urbes inundare? & repenti
        Tecta Deûm sonuisse fluctu?

Regumque turres, & pelago casas
Jam jam latentes? Jam video procul
    Mercesque differri, & natantem
        Oceano fluitare gazam.

Alterna rerum militat efficax
In damna mundus. Cladibus instruit,
    Bellisque, rixisque, & ruinis
        Sanguineam Libitina scenam;

Suprema donec stelligerum dies
Claudat theatrum. Quid morer hactenus
    Viator aurarum? & serenas
        Sole domos aditurus, usque

Humana mirer? Tollite praepetem
Festina Vatem: tollite, nubila,
    Quà solis & lunae labores
        Caeruleo vehit aethra campo.

Ludor? sequaces an subeunt latus
Feruntque venti? jamque iterum mihi
    Et regna decrevêre, & immensae
        Ante oculos periêre gentes:

Suoque semper terra minor globo
Jam jamque cerni difficilis suum
    Vanescit in punctum? O refusum
        Numinis Oceanum! o carentem

Mortalitatis portubus insulam!
O clausa nullis marginibus freta!
    Haurite anhelantem, & perenni
        Sarbivium glomerate fluctu.

BOOK II, ODE V
*A DEPARTURE FROM THINGS HUMANE**

Lift me up quickly on your wings,
   Ye Clouds, and Winds; I leave all earthly things.
How devious hills give way to mee!
   And the vast ayre brings under, as I fly,
Kingdomes and populous states! see how
   The Glytt'ring Temples of the Gods doe bow;
The glorious Tow'rs of Princes, and
   Forsaken townes, shrunke into nothing, stand:
And as I downward looke, I spy
   Whole Nations every where all scattred lye.
Oh the sad change that Fortune brings!
   The rise and fall of transitory things!
Here walled townes that threatned Heav'n,
   Now old and ruin'd, with earth lye even:
Here stately Pallaces, that thrust
   Their heads i'th'ayre, lye buried all in dust.
Here the Ayre Temp'rate is and mild,
   But the fierce people rush to warres, most wild:
Here in joyfull peace they rest,
   But Direfull Murraines their quiet fields lay wast.
Here the whole Land doth scorching lye
   Under the glitt'ring Armes o'th'Enemy:
Under the hovering stroke o'th'Fates
   The Armies yet both stand; and fury waites
With doubtfull steps, upon the warre;
   Fresh courage here, the mingled troopes prepare,
Each against other fiercely run,
   And mutually they worke destruction:
The slaughtered heapes in reeking gore
   With bloudy covering spread the fields all o're:
Here on safe Seas, as joyfull prize
   Is strip'd away th'Aegyptian Merchandize,
Whilst the full Havens thick beset,
   Doe furiously with fierce contention fret.
Mars hath his divers Causes, and
   His severall fashion'd weapons to command.
From the Adultresse smiling lookes
   Pleasure doth fight, and unto Warre provokes,

---

* This translation, in the original spelling, is from the collection of
Sarbiewski translations into English published in London in 1646 by G. H(ils)
under the title *Odes of Casimire*.

The doting world with *Helen* burnes.
   This sordid man, oh base advantage! turnes
Revenge of words to blowes;
   Mischiefe begets it selfe, from mischiefe growes.
Small sins by example higher dare,
   Nor doth all sin, alwaies like sin appeare.
There th'Easterne Sea lyes covered o're
   With warlike Fleets: *Thetis* begins to rore
With stormes of flaming Brasse, and here
   Th'astonish'd Rocks all trembling stand with feare.
The troubled Sea with winds beset
   Which stronger waves 'gainst the full shore doth beat.
Forbeare, cruell men to multiply
   With fire, Sword-wrack your single destiny.
Is the large Earth too narrow growne,
   Such slaughters, such dire tragedies to owne?
Large Kingdomes there, brought under thrall
   With Tumult, stagger, and for feare doe fall;
Where in one Ruine wee may see
   The dying people all o'rewhelmed lye,
The silent dust remaines, to let
   The weary Pilgrim this Inscription set
(In After times, as hee goes by)
   King, Kingdome, People here entombed lye.
What should I name the raging Seas,
   Whole Havens over-flowing, and with these
I'th'sudden floud whole Cities drown'd
   The shaken Temples of the Gods that sound?
Kings Pallaces what should I name
   Now sunke i'th'deepe, small Cottages i'th'same?
Vast wealth I see swept downe with th' tyde
   Rich treasure in the Ocean floting glyde.
The active world t'each others harmes
   Doth daily fight, and the pale Goddesse armes
The bloudy scene with slaughters, warrs,
   With utter ruins, and with deadly jarrs;
Thus there's no *Exit* of our woes,
   Till the last day the Theater shall close,
Why stay I then, when goe I may—
   To 'a house enlightned by the Suns bright ray?
Shall I still dote on things humane?
   Lift up your longing Priest, yee Clouds, oh deigne
Lift m'up where th'aire a splendour yields

Lights the sun's chariot through the azure fields.
Am I deceived? or doe I see
The following winds on their wings mounting me,
And now againe Great Kingdomes lye
Whole Nations perishing before mine eye?
The earth which alwayes lesse hath beene
Then's Globe, and now, just now can scarce be seene,
Into it's point doth vanish, see!
Oh the brim'd Ocean of the Deitie!
Oh Glorious Island richly free
From the cold Harbours of mortality!
Yee boundlesse seas, with endlesse flouds of rest
Girt round Sarbivius your panting Priest.

Maciej Kazimierz Sarbiewski (Sarbievius, "Casimir,"
"Casimire") (1595–1640)

§ *Czech*

POHRZENÍ POMÍJEJÍCÍHO SVĚTA

Co pomáhá světská sláva,
an pomíjí jako tráva?
Dým v povětří větrem hyne,
život náš dnes, zejtra mine.

Co trůn pánův, berla králův,
co koruny potentátův?
Všecko někdy vezme konec,
smrt poslední chce mít tanec.

Co spomáhá krásným býti,
třebas tvář andělskou míti?
Nejpěknější sprchá růže,
v hrobě hnije tělo, kůže.

Měj i oči křišťálový,
měj i pysky korálový,
bud' vlas žlutý víc než zlato,
v brzkém čase bude bláto.

Měj zlatohlav neb hedbáví
a co koli oči vábí:

zlato země jest červená,
marná jest u lidí cena.

Co jest roucho šarlatové?
krev jest, lejno hlemejžďové,
    pejše musi sloužit moře,
    bude někdy těžke hoře.

Co choditi v aksamitě,
ošaťte se jak umíte,
    pošlo z červíčkův přediva,
    nač se světa pejcha dívá?

Co červ z sebe vyhazuje
velice člověk šacuje,
    v tom se sadí a nadýmá,
    své kochání, rozkoš mívá.

Měj se dobře marný světe,
kratičký dým, jarní květe,
    nedám se tobě mámiti,
    volím věčnou rozkoš míti.

Čiň jak tě tvá vede libost,
já nestojím o tvou milost,
    vzdychám, dychtím po věčnosti,
    časně sahám k pobožnosti.

DISDAIN FOR THIS TRANSITORY WORLD

What avail is worldly glory?
Flesh like grass is transitory.
    Smoke we are, by rough winds carried,
    Here to stay, tomorrow buried.

What are royal throne and power,
Princely castle, knightly tower?
    All must come to dust and ashes:
    Death's last dance will end all passion.

What avail are youth and vigor,
Angel's face on fairest figure?
    E'en the rose must wilt and wither
    Grave rots bone and skin together.

Be your eyes of crystal lightness,
Be your lips of coral brightness,

Be your hair like red gold burning:
Soon to clay it will be turning.

Rustling silk or golden treasure,
All which to the eye gives pleasure:
   Gold is sand, like sand you spend it;
   Vain the price that humans lend it.

What are crimson robe and ermine?
Merely blood and slime and vermin.
   Pride and riches will be humbled,
   Greatness mercilessly tumbled.

Ye who walk in velvet breeches:
Poverty the Master teaches!
   Silk is but the worm's extrusion,
   Worldly pride is but illusion.

What the silkworm has excreted,
Worthless, horrible and fetid,
   Man counts precious and entrancing:
   Silk he wears for feast and dancing.

So adieu, world of the senses,
Tempting me with vain pretenses,
   Brief as smoke and flower vernal:
   I elect the joys eternal.

How the world behaves I care not,
In its vanity I share not:
   I am eager for salvation,
   Turn to pious meditation.

Adam Michna of Otradovice (c. 1600–76)
Trans. by E. Osers

FROM *CAPELLA REGIA MUSICALIS.
KAPLE KRÁLOVSKÁ ZPĚVNÍ.*

Kde jste, kde, císařové,
umřeli jste,
kde, světa mocnářové,
již víc nejste,
za vámi my půjdeme,
smrti neujdeme,
ach, půjdeme k vám do věčnosti.

Kde jste pak, kde, knížata,
zmizeli jste,
kde, přeslavná hrabata,
umřeli jste,
za vámi my půjdeme,
smrti neujdeme,
ach, půjdeme k vám do věčnosti.

Kde jste, krásné slečenky,
ach, zbledly jste,
kde, přepěkné panenky,
ach, shnily jste,
za vámi my půjdeme
smrti neujdeme,
ach, půjdeme k vám do věčnosti.

Kde jste, statečné paní,
již nejste nic,
žádný vás již ze spaní
nezbudí víc,
za vámi my půjdeme,
smrti neujdeme,
ach, půjdeme k vám do věčnosti.

Kde jste, kde, boháčové,
ach, schudli jste,
kde světa miláčkové,
ach, ustydli jste,
za vámi my půjdeme,
smrti neujdeme,
ach, půjdeme k vám do věčnosti.

Kde jste, kde, i měšťané,
ach, v kostnici,
jináče se nám nestane,
chtíc nechtící
za vámi my půjdeme,
smrti neujdeme,
ach, půjdeme k vám do věčnosti.

Robotní sedláčkové
přestali jsou,
všichni hospodářové
již domů jdou,
za vámi my půjdeme,

smrti neujdeme,
ach, půjdeme k vám do věčnosti.

I my všickni na světě
tam půjdeme,
snad v tom neb v druhém létě,
tam, tam všickni půjdeme,
smrti neujdeme,
ach, půjdeme k vám do věčnosti.

WHERE, WHERE ARE YOU, GREAT EMPERORS?

Where, where are you, great emperors?
all dead and gone.
And where are you, earth's noble sirs?
your lives are done.
And we shall follow you,
for death will claim us too.
Oh, we shall join you in eternity.

O where are you, great lords of earth?
long since passed on.
And you, you men of noble birth?
dead and gone.
And we shall follow you,
for death will claim us too.
Oh, we shall join you in eternity.

And you, fair maid? your lovely face
turned white and cold,
You too, fine ladies, filled with grace?
rotting mold.
And we shall follow you,
for death will claim us too,
Oh, we shall join you in eternity

O where are you, brave noblemen?
crumbled to dust,
and no one ever shall again
disturb your rest:
but we shall follow you,
for death will claim us too.
Oh, we shall join you in eternity.

Where, where are you, the wealthy ones?
Your wealth is fled.
And where are you, earth's favored sons?
cold and dead;
And we shall follow you,
for death will claim us too.
Oh, we shall join you in eternity.

You city folk, where, where are you?
within the tomb,
and we ourselves, what e'er we do
must share your doom:
for we shall follow you,
and death will claim us too.
Oh, we shall join you in eternity.

The labors of the serfs are spent
at close of day;
the bailiffs are all homeward bent
upon their way:
and we shall follow you,
for death will claim us too.
Oh, we shall join you in eternity.

All creatures of this worldly place
shall follow you,
this year, or in a little space,
we all, we all shall follow you:
for death will claim us too.
Oh, we shall join you in eternity.

Václav Karel Holan Rovenský
Trans. by A. French

§ *Croatian*

LJUDSKI ŽIVOT

Budi nam spomena, ljudska su godišta:
   Vihar, plam i sjena, san, magla i ništa
Vihar se zameće sred ljetne tišine
   Sviem svijetom uskreće, nu do čas pak mine.
Plam slame uzgori k nebesima ulazi,
   Nu brzo dogori, i sam se ugasi.

Sjena nas svedj slidi, nu kad smo u tmini
Tere se ne vidi, i sjene s nami nij.
San ludu kaže, da ima što žudi,
Nu pozna da laže, kad se lud probudi.
Magla sve pokrije o zori, danu pak
Sva se opet sakrije, kad sine sunčan zrak.
Ništa je sve vrime, za danom noć hodi,
Za ljetom zle zime, svaka stvar prohodi.
Budi nam spomena, ljudska su godišta:
Vihar, plam i sjena, san, magla i ništa.

HUMAN LIFE

Let us remember that man's years on earth
Are tempest, fire and shadow, dream, mist, naught.
The tempest scatters 'midst the summer's still;
It flashes brilliantly, but quickly fades.
The fire of burning straw climbs to the skies,
But burns up soon and of itself expires.
Shadows e'er follow us, but in the dark
They disappear and are with us no more.
A madman's dream reveals a yearning, too,
But when he wakes still mad he grasps the lie.
Mist covers everything at dawn, and then
The shining rays of sun hide all again.
Nothing is its own time; night follows day,
Harsh winters, summer, all things pass away.
Let us remember that man's years on earth
Are tempest, fire and shadow, dream, mist, naught.

Dživo Bunić-Vučić (Ivan Bunič-Vučićević)
(1591–1658)

C. TIME

§ *English*

TO HIS WATCH,
WHEN HE COULD NOT SLEEP

Uncessant Minutes, whil'st you move you tell
The time that tells our life, which though it run

Never so fast or farr, your new begun
Short steps shall overtake; for though life well

May scape his own Account, it shall not yours,
   You are Death's Auditors, that both divide
And summ what ere that life inspir'd endures
   Past a beginning, and through you we bide

The doom of Fate, whose unrecall'd Decree
   You date, bring, execute; making what's new,
Ill and good, old, for as we die in you,
   You die in Time, Time in Eternity.

          Edward, Lord Herbert of Cherbury (1583–1648)

TIME

Meeting with Time, Slack thing, said I,
Thy sithe is dull; whet it for shame.
No marvell Sir, he did replie,
If it at length deserve some blame:
   But where one man would have me grinde it,
   Twentie for one too sharp do finde it.

Perhaps some such of old did passe,
Who above all things lov'd this life;
To whom thy sithe a hatchet was,
Which now is but a pruning-knife.
   Christs coming hath made man thy debter,
   Since by thy cutting he grows better.

And in his blessing thou art blest:
For where thou onely wert before
An executioner at best,
Thou art a gard'ner now, and more,
   An usher to convey our souls
   Beyond the utmost starres and poles.

And this is that makes life so long,
While it detains us from our God.
Ev'n pleasures here increase the wrong,
And length of dayes lengthen the rod.
   Who wants the place, where God doth dwell,
   Partakes already half of hell.

Of what strange length must that needs be,
Which ev'n eternitie excludes!
Thus farre Time heard me patiently:
Then chafing said, This man deludes:
 What do I here before his doore?
 He doth not crave lesse time, but more.

George Herbert

ALL THINGS DECAY AND DIE

All things decay with Time: The Forrest sees
The growth, and down-fall of her aged trees:
That Timber tall, which three-score *lusters* stood
The proud *Dictator* of the State-like wood:
I meane (the Soveraigne of all Plants) the Oke
Droops, dies, and falls without the cleavers stroke.

Robert Herrick

MY MIDNIGHT MEDITATION

Ill busi'd man! why should'st thou take such care
To lengthen out thy lifes short Kalendar?
When ev'ry spectacle thou lookst upon
Presents and acts thy execution.
 Each drooping season and each flower doth cry,
 Fool! as I fade and wither, thou must dy.

The beating of thy pulse (when thou art well)
Is just the tolling of thy Passing Bell:
Night is thy Hearse, whose sable Canopie
Covers alike deceased day and thee.
 And all those weeping dewes which nightly fall,
 Are but the tears shed for thy funerall.

Henry King

ON TIME

Fly envious *Time*, till thou run out thy race,
Call on the lazy leaden-stepping hours,

Whose speed is but the heavy Plummets pace;
And glut thy self with what thy womb devours,
Which is no more than what is false and vain,
And merely mortal dross;
So little is our loss,
So little is thy gain.
For when as each thing bad thou hast entomb'd,
And last of all, thy greedy self consum'd,
Then long eternity shall greet our bliss
With an individual kiss;
And Joy shall overtake us as a flood,
When every thing that is sincerely good
And perfectly divine,
With Truth, and Peace, and Love shall ever shine
About the supreme Throne
Of him, t'whose happy-making sight alone,
When once our heav'nly guided soul shall clime,
Then all this Earthy grosnes quit,
Attir'd with Stars, we shall for ever sit,
  Triumphing over Death, and Chance, and thee o Time.

John Milton (1608–74)

§ *American*

FROM   *CONTEMPLATIONS*

18
When I behold the heavens as in their prime,
And then the earth (though old) stil clad in green,
The stones and trees, insensible of time,
Nor age nor wrinkle on their front are seen;
If winter come, and greeness then do fade,
A Spring returns, and they more youthfull made;
But Man grows old, lies down, remains where once he's laid.

19
By birth more noble than those creatures all,
Yet seems by nature and by custome curs'd,
No sooner born, but grief and care makes fall
That state obliterate he had at first:
Nor youth, nor strength, nor wisdom spring again

Nor habitations long their names retain,
But in oblivion to the final day remain.

20

Shall I then praise the heavens, the trees, the earth
Because their beauty and their strength last longer
Shall I wish there, or never to had birth,
Because they're bigger, and their bodyes stronger?
Nay, they shall darken, perish, fade and dye,
And when unmade, so ever shall they lye,
But man was made for endless immortality.

29

Man at the best a creature frail and vain,
In knowledg ignorant, in strength but weak,
Subject to sorrows, losses, sickness, pain,
Each storm his state, his mind, his body break,
From some of these he never finds cessation,
But day or night, within, without, vexation,
Troubles from foes, from friends, from dearest, near'st Relation.

30

And yet this sinfull creature, frail and vain,
This lump of wretchedness, of sin and sorrow,
This weather-beaten vessel wrackt with pain,
Joyes not in hope of an eternal morrow;
Nor all his losses, crosses and vexation,
In weight, in frequency and long duration
Can make him deeply groan for that divine Translation.

31

The Mariner that on smooth waves doth glide,
Sings merrily, and steers his barque with ease,
As if he had command of wind and tide,
And now become great Master of the seas;
But suddenly a storm spoiles all the sport,
And makes him long for a more quiet port,
Which 'gainst all adverse winds may serve for fort.

32

So he that saileth in this world of pleasure,
Feeding on sweets, that never bit of th' sowre,
That's full of friends, of honour and of treasure,
Fond fool, he takes this earth ev'n for heav'ns bower.
But sad affliction comes and makes him see

Here's neither honour, wealth, nor safety;
Only above is found all with security.

      33
O Time the fatal wrack of mortal things,
That draws oblivions curtains over kings,
Their sumptuous monuments, men know them not,
Their names without a Record are forgot,
Their parts, their ports, their pomp's all laid in th' dust
Nor wit nor gold, nor buildings scape times rust;
But he whose name is grav'd in the white stone*
Shall last and shine when all of these are gone.

                          Anne Bradstreet (c. 1612–72)

§ *Dutch*

DE HOROLOGIEMAAKER
DAT MEN BEREID IS TERWYL HET TYD IS.

   ô Mens, beschik uw zielenstaat,
      Terwyl des levens uurwerk gaat;
Want als 't gewigt is afgeloopen
      Van deezen korten leevenstyd,
Daar is geen ophaal weêr te koopen,
      Voor konst, noch geld, noch achtbaarheid.

THE CLOCKMAKER
THAT MAN PREPARE HIMSELF
WHILE THERE IS TIME.

   O Man, set straight your soul's abode
      While life's clock ticks its measured road;
For when the pendulum runs down,
      Which marks the span of life's short round,
There is no upstroke to be found
      For art, or money, or renown.

                          Jan Luyken

   * Rev. 2:17: "To him that overcometh will I give to eat of the hidden
manna, and will give him a white stone, and in the stone a new name written,
which no man knoweth saving he that receiveth it."

§ *German*

BETRACHTUNG DER ZEIT

Mein sind die Jahre nicht, die mir die Zeit genommen;
Mein sind die Jahre nicht, die etwa möchten kommen;
Der Augenblick ist mein, und nehm ich den in acht,
So ist der mein, der Jahr und Ewigkeit gemacht.

CONTEMPLATION OF TIME

Not mine the years which plundered me of time;
Not mine the years which may yet come sometime;
The moment's mine, on it I concentrate,
Thus mine who year and life eternal made.

Andreas Gryphius

GEDANKEN ÜBER DER ZEIT

Ihr lebet in der Zeit und kennt doch keine Zeit;
So wisst ihr Menschen nicht, von und in was ihr seid.
Dies wisst ihr, dass ihr seid in einer Zeit geboren
Und dass ihr werdet auch in einer Zeit verloren.

Was aber war die Zeit, die euch in sich gebracht?
Und was wird diese sein, die euch zu nichts mehr macht?
Die Zeit ist was und nichts, der Mensch in gleichem Falle;
Doch was dasselbe was und nichts sei, zweifeln alle.

Die Zeit, die stirbt in sich und zeugt sich auch aus sich.
Dies kömmt aus mir und dir, von dem du bist und ich.
Der Mensch ist in der Zeit; sie ist in ihm ingleichen,
Doch aber muss der Mensch, wenn sie noch bleibet, weichen.

Die Zeit ist, was ihr seid, und ihr seid, was die Zeit,
Nur dass ihr wen'ger noch, als was die Zeit ist, seid.
Ach! dass doch jene Zeit, die ohne Zeit ist, käme
Und uns aus dieser Zeit in ihre Zeiten nähme,
Und aus uns selbsten uns, dass wir gleich könnten sein,
Wie der itzt, jener Zeit, die keine Zeit geht ein!

THOUGHTS ON TIME

You live in time yet know not any time;
Nor do you grasp of what, in what you are.
You only know that one time you were born
And that one time you also will be lost.

What was the time which brought you in itself?
And what the time which makes you nothing more?
Time is and yet is not, like man himself;
All doubt what is itself and yet is not.

Time dies in time but from itself bears time;
It comes from me and you, and we from it.
Man lives in time, and likewise time in man,
But man must yield, while time continues on.

Time's what you are, and you are what time is,
Except that you are less than what time is.
Oh! let the other time, which has no time,
Come take us from this time to its own times,
And us from out ourselves that we be like,
As He, the other time that no time dies.

                                        Paul Fleming

DIE ZEIT

Ich kugelrundes Haus, das in dem Luft bestehet,
verschleuss, was lebt und bebt, dass es beharrlich gehet.
Was ich gewesen bin, das werd ich nach und nach:
Wer mich einmal verliert, gewinnet Weh und Ach!

TIME

Round house midst heaven's realm, I seal on high
What lives and quakes, that all may steadfast be.
What I have been, I shall be by and by,
Who loses me wins grief and misery.

                    Georg Philipp Harsdörffer (1607–58)

§ *Italian*

OROLOGI DA RUOTE, DA POLVE E DA SOLE

Quei che le vite altrui tradisce e fura,
qual reo su cento rote ecco si volve,
e lui, che scioglier suol gli uomini in polve,
con poca polve or l'uom lega e misura.
E se con l'ombre i nostri giorni oscura,
se stesso in ombra ai rai del sol risolve;
quinci apprendi, o mortal, come dissolve
ogni cosa qua giù tempo e natura.
Su quelle rote egli trionfa e regna;
con quella polve ad acciecarti aspira;
e tra quell'ombra ucciderti disegna.
Su quelle rote i tuoi pensier martira;
in quella polve i tuoi diletti ei segna;
e tra quell'ombra ombre di morte aggira.

CLOCKS OF WHEELS, SAND AND SUN

He [i.e. time] who betrays and plunders others' lives,
how cruel he turns upon a hundred wheels,
and he, whose lust is grinding men to dust,
with little dust now binds and measures man.
And if with shadows he obscures our days,
in shadow he himself melts 'neath sun's rays.
Therefore, O mortal, learn how here below,
all things by Time and Nature are dissolved.
Upon those wheels he triumphs and holds sway;
'tis with that dust he seeks to make you blind;
and 'midst that shadow plots you low to lay.
Upon those wheels he torments all your thoughts;
'tis in that dust your pleasures duly marks;
and 'midst that shadow shadows of death spins.

Giovan Leone Sempronio

§ *Spanish*

MIRÉ LOS MUROS
DE LA PATRIA MÍA

Miré los muros de la patria mía,
si un tiempo fuertes, ya desmoronados,
de la carrera de la edad cansados
por quien caduca ya su valentía.

Salíme al campo, vi que el Sol bebía
los arroyos del yelo desatados;
y del monte quejosos los ganados
que con sombras hurtó su luz al día.

Entré en mi casa; vi que, amancillada,
de anciana habitación era despojos;
mi báculo, más corvo y menos fuerte.

Vencida de la edad sentí mi espada,
y no hallé cosa en que poner los ojos
que no fuese recuerdo de la muerte.

I GAZED UPON THE WALLS
OF MY OWN LAND

I gazed upon the walls of my own land,
which were so mighty once, now crumbled lay,
exhausted by the passage of the years
by which their valor now falls to decay.

I went out to the fields, the sun saw drinking
the streams at last released from bonds of ice,
and cattle 'gainst the woods all clam'ring
that they by shadows stole their light of day.

I entered next my house; I saw that, blotched,
the ruins it was of ancient dwelling place;
that now my staff more bent was and less strong.

I felt my sword defeated too by time
and found no thing on which to rest my eyes
that was itself no memory of death.

Francisco de Quevedo

§ *Mexican*

PÍDEME DE MÍ MISMO EL TIEMPO CUENTA

Pídeme de mí mismo el tiempo cuenta;
si a darla voy, la cuenta pide tiempo:
que quien gastó sin cuenta tanto tiempo,
¿cómo dará, sin tiempo, tanta cuenta?

Tomar no quiere el tiempo tiempo en cuenta,
porque la cuenta no se hizo en tiempo;
que el tiempo recibiera en cuenta tiempo
si en la cuenta del tiempo hubiera cuenta.

¿Qué cuenta ha de bastar a tanto tiempo?
¿Qué tiempo ha de bastar a tanta cuenta?
Que quien sin cuenta vive, está sin tiempo.

Estoy sin tener tiempo y sin dar cuenta,
sabiendo que he de dar cuenta del tiempo
y ha de llegar el tiempo de la cuenta.

TIME REQUIRES ME TO GIVE ACCOUNT

Time requires me to give account;
the account, if I would give it, requires time:
for he, without account, who lost such time,
how shall he, without time, give such account?

Time cares not to take time into account,
for the account was not made up in time;
for time would only take account of time
if in the account of time time found account.

What account shall suffice for so much time?
What time suffice for so great an account?
Life careless of account is shorn of time.

I live, I have no time, give no account,
knowing that I must give account of time
and that the time must come to give account.

Miguel de Guevara
Trans. by Samuel Beckett

§ *Portuguese*

O TEMPO ACABA O ANO, O MÊS E A HORA

O tempo acaba o ano, o mês e a hora,
  A fôrça, a arte, a manha, a fortaleza;
  O tempo acaba a fama e a riqueza,
  O tempo o mesmo tempo de si chora;
O tempo busca e acaba o onde mora
  Qualquer ingratidão, qualquer dureza;
  Mas não pode acabar minha tristeza,
  Enquanto não quiserdes vós, Senhora.
O tempo o claro dia torna escuro,
  E o mais ledo prazer em chôro triste;
  O tempo, a tempestade em grão bonança.
Mas de abrandar o tempo estou seguro
  O peito de diamente, onde consiste
  A pena e o prazer desta esperança.

TIME MARKS AN END OF YEARS, OF MONTHS, OF HOURS

Time marks an end of years, of months, of hours,
  Of might, of art, of wit, of manly strength;
  Time marks an end of fame and earthly wealth,
  Time time itself bemoaning in its course.
Time seeks their dwelling place and makes an end
  Of all ingratitude, all stubbornness.
  But time, alas, my sadness cannot end
  So long as you withhold your love, my dear.
Time turns the clearest day to night obscure,
  The gayest pleasures into sad lament;
  Time tempests to tranquillity transforms.
But time ne'er soften will, of this I'm sure,
  That diamantine heart, wherein consist
  The pain and pleasure of this hope of mine.

Luís de Camões

§ *Polish*

CO CZAS ZNAJDZIE, CZAS GUBI

Ktoś powiedział: nic nad czas mędrszego, a drugi:
  Nic głupszego. Cóż tedy po dyspucie długiej?
Tamten różne rzemiosła i nauki liczy,
  W których czas ludzi ćwiczył i dotychczas ćwiczy.
Ten króle, mędrce, męże, rycerze, narody,
  Zamki, miasta, pałace, które nie bez szkody
Zostawiwszy przy jednym niepewnym imieniu,
  W wiecznym, nie wetowanym pogrążył milczeniu.
Pytasz: jaki ta koniec kwestyja odniesie?
  Cokolwiek z czasem wyszło, wszytko ginie w czesie.

WHAT TIME FINDS, TIME RUINS

Someone once said, Time's wisdom has no peer.
  Another, Time's stupidity. And so?
The former counted divers trades and arts,
  Which time did exercise men in—and does;
The latter—statesmen, states, kings, sages, knights,
  Towns, castles, palaces, which to their harm
Bequeathed the same uncertain legacy,
  Sank in the silence of eternity.
You ask, The question then is how resolved?
  Whatever came with time shall in time die.

                                   Wacław Potocki

D. DEATH

§ *English*

DEATH

Death, thou wast once an uncouth hideous thing,
            Nothing but bones,
        The sad effect of sadder grones:
Thy mouth was open, but thou couldst not sing.

For we consider'd thee as at some six
            Or ten yeares hence,

After the losse of life and sense,
Flesh being turn'd to dust, and bones to sticks.

We lookt on this side of thee, shooting short;
Where we did finde
The shells of fledge souls left behinde,
Dry dust, which sheds no tears, but may extort.

But since our Saviours death did put some bloud
Into thy face;
Thou art grown fair and full of grace,
Much in request, much sought for as a good.

For we do now behold thee gay and glad,
As at dooms-day;
When souls shall wear their new aray,
And all thy bones with beautie shall be clad.

Therefore we can go die as sleep, and trust
Half that we have
Unto an honest faithfull grave;
Making our pillows either down, or dust.

George Herbert

§ *German*

AN SICH SELBST

Mir grauet vor mir selbst; mir zittern alle Glieder,
Wenn ich die Lipp und Nas und beider Augen Kluft,
Die blind vom Wachen sind, des Atems schwere Luft
Betracht und die nun schon erstorbnen Augenlieder.

Die Zunge, schwarz von Brand, fällt mit den Worten nieder
Und lallt, ich weiss nicht was; die müde Seele ruft
Dem grossen Tröster zu, das Fleisch reucht nach der Gruft,
Die Ärzte lassen mich, die Schmerzen kommen wieder.

Mein Körper ist nicht mehr als Adern, Fell und Bein.
Das Sitzen ist mein Tod, das Liegen meine Pein.
Die Schenkel haben selbst nun Träger wohl vonnöten.

Was ist der hohe Ruhm und Jugend, Ehr und Kunst?
Wenn diese Stunde kommt, wird alles Rauch und Dunst,
Und eine Not muss uns mit allem Vorsatz töten.

TO HIMSELF

I sicken of myself, my members are all shaking,
When I my lip and nose, my breathing's heavy wave,
My lids already numb, and next my two eyes' cave
Will contemplate, which last are blind from too long waking.

My tongue, with fever black and sense of words forsaking,
Babbles I know not what, my spent soul can but crave
The great consoler's aid, my flesh smells of the grave.
The doctors leave me now whom pains again are taking.

My body is no more than skin and bone and vein;
To sit my certain death, and yet to lie my pain,
My thighs themselves are come into the need of bearers.

Of what do lofty fame, youth, honor, art consist?
When this hour has approached, all turns to smoke and mist,
One curse with all design must slay us through its terrors.

Andreas Gryphius
Trans. by George C. Schoolfield

§ *French*

FROM *SONNETS DE LA MORT*

Mais si faut-il mourir, et la vie orgueilleuse,
Qui brave de la mort, sentira ses fureurs
Les soleils hâleront ces journalières fleurs
Et le temps crèvera cette ampoule venteuse;

Ce beau flambeau, qui lance une flamme fumeuse,
Sur le vert de la cire éteindra ses ardeurs,
L'huile de ce tableau ternira ses couleurs
Et ces flots se rompront à la rive écumeuse.

J'ai vu ces clairs éclairs passer devant mes yeux,
Et le tonnerre encor qui gronde dans les cieux,
Où d'une ou d'autre part éclatera l'orage.

J'ai vu fondre la neige et ses torrents tarir,
Ces lions rugissants je les ai vus sans rage:
Vivez, hommes, vivez, mais si faut-il mourir.

FROM *SONNETS ON DEATH*

Yet man is doomed to die, and this proud life,
Which death defies, will come to know its wrath;
The suns will fade those flowers of a day
And time will crack this ampulla of wind.

This lovely candle casting smoking flame
Will burn its ardor in the wax's green;
This picture's oil will dim its brilliant hues,
And on the foamy shore will break the waves.

I've seen bright lightnings pass before my eyes
And thunder rumbling in the skies again
Somewhere from which the storm will surely burst.

I've seen the snows melt and the streams run dry;
These roaring lions seen bereft of rage:
Do live, men, live, yet man is doomed to die.

Jean de Sponde (1557–95)

FROM *SONNETS DE LA MORT*

Qui sont, qui sont ceux-là dont le coeur idolâtre
Se jette aux pieds du monde et flatte ses honneurs,
Et qui sont ces valets, et qui sont ces seigneurs?
Et ces âmes d'ébène et ces faces d'albâtre?

Ces masques déguisés, dont la troupe folâtre
S'amuse à caresser je ne sais quels donneurs
De fumées de cour, et ces entrepreneurs
De vaincre encor le ciel qu'ils ne peuvent combattre?

Qui sont ces louvoyeurs qui s'éloignent du port,
Hommagers à la vie et félons à la mort,
Dont l'étoile est leur bien, le vent leur fantaisie?

Je vogue en même mer et craindrais de périr,
Si ce n'est que je sais que cette même vie
N'est rien que le fanal qui me guide au morir.

FROM *SONNETS ON DEATH*

Who are they, the idolatrous of heart,
Who at the world's feet, prone, its honors praise?

And who these lackeys, who these noblemen?
These ebon souls, these alabaster faces?

These maskers in disguise whose playful band
Its time spends heaping praise on vague dispensers
Of courtly vanities, and those who scheme
Again to conquer heaven they can't fight?

Who are these tackers sailing far from port,
Who homage render life, and death deceit,
Whose star is their own good, the wind their whim.

I sail the same sea too and should fear death,
Did I not know that this same life
Is just the beacon showing me death's way.

                                        Jean de Sponde

FROM *LE MÉPRIS DE LA VIE
ET CONSOLATION CONTRE LA MORT*

Assieds-toi sur le bord d'une ondante rivière:
Tu la verras fluer d'un perpétuel cours,
Et flots sur flots roulant en mille et mille tours
Décharger par les prés son humide carrière.

Mais tu ne verras rien de cette onde première
Qui naguère coulait; l'eau change tous les jours,
Tous les jours elle passe, et la nommons toujours
Même fleuve, et même eau, d'une même manière.

Ainsi l'homme varie, et ne sera demain
Telle comme aujourd'hui du pauvre corps humain
La force que le temps abrévie et consomme:

Le nom sans varier nous suit jusqu'au trépas,
Et combien qu'aujourd'hui celui ne sois-je pas
Qui vivais hier passé, toujours même on me nomme.

FROM *THE SCORN FOR LIFE
AND SOLACE AGAINST DEATH*

Sit down beside a river rippling by:
You'll see it flowing in eternal stream,

And rolling wave on wave in countless turns
In meadowlands its watery course outpours.

But nothing will you see of that first wave
Which erstwhile flowed; each day its waters change,
Each day it passes, and we call it still
Same river, and same water, just the same.

So varies man, and his poor human strength,
Which time, like all things, shortens and consumes,
Tomorrow will not be as is today.

The name unchanging follows us till death,
And though the same man I am not today
As yesterday, I'm always called the same.

Jean-Baptiste Chassignet (c. 1570–c. 1635)

§ *Italian*

LA MORTE ESSER INEVITABILE

Alzi pur d'oro e cinga il letto intorno
scolpito argento, e le cortine intessa
nube di gemma a meraviglia espressa
di fregio illustre oltr'ogni stile adorno,
   pur vi morrai, superbo, e pur d'un giorno
non fia dimora al tuo pregar concessa,
che nulla val, quando la morte appressa,
della ricca Amaltea versare il corno.
   Crescere un palmo alla statura umana
chi può vivendo? E cerchi pur d'alzarsi
fasto terren, ch'ogni sua prova è vana.
   Né la morte un sol dì lontana farsi
può per tesoro, e non fu mai lontana
più d'un momento; ahi dì fugaci e scarsi!

INVINCIBLE DEATH

Although you raise a bed of gold and gird
it round with sculptured silver, and weave drapes
of clouds and gems, to dazzle mortal eyes,
surpassing in exquisiteness all styles,

you still will die, proud person, and one day
no refuge will be granted to your pleas,
for nothing matters then when death draws near
to spill the wealthy Amalthea's horn.
Who can, while live, man's stature raise a palm?
For though it seek to lift itself on high
each effort of terrestrial pomp is naught.
Death cannot be by riches held at bay
a single day; and ne'er was farther than
a moment—Ah, days fleeting and so few!

Francesco Bracciolini

§ *Mexican*

A UNA CÓMICA DIFUNTA

Aquí yace la púrpura dormida;
aquí el garbo, el gracejo, la hermosura,
la voz de aquel clarín de la dulzura
donde templó sus números la vida.

Trompa de amor, ya no a la lid convida
el clarín de su música blandura;
hoy aprisiona en la tiniebla obscura
tantas sonoras almas una herida.

La representación, la vida airosa
te debieron los versos y más cierta.
Tan bien fingiste—amante, helada, esquiva—,

que hasta la Muerte se quedó dudosa
si la representaste como muerta
o si la padeciste como viva.

TO A DEAD ACTRESS

Here lies the purple sleeping and here lie
elegance and grace and loveliness,
and here that clarion of dulcitude
whose voice was lent to life's harmonious numbers.

Trumpet of love, no more thy clamant strain
with sonorous softness summons to the fray;

now in the tenebrous obscurity
with thine lies stricken many a tuneful soul.

Poesy thanks to thee was manifest
and with a fairer, surer life endued;
and—loving, cold, disdainful—thou didst feign

so well that even Death was unresolved
if thou didst simulate him as one dead
or didst submit to him as one alive.

Luis de Sandoval y Zapata
Trans. by Samuel Beckett

§ *Portuguese*

—QUE LEVAS, CRUEL MORTE?
—UM CLARO DIA*

—Que levas, cruel Morte?—Um claro dia.
—A que horas o tomaste?—Amanhecendo.
—Entendes o que levas?—Não o entendo.
—Pois quem to faz levar?—Quem o entendia.
—Seu corpo quem o goza?—A terra fria.
—Como ficou sua luz?—Anoitecendo.
—Lusitânia que diz?—Fica dizendo:
Enfim, não mereci Dona Maria.
—Mataste quem a viu?—Já morto estava.
—Que diz o cru Amor?—Falar não ousa.
—E quem o faz calar?—Minha vontade.
—Na corte que ficou?—Saudade brava.
—Que fica lá que ver?—Nenhũa cousa;
Mas fica chorar sua beldade.

WHAT BEAR YOU, CRUEL DEATH?
—"A SPLENDID DAY"

—What bear you, cruel Death?—"A splendid day."
—At what hour did you take it?—"At the dawn."
—Do you know what you carry?—"I know not."
—Pray, whose will do you heed?—"Who willed this deed."

* Written on the death of the Infanta D. Maria, 1578.

—Who now enjoys her body?—"Cold damp earth."
    —What of her light was left?—"Naught but the dark."
    —What words has Portugal to say?—"She says:
Dona Maria's death was undeserved."
—You slew whoe'er beheld her?—"Dead they were."
    —Cruel Love has what to say?—"He dares not speak."
    —What holds his speech restrained?—"My will alone."
—What still abides at court?—"A brave despair."
    —What there remains to see?—"No thing, alas."
There but remains to grieve her beauty's loss.

Luís de Camões

II

The World of the Senses

§ *English*

ELEGY 19
GOING TO BED

Come, Madam, come, all rest my powers defie,
Until I labour, I in labour lie.
The foe oft-times having the foe in sight,
Is tir'd with standing though he never fight.
Off with that girdle, like heavens Zone glittering,
But a far fairer world incompassing,
Unpin that spangled breastplate which you wear,
That th'eyes of busie fooles may be stopt there.
Unlace your self, for that harmonious chyme,
Tells me from you, that now it is bed time.
Off with that happy busk, which I envie,
That still can be, and still can stand so nigh.
Your gown going off, such beautious state reveals,
As when from flowry meads th'hills shadow steales.
Off with that wyerie Coronet and shew
The haiery Diademe which on you doth grow:
Now off with those shooes, and then safely tread
In this loves hallow'd temple, this soft bed.
In such white robes, heaven's Angels us'd to be
Receavd by men; Thou Angel bringst with thee
A heaven like Mahomets Paradise; and though
Ill spirits walk in white, we easly know,

By this these Angels from an evil sprite,
Those set our hairs, but these our flesh upright.
   Licence my roaving hands, and let them go,
Before, behind, between, above, below,
O my America! my new-found-land,
My kingdome, safeliest when with one man man'd,
My Myne of precious stones, My Emperie,
How blest am I in this discovering thee!
To enter in these bonds, is to be free;
Then where my hand is set, my seal shall be.
   Full nakedness! All joyes are due to thee,
As souls unbodied, bodies uncloth'd must be,
To taste whole joyes. Gems which you women use
Are like Atlanta's balls, cast in mens views,
That when a fools eye lighteth on a Gem,
His earthly soul may covet theirs, not them.
Like pictures, or like books gay coverings made
For lay-men, are all women thus array'd;
Themselves are mystick books, which only wee
(Whom their imputed grace will dignifie)
Must see reveal'd. Then since that I may know;
As liberally, as to a Midwife, shew
Thy self: cast all, yea, this white lynnen hence,
There is no pennance due to innocence.
   To teach thee, I am naked first; why than
What needst thou have more covering than a man.

John Donne

A VALEDICTION: OF WEEPING

    Let me poure forth
My teares before thy face, whil'st I stay here,
For thy face coines them, and thy stampe they beare,
And by this Mintage they are something worth,
    For thus they bee
    Pregnant of thee;
Fruits of much griefe they are, emblemes of more,
When a teare falls, that thou falst which it bore,
So thou and I are nothing then, when on a divers shore.

    On a round ball
A workeman that hath copies by, can lay

An Europe, Afrique, and an Asia,
And quickly make that, which was nothing, *All*,
    So doth each teare,
    Which thee doth weare,
A globe, yea world by that impression grow,
Till thy teares mixt with mine doe overflow
This world, by waters sent from thee, my heaven dissolved so.

    O more than Moone,
Draw not up seas to drowne me in thy spheare,
Weepe me not dead, in thine armes, but forbeare
To teach the sea, what it may doe too soone;
    Let not the winde
    Example finde,
To doe me more harme, then it purposeth;
Since thou and I sigh one anothers breath,
Who e'er sighs most, is cruellest, and hasts the others death.

John Donne

THE FLEA

Marke but this flea, and marke in this,
How little that which thou deny'st me is;
It suck'd me first, and now sucks thee,
And in this flea, our two bloods mingled bee;
Thou know'st that this cannot be said
A sinne, nor shame, nor losse of maidenhead,
    Yet this enjoyes before it wooe,
    And pamper'd swells with one blood made of two,
    And this, alas, is more then wee would doe.

Oh stay, three lives in one flea spare,
Where wee almost, yea more then maryed are,
This flea is you and I, and this
Our marriage bed, and marriage temple is;
Though parents grudge, and you, w'are met,
And cloysterd in these living walls of Jet.
    Though use make you apt to kill mee,
    Let not to that, selfe murder added bee,
    And sacrilege, three sinnes in killing three.

Cruell and sodaine, hast thou since
Purpled thy naile, in blood of innocence?

Wherein could this flea guilty bee,
Except in that drop which it suckt from thee?
Yet thou triumph'st, and saist that thou
Find'st not thy selfe, nor mee the weaker now;
   'Tis true, then learne how false, feares bee;
   Just so much honor, when thou yeeld'st to mee,
   Will wast, as this flea's death tooke life from thee.

                          John Donne

THE EXTASIE

Where, like a pillow on a bed,
   A Pregnant banke swel'd up, to rest
The violets reclining head,
   Sat we two, one anothers best.
Our hands were firmely cimented
   With a fast balme, which thence did spring,
Our eye-beames twisted, and did thred
   Our eyes, upon one double string;
So to'entergraft our hands, as yet
   Was all the meanes to make us one,
And pictures in our eyes to get
   Was all our propagation.
As 'twixt two equal Armies, Fate
   Suspends uncertaine victorie,
Our soules, (which to advance their state
   Were gone out) hung 'twixt her, and mee.
And whil'st our soules negotiate there,
   Wee like sepulchrall statues lay;
All day, the same our postures were,
   And wee said nothing, all the day.
If any, so by love refin'd,
   That he soules language understood,
And by good love were growen all minde,
   Within convenient distance stood,
He (though he knew not which soule spake,
   Because both meant, both spake the same)
Might thence a new concoction take,
   And part farre purer than he came.
This Exstasie doth unperplex
   (We said) and tell us what we love,

Wee see by this, it was not sexe,
    Wee see, we saw not what did move:
But as all severall soules containe
    Mixture of things, they know not what,
Love, these mixt soules doth mixe againe,
    And makes both one, each this and that.
A single violet transplant,
    The strength, the colour, and the size,
(All which before was poore, and scant,)
    Redoubles still, and multiplies.
When love, with one another so
    Interinanimates two soules,
That abler soule, which thence doth flow,
    Defects of loneliness controules.
Wee then, who are this new soule, know
    Of what we are compos'd, and made,
For, th'Atomies of which we grow,
    Are soules, whom no change can invade.
But O alas, so long, so farre
    Our bodies why doe wee forbeare?
They'are ours, though they'are not wee; Wee are
    The intelligences, they the spheare.
We owe them thankes, because they thus,
    Did us, to us, at first convay,
Yeelded their forces, sense, to us,
    Nor are drosse to us, but allay.
On man heavens influence workes not so,
    But that it first imprints the ayre,
Soe soule into the soule may flow,
    Though it to body first repaire.
As our blood labours to beget
    Spirits, as like soules as it can,
Because such fingers need to knit
    That subtile knot, which makes us man:
So must pure lovers' soules descend
    T'affections, and to faculties,
Which sense may reach and apprehend,
    Else a great Prince in prison lies.
To'our bodies turne wee then, that so
    Weake men on love reveal'd may looke;
Loves mysteries in soules doe grow,
    But yet the body is his booke.
And if some lover, such as wee,

Have heard this dialogue of one,
Let him still marke us, he shall see
  Small change, when we'are to bodies gone.

John Donne

TO HIS COY MISTRESS

  Had we but World enough, and Time,
This coyness Lady were no crime.
We would sit down, and think which way
To walk, and pass our long Loves Day.
Thou by the *Indian Ganges* side
Should'st Rubies find: I by the Tide
Of *Humber* would complain. I would
Love you ten years before the Flood:
And you should if you please refuse
Till the conversion of the *Jews*.
My vegetable Love should grow
Vaster than Empires, and more slow.
An hundred years should go to praise
Thine Eyes, and on thy Forehead Gaze.
Two hundred to adore each Breast:
But thirty thousand to the rest.
An Age at least to every part,
And the last Age should show your Heart.
For Lady you deserve this State;
Nor would I love at lower rate.
  But at my back I alwaies hear
Times winged Charriot hurrying near:
And yonder all before us lye
Desarts of vast Eternity.
Thy Beauty shall no more be found;
Nor, in thy marble Vault, shall sound
My ecchoing Song: then Worms shall try
That long preserv'd Virginity:
And your quaint Honour turn to dust;
And into ashes all my Lust.
The Grave's a fine and private place,
But none I think do there embrace.
  Now therefore, while the youthful hew
Sits on thy skin like morning dew,
And while thy willing Soul transpires

At every pore with instant Fires,
Now let us sport us while we may;
And now, like am'rous birds of prey,
Rather at once our Time devour,
Than languish in his slow-chapt pow'r.
Let us roll all our Strength, and all
Our sweetness, up into one Ball:
And tear our Pleasures with rough strife,
Thorough the Iron gates of Life.
Thus, though we cannot make our Sun
Stand still, yet we will make him run.

Andrew Marvell (1621–78)

THE KISSES. A DIALOGUE.

1. Among thy Fancies, tell me this,
    What is the thing we call a kisse?
2. I shall resolve ye, what it is.

    It is a creature born and bred
    Between the lips, (all cherrie-red,)
    By love and warme desires fed,
Chor. And makes more soft the Bridall bed.

2. It is an active flame, that flies,
    First, to the Babies of the eyes;
    And charmes them there with lullabies;
Chor. And stils the Bride too, when she cries.

2. Then to the chin, the cheek, the eare,
    It frisks, and flyes, now here, now there,
    'Tis now farre off, and then tis nere;
Chor. And here, and there, and every where.

1. Ha's it a speaking virtue? 2. Yes;
1. How speak's it, say? 2. Do you but this,
    Part your joyn'd lips, then speaks your kisse;
Chor. And this loves sweetest language is.

1. Has it a body? 2. I, and wings
    With thousand rare encolourings:
    And as it flyes, it gently sings,
Chor. Love, honie yeelds; but never stings.

Robert Herrick

KISSES LOATHSOME

I abhor the slimie kisse,
(Which to me most loathsome is.)
Those lips please me which are plac't
Close, but not too strictly lac't:
Yielding I wo'd have them; yet
Not a wimbling Tongue admit:
What sho'd poking-sticks make there,
When the ruffe is set elsewhere?

Robert Herrick

TO DIANEME

Shew me thy feet; shew me thy legs, thy thighes;
Shew me Those *Fleshie Principalities;*
Shew me that Hill (where smiling Love doth sit)
Having a living Fountain under it.
Shew me thy waste; Then let me there withall,
By the *Assention* of thy Lawn, see All.

Robert Herrick

THE VINE

I dream'd this mortal part of mine
Was Metamorphoz'd to a Vine;
Which crawling one and every way,
Enthrall'd my dainty *Lucia.*
Me thought, her long small legs & thighs
I with my *Tendrils* did surprize;
Her Belly, Buttocks, and her Waste
By my soft *Nerv'lits* were embrac'd:
About her head I writhing hung,   ⎫
And with rich clusters (hid among   ⎬
The leaves) her temples I behung: ⎭
So that my *Lucia* seem'd to me
Young *Bacchus* ravisht by his tree.
My curls about her neck did craule,
And armes and hands they did enthrall:
So that she could not freely stir,

(All parts there made one prisoner.)
But when I crept with leaves to hide
Those parts, which maids keep unespy'd,
Such fleeting pleasures there I took,
That with the fancie I awook;
And found (Ah me!) this flesh of mine
More like a *Stock*, than like a *Vine*.

Robert Herrick

UPON A BLACK TWIST, ROUNDING THE ARME OF THE COUNTESSE OF CARLILE

I saw upon her spotlesse wrist,
Of blackest silk, a curious twist;
Which, circumvolving gently, there
Enthrall'd her Arme, as Prisoner.
Dark was the Jayle; but as if light
Had met t'engender with the night;
Or so, as Darknesse made a stay
To shew at once, both night and day.
I fancie none! but if there be
Such Freedome in Captivity;
I beg of Love, that ever I
May in like Chains of Darknesse lie.

Robert Herrick

§ *Dutch*

SONNET

Mijn lief, mijn lief, mijn lief; soo sprack mijn lief mij toe,
Dewijl mijn lippen op haer lieve lipjes weiden.
De woordtjes alle drie wel claer en wel bescheiden
Vloeiden mijn ooren in, en roerden ('ck weet niet hoe)
Al mijn gedachten om staech maelend nemmer moe;
Die 't oor mistrouwden en de woordtjes wederleiden.
Dies jck mijn vrouwe bad mij claerder te verbreiden
Haer onverwachte reên; en sij verhaelde' het doe.

O rijckdoom van mijn hart dat over liep van vreuchden!
Bedoven viel mijn siel in haer vol hart van deuchden.
Maer doe de morgenstar nam voor den dach haer wijck,
Is, met de claere son, de waerheit droef verresen.
Hemelsche Goôn, hoe comt de Schijn soo naer aen 't Wesen,
Het leven droom, en droom het leven soo gelijck?

SONNET

My love, my love, thus spoke my love to me,
While on her delicate lips my lips were browsing.
Those words, too clear to be in need of glozing,
    Entered my ears and stirred mysteriously
    My inmost thoughts into tumultuous stress.
They did not trust the ear and, at their pressure,
I begged my dearest for a fuller measure
    Of that confession, and she did confess.
Oh bounty of the heart that overflows!
Entranced, each heart did other's heart imprison.
    But when the morning star fled for the risen
Light of the sun, the sad truth too arose:
Oh Gods, how close are things that are and seem.
    How like the dream is life, like life the dream.

Pieter Corneliszoon Hooft (1581–1647)
Trans. by Adriaan J. Barnouw

§ *German*

BESCHREIBUNG VOLLKOMENER SCHÖNHEIT

Ein Haar, so kühnlich Trotz der Berenice spricht,
Ein Mund, der Rosen führt und Perlen in sich heget,
Ein Zünglein, so ein Gift vor Tausend Herzen träget,
Zwo Brüste, wo Rubin durch Alabaster bricht.
Ein Hals, der Schwänenschnee weit, weit zurücke sticht,
Zwei Wangen, wo die Pracht der Flora sich beweget,
Ein Blick, der Blitze führt und Männer niederleget,
Zwei Armen, derer Kraft oft Leuen hingericht,
Ein Herz, aus welchem nichts als mein Verderben quillet,
Ein Wort, so himmlisch ist und mich verdammen kann,

Zwei Hände, derer Grimm mich in den Bann getan
Und durch ein süsses Gift die Seele selbst umhüllet,
Ein Zierat, wie es scheint, im Paradies gemacht,
Hat mich um meinen Witz und meine Freiheit bracht.

DESCRIPTION OF PERFECT BEAUTY

A hair which boldly speaks in Bernice's despite,
A mouth which starts with rose and pearls within it hides,
A tonguelet where a bane for thousand hearts resides,
Two breasts where ruby breaks through alabaster's white.
A throat which snow of swans has put to distant flight,
Two cheeks within whose veins the pomp of Flora glides,
A glance which conquers men and lightning's weapon guides,
Two arms whose power has oft wild lions slain in fight,
A heart from which alone my ruination flows,
A word which both can damn and yet from Heaven stem,
Two hands, whose awful rage can me to death condemn
And through sweet bane a cloak about the spirit throws,
An ornament, it seems, born out of Paradise,
Has made me both my sense and freedom sacrifice.

Christian Hofmann von Hofmannswaldau
Trans. by George C. Schoolfield

ER SCHAUET DER LESBIE
DURCH EIN LOCH ZU

Es dachte Lesbie, sie sässe ganz allein,
Indem sie wohl verwahrt die Fenster und die Türen,
Doch liess sich Sylvius den geilen Fürwitz führen
Und schaute durch ein Loch in ihr Gemach hinein.

Auf ihrem linken Knie lag ihr das rechte Bein,
Die Hand war höchst bemüht, den Schuh ihr zuzuschnüren,
Er schaute, wie das Moos Zinnober weiss zu zieren,
Und wo Cupido will mit Lust gewieget sein.

Es rufte Sylvius: wie zierlich sind die Waden
Mit warmen Schnee bedeckt, mit Elfenbein beladen!
Er sahe selbst den Ort, wo seine Hoffnung stund.

Es lachte Sylvius. Sie sprach: du bist verloren,
Zum Schmerze bist du dir und mir zur Pein erkoren,
Denn deine Hoffnung hat ja gar zu schlechten Grund.

HE OBSERVES LESBIA THROUGH A HOLE

It seemed to Lesbia that she all lonely stayed
Since she so tight had put the doors and windows to,
Yet Sylvius could not his clever lust subdue,
And through a little hole her chamber he surveyed.

Upon her knee (the left) her leg (the right) she laid,
Her hand was all engaged to buckle up her shoe,
He saw how dainty moss around vermilion grew,
He saw where Cupid would with joy his head have laid.

Then Sylvius exclaimed: how lovely are those thighs,
Where warming snow is piled and where sweet ivory lies!
He saw indeed the place toward which his hope was bound.

He laughed aloud—she said: "Now you are surely lost.
What pains you have yourself and me what torments cost.
In truth your confidence has but a faulty ground."

Christian Hofmann von Hofmannswaldau
Trans. by George C. Schoolfield

AUF DEN MUND

Mund! der die Seelen kann durch Lust zusammen hetzen,
Mund! der viel süsser ist als starker Himmelswein,
Mund! der du Alikant des Lebens schenkest ein,
Mund! den ich vorziehn muss der Juden reichen Schätzen,
Mund! dessen Balsam uns kann stärken und verletzen,
Mund! der vergnügter blüht als aller Rosen Schein,
Mund! welchem kein Rubin kann gleich und ähnlich sein,
Mund! den die Gratien mit ihren Quellen netzen;
Mund! ach Korallenmund, mein einziges Ergetzen,
Mund! lass mich einen Kuss auf deinen Purpur setzen!

ON THE MOUTH

Mouth! which all hearts through lust can captivate,
Mouth! sweeter far than heaven's stronger wine,
Mouth! who makes present of life's elixir,
Mouth! whom I must prefer to Jews' rich stores,
Mouth! balsam whose can make us strong and weak,
Mouth! lovelier in form than rose's blooms,
Mouth! whom no ruby can hold semblance to,
Mouth! whom the Graces sprinkled from their founts:
Mouth! ah, mouth made of coral, my sole joy,
Mouth! let me 'pon your crimson press a kiss!

Christian Hofmann von Hofmannswaldau

WIE ER WOLLE GEKÜSSET SEIN

Nirgends hin als auf den Mund,
Da sinkts in des Herzen Grund.
Nicht zu frei, nicht zu gezwungen,
Nicht mit gar zu fauler Zungen.

Nicht zu wenig, nicht zu viel,
Beides wird sonst Kinderspiel.
Nicht zu laut und nicht zu leise,
Bei der Mass ist rechte Weise.

Nicht zu nahe, nicht zu weit;
Dies macht Kummer, jenes Leid,
Nicht zu trucken, nicht zu feuchte,
Wie Adonis Venus reichte.

Nicht zu harte, nicht zu weich,
Bald zugleich, bald nicht zugleich.
Nicht zu langsam, nicht zu schnelle,
Nicht ohn Unterscheid der Stelle.

Halb gebissen, halb gehaucht,
Halb die Lippen eingetaucht.
Nicht ohn Unterscheid der Zeiten,
Mehr alleine, denn bei Leuten.

Küsse nun ein jedermann,
Wie er weiss, will, soll und kann!
Ich nur und die Liebste wissen,
Wie wir uns recht sollen küssen.

HOW HE SHOULD LIKE TO BE KISSED

Nowhere else but on the mouth,
So that it heart's depths should touch.
Not too free, not too constrained,
Not with tongues too soiled and stained.

Not too little, not too much,
Children's play would each be such.
Not too loud and not too soft,
Moderation keep aloft.

Not too near and not too far,
One brings grief, the other harm.
Not too dry, and not too wet,
As Adonis Venus met.

Not too tender, not too hard,
Now together, now apart.
Not too fast, and not too slow,
Mind you where you pleasures sow.

Half a whisper, half a bite,
Half immersed, the lips unite.
Mind you keep the times in view,
Most alone, 'midst people few.

Kiss indeed let every man,
As he knows, wants, ought and can.
Only my belov'd and I
Know the kissing we would try.

Paul Fleming

§ *French*

SUR LES YEUX DE MADAME LA DUCHESSE DE BEAUFORT

Ce ne sont pas des yeux, ce sont plutôt des dieux:
Ils ont dessus les rois la puissance absolue.
Dieux? non, ce sont des cieux: ils ont la couleur bleue
Et le mouvement prompt comme celui des cieux.

Cieux? non, mais deux soleils clairement radieux,
Dont les rayons brillants nous offusquent la vue.
Soleils? non, mais éclairs de puissance inconnue,
Des foudres de l'Amour signes présagieux.

Car s'ils étaient des dieux, feraient-ils tant de mal?
Si des cieux, ils auraient leur mouvement égal.
Deux soleils ne se peut: le soleil est unique.

Eclairs? non, car ceux-ci durent trop et trop clairs.
Toutefois je les nomme, afin que je m'explique,
Des yeux, des dieux, des cieux, des soleils, des éclairs.

ON THE EYES OF
THE DUCHESS OF BEAUFORT

These are not eyes, no, rather are they gods:
O'er kings the power they hold is absolute.
Gods? No, but skies: they have the color blue
And rapid movement of the skies themselves.

Skies? No, instead two clearly radiant suns,
The dazzling rays of which obscure our view.
Sun? No, but flashes of an unknown force
Foretelling signs of thunderbolts of love.

For were they gods, would they inflict such pain?
If skies, would not their movement be the same?
Two suns they cannot be, the sun is one.

Rays? No, these longer last and brighter burn—
Yet I shall name them, so I may explain,
Eyes, gods, skies, suns, and rays—each one in turn.

Honorat Laugier de Porchères (1572–1653)

A UNE DEMOISELLE
QUI AVAIT LES MANCHES DE SA CHEMISE
RETROUSSÉES ET SALES

Vous, qui tenez incessamment
Cent amants dedans votre manche,
Tenez-les au moins proprement,
Et faites qu'elle soit plus blanche.

Vous pouvez bien avec raison,
Usant des droits de la victoire,
Mettre vos galants en prison,
Mais qu'elle ne soit pas si noire.

Mon coeur, qui vous est si dévot,
Et que vous réduissez en cendre,
Vous le tenez dans un cachot
Comme un prisonnier qu'on va pendre.

Est-ce que, brûlant nuit et jour,
Je remplis ce lieu de fumée,
Et que le feu de mon amour
En a fait une cheminée?

TO A YOUNG LADY WHO HAD THE SLEEVES OF HER SHIFT ROLLED UP AND DIRTY

You who keeps constantly
A hundred lovers up your sleeve,
Why, see at least they're cleanly kept
And that your sleeve is whiter.

You may, quite justifiably,
Resorting to the victor's rights,
Throw all your suitors into jail,
But make it one that's lighter.

My heart, which is so true to you,
And which to ashes you reduce,
You keep within a dungeon's walls
Like some poor convict to be hanged.

Can it be, burning night and day,
I fill this place with smoke,
And that the fire of my love
Has made of it a chimney?

Vincent Voiture (1597–1648)

L'EXTASE D'UN BAISER

Au point où j'expirais, tu m'as rendu le jour,
Baiser, dont jusqu'au coeur le sentiment me touche,

Enfant délicieux de la plus belle bouche
Qui jamais prononça les oracles d'amour.

Mais tout mon sang s'altère, une brûlante fièvre
Me ravit la couleur et m'ôte la raison;
Cieux! j'ai pris à la fois sur cette belle lèvre
D'un céleste nectar et d'un mortel poison.

Ah! mon âme s'envole en ce transport de joie!
Ce gage de salut dans la tombe m'envoie;
C'est fait! Je n'en puis plus, Élise, je me meurs.

Ce baiser est un sceau par qui ma vie est close:
Et comme on peut trouver un serpent sous des fleurs,
J'ai recontré ma mort sur un bouton de rose.

THE ECSTASY OF A KISS

At point of death, you gave me back the day,
A kiss, whose feeling reaches to the heart,
Delicious child of that most lovely mouth
Which e'er pronounced the oracles of love.

But all my blood grows weak, a feverish heat
My color steals, my reason captivates.
My God! I've taken from these lovely lips
Both heav'nly nectar and a mortal bane.

This joyous transport wings my soul on high!
This pledge of health sends me unto the tomb;
'Tis done. I can no more, Elise, I die.

This kiss—a seal through which my life is closed.
And as 'midst flowers one may find a snake,
So have I 'pon a rosebud found my death.

                                    Tristan L'Hermite (1601?–55)

STANCES DE MARQUIS

Estes-vous un soleil, bel astre de ma vie?
Vos yeux comme les siens embrasent l'horizon:
Mais par votre inconstance, on a juste raison
De vous dire une lune, adorable Silvie;

Ainsi je doute encore, bel objet non pareil,
Si je vous dois nommer le lune ou le soleil?

Vos lèvres de corail et vos joües pourprines
Vous font estre une rose, aimable et douce fleur;
Mais quoi? votre rigueur, cause de mon malheur,
Vous compare au rosier qui porte des espines;
Ainsi je doute encore, source de mon brasier,
Si je vous dois nommer la rose ou le rosier?

Enfin vous estes feu, vous estes enfin onde,
Rocher où l'on se perd, très agréable port;
Et, pour conclusion, arbitre de mon sort,
Mes vers vous nommeront par tous les coins du monde:
Le rocher et le port, l'onde avec le brasier,
La lune et le soleil, la rose et le rosier!

STANZAS OF A MARQUIS

Are you a sun, fair star of my wan life?
Your eyes, like suns, illumine the horizon.
But by your fickleness, one rightly can
Bespeak you moon, my lovely Sylvia.
Thus still I doubt, fair object without peer,
If I should name you moon or sun instead.

Your coral lips, your cheeks of purplish hue,
Make you appear a rose, sweet pleasant bloom;
But why? Your coldness, cause of my despair,
Compares you to a rosebush filled with thorns.
Thus still I doubt, my burning ardor's source,
If rose or rosebush I should christen you.

You are, *in fine*, a fire, *in fine*, a wave,
A crag where one gets lost, most pleasant port;
And in conclusion, O sovereign of my fate,
My verse will name you in the earth's far ends
Both crag and port, and wave and furnace,
Both moon and sun, and rose and rosebush.

Jean-François Sarasin (1615–54)

§ *Italian*

LA CANZONE DEI BACI

O baci avventurosi,
ristoro de'miei mali,
che di nettare al cor cibo porgete;
spiriti rugiadosi,
sensi d'amor vitali,
che 'n breve giro il viver mio chiudete;
in voi le più secrete
dolcezze e più profonde
provo, talor che con sommessi accenti
interrotti lamenti,
lascivetti desiri,
languidetti sospiri
tra rubino e rubino Amor confonde,
e più d'un'alma in una bocca asconde!

Una bocca omicida,
dolce d'Amor guerrera,
cui natura di gemme arma ed inostra,
dolcemente mi sfida,
e schiva e lusinghiera,
ed amante e nemica a me si mostra.
Entran scherzando in giostra
le lingue innamorate;
baci le trombe son, baci l'offese,
baci son le contese;
quelle labra, ch'io stringo,
son l'agone e l'arringo;
vezzi son l'onte, e son le piaghe amate,
quanto profonde più, tanto più grate.

Tranquilla guerra e cara,
ove l'ira è dolcezza,
Amor lo sdegno, e ne le risse è pace;
ove 'l morir s'impara,
l'esser prigion s'apprezza,
né men che la vittoria il perder piace!
Quel corallo mordace,
che m'offende, mi giova;
quel dente, che mi fère ad ora ad ora,
quel mi risana ancora;

quel bacio, che mi priva
di vita, mi raviva;
ond'io, c'ho nel morir vita ognor nova,
per ferito esser più, ferisco a prova.

   Or tepid'aura e leve,
or accento or sorriso,
pon freno al bacio, a pien non anco impresso.
Spesso un sol bacio beve
sospir, parola e riso;
spesso il bacio vien doppio, e 'l bacio spesso
tronco è dal bacio stesso.
Né sazio avien che lasce
pur d'aver sete il desir troppo ingordo:
suggo, mordo, rimordo
un bacio fugge, un riede,
un ne more, un succede;
de la morte di quel questo si pasce,
e, pria che mora l'un, l'altro rinasce.

   L'asciutto è caro al core,
il molle è più soave,
men dolce è quel che mormorando fugge.
Ma quel, che stampa Amore
d'ambrosia umido e grave,
i vaghi spiriti dolcemente sugge.
Lasso! ma chi mi strugge
ristrosa il mi contende
in atto si gentil, che 'nvita e nega,
ricusa insieme e prega.
Pur amata ed amante,
e baciata e baciante,
alfin col bacio il cor mi porge e prende,
e la vita col cor mi fura e rende.

   Miro, rimiro ed ardo,
bacio, ribacio e godo,
e mirando e baciando mi disfaccio.
Amor tra 'l bacio e 'l guardo
scherza e vaneggia in modo,
ch'ebro di tanta gloria i' tremo e taccio;
ond'ella che m'ha in braccio,
lascivamente onesta,
gli occhi mi bacia, e fra le perle elette
frange due parolette:

—Cor mio!—dicendo, e poi,
baciando i baci suoi,
di bacio in bacio a quel piacer mi desta,
che l'alme insieme allaccia e i corpi innesta.

Vinta allor dal diletto
con un sospir se 'n viene
l'animal al varco, e 'l proprio albergo oblia;
ma con pietoso affetto
la 'ncontra ivi e ritiene
l'anima amica, che s'oppon tra via;
e 'n lei, ch'arde e desia
già languida e smarrita,
d'un vasel di rubin tal pioggia versa
di gioia, che sommersa
in quel piacer gentile,
cui presso ogni altro è vile,
baciando l'altra, ch'a baciar la 'nvita,
alfin ne more, e quel morire è vita.

Deh taci, o lingua sciocca;
senti la dolce bocca,
che t'appella e ti dice:—Or godi, e taci!—
E, per farti tacer, raddoppia i baci.

THE SONG OF THE KISSES

O daring kisses,
healers of my ills,
who offer food of nectar to my heart;
dewy spirits,
vital senses of love,
who in a brief circling enclose my life;
in you the most secret
and profound sweetness,
I taste when, midst humble tones,
broken moans,
lascivious little desires,
and languid sighs,
love grows confused between ruby and ruby,
and hides more than one soul in a single mouth!

A murderous mouth,
sweet warrior of Love,

whom nature arms and adorns with jewels,
sweetly challenges me,
and, both shy and enticing,
loving and hostile, displays herself before me.
The enamored tongues
enter the lists playfully;
kisses are the trumpets, kisses the thrusts,
kisses the fray;
those lips which I press
are the field and the arena;
lovely the charges and loving the wounds,
the deeper they are, the more the pleasing.

Tranquil and precious battle,
wherein anger is sweetness,
disdain love, and clashes are peace;
wherein dying is learned,
imprisonment is esteemed,
and defeat pleases no less than victory!
That biting coral
that hurts me also helps me;
those same teeth which wound me again and again
still cure me;
that kiss which deprives me
of life revives me;
so that I, who in dying have ever new life,
hoping to be wounded again thrust provokingly.

Now tepid and light breezes,
now sound or smile
rein in the kiss, before it is hardly pressed.
Often a single kiss drinks
sighs, words, and laughter;
often a kiss is redoubled, and a kiss
is often interrupted by a kiss itself.
Nor does too greedy desire
become sated enough to allow for thirst:
I suck and bite and bite again,
one kiss flees and another returns,
one dies and another replaces it;
on the death of one another feeds,
and hardly is one dead when another is born.

The dry kiss is dear to the heart,
but the damp one is smoother,

and less delightful is the one that flees murmuring.
But the dewy and grave one,
which Love presses from ambrosia,
the longing spirits sweetly sip.
Alas! But she who consumes me
contends with me
in so sweet a manner that she beckons and refuses,
at the same time reluctant and begging.
Both loved and loving,
kissed and kissing,
at last with a kiss she both gives and takes my heart,
and my life with my heart she steals and returns.

   I gaze, gaze again, and burn,
I kiss, kiss again, and revel;
and in kissing and gazing I destroy myself.
Midst kiss and glance Love
prances and boasts in such wise
that, drunk with so much glory, I tremble and am silent;
whence she who holds me in her arms,
lasciviously chaste,
kisses my eyes and crushes
two little words in the midst of precious pearls,
saying: "My heart!" and then,
kissing her own kisses,
from kiss to kiss taking me to that pleasure
which ties souls together and blends bodies in one.

   Conquered now by delight,
my soul comes sighing
to the gateway, and forgets its own home;
but, with piteous feeling,
my beloved's soul, encountered on the way,
meets and holds it there;
and on my burning and desirous soul,
now languishing and dazed,
she pours from a goblet of ruby a shower
so joyous that, drowning,
in that gentle pleasure
beside which all other is vulgar,
and kissing the other, who has invited the kiss,
it finally dies—and that death is life.

   There, be silent, O foolish tongue;
listen to that sweet mouth

which calls you and says: "Now enjoy, and be still!"
—And to make you be still redoubles its kisses.

Giambattista Marino (1569–1625)
Trans. by James V. Mirollo

LA BELLA SCHIAVA

Nera sì, ma se'bella, o di natura
fra le belle d'amor leggiadro mostro;
fosca è l'alba appo te, perde e s'oscura
presso l'ebeno tuo l'avorio e l'ostro.

Or quando, or dove il mondo antico o il nostro
vide sì viva mai, sentì sì pura
o luce uscir di tenebroso inchiostro,
o di spento carbon nascere arsura?

Serva de chi m'è serva, ecco ch'avolto
porto di bruno laccio il core intorno,
che per candida man non fia mai sciolto.

Là've più arde, o Sol, sol per tuo scorno
un sole è nato; un sol, che nel bel volto
porta la notte, ed ha negli occhi il giorno.

THE BEAUTIFUL SLAVE

Black you are, yet beautiful, of nature
a lovely marvel 'midst love's beauties fair.
Dark is the dawn compared to you; beside
your ebony and purple ivory dims.

Now when, now where did our world or the old
so vivid light to flow from murky ink
ever behold, or feel so pure a fire
to which extinguished carbon did give birth?

A servant of my servant, see, I bear
my heart, all twisted 'round with cords of brown,
which ne'er can loosened be by snow-white hand.

There where, O Sun, you brighter burn, a Sun
is born to bear you solely scorn; a Sun
whose face the Night, whose eyes the Day convey.

Giambattista Marino

BELLISSIMA MENDICA

Sciolta il crin, rotta i panni e nuda il piede,
donna, cui fe' lo ciel povera e bella,
con fioca voce e languida favella
mendicava per Dio poca mercede.
Fa di mill'alme, intanto, avare prede
al fulminar de l'una e l'altra stella;
e di quel biondo crin l'aurea procella
a la sua povertà togliea la fede.
—A che fa—le diss'io—sì vil richiesta
la bocca tua d'oriental lavoro,
ov'Amor sul rubin la perla inesta?
Ché se vaga sei tu d'altro tesoro,
china la ricca e preziosa testa
che pioveran le chiome i nembi d'oro.

A MOST BEAUTIFUL MENDICANT

Her hair disheveled, garments torn, feet bare,
a lady, made by heaven poor and fair,
was begging alms for God with small success
in weakened voice and languid eloquence.
Of thousand souls she makes yet avid prey
with flashing of one and another star;
the golden tempest of that lustrous hair
thus to her poverty did put the lie.
Why makes—I asked—so lowly a request
your mouth of Oriental workmanship
where love the pearl and ruby interweave?
For if 'tis other treasure you desire,
incline your sumptuous and precious head,
that showers of gold your tresses may rain down.

Claudio Achillini (1574–1640)

§ *Spanish*

OH CLARO HONOR DEL LÍQUIDO ELEMENTO

¡Oh claro honor del líquido elemento,
dulce arroyuelo de corriente plata

cuya agua entre la yerba se dilata
con regalado son, con paso lento!

Pues la por quien helar y arder me siento,
(mientras en ti se mira). Amor retrata
de su rostro la nieve y la escarlata
en tu tranquilo y blando movimiento,

vete como te vas; no dejes floja
la undosa rienda al cristalino freno
con que gobiernas tu veloz corriente;

que no es bien que confusamente acoja
tanta belleza en su profundo seno
el gran Señor del húmido tridente.

PRIDE OF THE FOURTH AND LIQUID ELEMENT

Pride of the fourth and liquid element,
sweet brook whose waters with soft music pass,
stretching, pellucid and pre-eminent,
their ribbon of bright silver through the grass,

since Cupid on your smooth and quiet stream,
as she looks into it, portrays the snow
and scarlet of her face, for whom I seem
at times to freeze, at other times to glow,

watch how you move; be careful to keep taut
the crystal bridle's wavy rein with which
you curb your current's striving to run faster.

It would be wrong if beauty should be caught,
confused, in that deep breast, beauty so rich,
caught by the watery trident's mighty master.

Luis de Góngora
Trans. by J. M. Cohen

FROM *SONETOS*

VARIOS EFECTOS DEL AMOR

Desmayarse, atreverse, estar furioso,
aspero, tierno, liberal, esquivo,

alentado, mortal, difunto, vivo,
leal, traidor, cobarde y animoso;

no hallar fuera del bien centro y reposo,
mostrarse alegre, triste, humilde, altivo,
enojado, valiente, fugitivo,
satisfecho, ofendido, receloso;

huir el rostro al claro desengaño,
beber veneno por licor suave,
olvidar el provecho, amar el daño;

creer que un cielo en un infierno cabe,
dar la vida y el alma a un desengaño,
esto es amor, quien lo probó lo sabe.

FROM *SONNETS*
THE VARIOUS EFFECTS OF LOVE

Fall faint, be insolent, or furious,
gruff-mannered, tender, generous, reserved,
encouraged, wounded, living, or deceased,
unfailing, cowardly, brave, traitorous;

not find, not only good, but calm repose;
appear happy, mournful, humble, proud,
annoyed to anger, valiant, fugitive,
offended, satisfied, suspicious;

your face turn from an evident deceit,
drink venom for a soothing beverage,
forget advantage, and pay court to harm;

believe that hell for heaven can make room,
deliver life and soul to blighted hope;
that's love. Who's tasted it, knows well enough.

Lope de Vega (1562–1635)

FROM *SONETOS*
IR Y QUEDARSE Y CON QUEDAR PARTIRSE

Ir y quedarse y con quedar partirse,
partir sin alma e ir con alma ajena,

oir la dulce voz de una sirena
y no poder del árbol desasirse;

arder como la vela y consumirse
haciendo torres sobre tierna arena;
caer de un cielo y ver demonio en pena
y de serlo jamás arrepentirse;

hablar entre las mudas soledades,
pedir pues resta sobre fé paciencia,
y lo que es temporal llamar eterno;

creer sospechas y negar verdades,
es lo que llaman en el mundo ausencia,
fuego en la alma y en la vida infierno.

FROM *SONNETS*

TO GO AND STAY AND BY REMAINING PART

To go and stay and by remaining part,
soulless depart and with another's leave;
to hear the sweet voice of a siren call
and be unable to let go the tree;

to burn as though a candle and burn out
constructing towers on a sand still soft;
fall from a heaven and a devil see
in toil and for it ne'er repentant be;

to speak among the silent solitudes,
to make request of patience then on faith,
and what is temporal eternal call;

to trust suspicions and negate the truth,
is what is known as absence in the world,
the soul ablaze with fire but life a hell.

Lope de Vega

DEFINIENDO EL AMOR

Es yelo abrasador, es fuego helado,
es herida que duele y no se siente,
es un soñado bien, un mal presente,
es un breve descanso muy cansado.

Es un descuido que nos da cuidado,
un cobarde, con nombre de valiente,.
un andar solitario entre la gente,
un amar solamente ser amado.

Es una libertad encarcelada,
que dura hasta el postrero parasismo;
enfermedad que crece si es curada.

Este es el niño Amor, este es su abismo.
¡Mirad cual amistad tendrá con nada
el que en todo es contrario de sí mismo!

DEFINING LOVE

It is a freezing fire, a burning ice,
it is a wound that hurts yet is not felt,
it is a pleasant dream, an evil force,
it is a short rest very tiring.

It is a carelessness that gives us care,
a coward who is known as someone brave,
a walking all alone among the crowd,
a loving solely for the sake of love.

It is a liberty made prisoner,
until the last convulsion sets it free;
a sickness growing ever as it's cured.

This is the Cupid child, this its abyss.
Behold what friendship he will have with none
who is contrary to himself in all.

Francisco de Quevedo

§ *Mexican*

YO NO PUEDO TENERTE NI DEJARTE

Yo no puedo tenerte ni dejarte,
ni sé por qué, al dejarte o al tenerte,
se encuentra un no sé que para quererte
y muchos sí sé qué para olvidarte.

Pues ni quieres dejarme ni enmendarte,
yo tenmplaré mi corazon de suerte

que la mitad se incline a aborrecerte
aunque la otra mitad se incline a amarte.

Si ello es fuerza querernos, haya modo,
que es morir el estar siempre riñendo;
no se hable más en celo y en sospecha,

y quien da la mitad, no quiera el todo;
y cuando me la estás allá haciendo
sabe que estoy haciendo la deshecha.

I CANNOT HOLD YOU FAST, NOR LET YOU GO

I cannot hold you fast, nor let you go.
I know not why so desperately I cling.
As reason for such love I find one thing,
but many reasons to forget I know.

Since you will neither leave me nor amend,
the temper of my heart I'll so design
that half of it to hatred will incline,
although the other half would be your friend.

If we must love, our course must be this one:
leave off eternal quarrels and dissidence,
and jealous words and all suspicion shun.

The giver must not seek in recompense.
And when I see that for my sake you've done
all this, I'll know I'm living in pretense.

Sor Juana Inés de la Cruz
Trans. by Pauline Cook

DETENTE, SOMBRA DE MI BIEN ESQUIVO

Detente, sombra de mi bien esquivo,
imagen del hechizo que más quiero,
bella ilusión por quien alegre muero,
dulce ficción por quien penoso vivo.

Si al imán de tus gracias, atractivo,
sirve mi pecho de obediente acero,

¿para qué me enamoras lisonjero
si has de burlarme luego fugitivo?

Mas blasonar no puedas, satisfecho,
de que triunfa de mí tu tiranía;
que aunque dejas burlado el lazo estrecho

que tu forma fantástica ceñía,
poco importa burlar brazos y pecho
si te labra prisión mi fantasía.

ELUSIVE SHADOW OF MYSELF, REMAIN

Elusive shadow of myself, remain,
enchanting image for whose love I sigh,
illusion fair, for whom I gladly die,
sweet fiction, for whose sake I live in pain.

If to your magnet of attractive grace
my heart delights to play obedient steel,
why, flattering, did you lead me on to feel
new love, if mocking now you flee my face?

You cannot smugly boast that by your art
your tyranny is conqueror at last;
for though you burst the narrow cord apart,

which your fantastic form one time held fast,
if naught avails to mock my arms and heart
if fancy makes a prison of the past.

Sor Juana Inés de la Cruz
Trans. by Pauline Cook

QUÉ ES ESTO, ALCINO, CÓMO TU CORDURA

Qué es esto, Alcino, cómo tu cordura
se deja así vencer de un mal celoso,
haciendo con extremos de furioso
demostraciones más que de locura?

¿En qué te ofendió Celia, si se apura?
¿O por qué al amor culpas de engañoso
si no aseguró nunca poderoso
la eterna posesión de su hermosura?

La posesión de cosas temporales,
temporal es, Alcino, y es abuso
el querer conservarlas siempre iguales.

Con que tu error o tu ignorancia acuso,
pues fortuna y amor de cosas tales
la propiedad no han dado, sino el uso.

ALCINO, WHAT IS THIS...

Alcino, what is this; Do you permit
wild jealousy to mar your prudent care?
Your furious extremes assume the air
of madness worse than any frenzied fit.

In what did I offend you that you grieve?
Or why do you condemn love's influence
as traitorous? For to make pretense
that you can keep its beauty is naïve.

The ownership of any temporal thing
is temporal. Its nature you abuse
when to its constancy you try to cling.

Your error or your ignorance I accuse.
If fortune comes with love as offering,
you may not own it; you may only use.

Sor Juana Inés de la Cruz
Trans. by Pauline Cook

ROSA DIVINA QUE EN GENTIL CULTURA

Rosa divina que en gentil cultura
eres, con tu fragante sutileza,
magisterio purpúreo en la belleza,
enseñanza nevada a la hermosura.

Amago de la humana arquitectura,
ejemplo de la vana gentileza
en cuyo sér unió naturaleza
la cuna alegre y triste sepultura.

¡Cuan altiva en tu pompa, presumida,

soberbia, el riesgo de morir desdeñas,
y luego desmayada y encogida

de tu caduco sér das mustias señas
con que con docta muerte y necia vida,
viviendo engañas y muriendo enseñas!

O ROSE DIVINE, WITH CULTIVATED AIR

O rose divine, with cultivated air
and slender throat, for very beauty's sake
the academic purple you may take,
or, decked with white, be lesson to the fair.

An empty promise for the hopes of man,
example of a vain but noble grace
within whose being first and last embrace:—
the cradle and the grave in one short span.

How naughty in your splendor now arrayed,
disdainful, arrogant in death's quick reach.
Then suddenly dim-lustered and afraid,

the frailty of your being utters speech.
So that with foolish life and learned death displayed,
while living you deceive, but dying, you may teach.

Sor Juana Inés de la Cruz
Trans. by Pauline Cook

§ *Portuguese*

TRANSFORMA-SE
O AMADOR NA COUSA AMADA

Transforma-se o amador na cousa amada,
    Por virtude do muito imaginar;
    Não tenho logo mais que desejar,
    Pois em nim tenho a parte desejada.
¿Se nela está minha alma transformada,
    Que mais deseja o corpo de alcançar?
    Em si sòmente pode descansar,
    Pois consigo tal alma está liada.

Mas esta linda e pura semideia,
  Que, como o acidente em seu sujeito,
  Assim com a alma minha se conforma,
Está no pensamento como idéia;
  [E]o vivo e puro amor de que sou feito,
  Como a matéria simples busca a forma.

THE LOVER TO BELOVÈD
IS TRANSFORMED

The lover to belovèd is transformed
  By virtue of a rich imagination.
  Then I have nothing left me to desire,
  For in me do I have the thing desired.
If my soul is transformed to her I love,
  What else is there my body yearns to reach?
  Repose it finds alone within itself,
  Since that same spirit did my form infuse.
But this half-goddess, beautiful and chaste,
  Who in her subject like an accident
  Conforms thus with my soul in all respects,
In very thought exists like an idea.
  The living and pure love of which I'm made
  Like simple matter seeks its proper form.

Luís de Camões

AMOR É FOGO QUE ARDE SEM SE VER

Amor é fogo que arde sem se ver;
  É ferida que dói e não se sente;
  É um contentamento descontente;
  É dor que desatina sem doer;
É um não querer mais que bem querer;
  É solitário andar por entre a gente;
  É nunca contentar-se de contente;
  É cuidar que se ganha em se perder;
É querer estar prêso por vontade;
  É servir a quem vence, o vencedor;
  É ter com quem nos mata lealdade.
¿Mas como causar pode seu favor

Nos corações humanos amizade,
Se tão contrário a si é o mesmo Amor?

LOVE IS A FIRE THAT BURNS INVISIBLE

Love is a fire that burns invisible;
    It is a wound that aches yet is not felt;
    It is a long contented discontent;
    It is a pain that maddens without pain;
It is to want no more than to want well;
    It is a strolling hermit-like through crowds;
    It is to never be content content;
    It is a caring to reap gain in loss;
It is to be enchained of one's own will;
    It is the victor serving vanquished fain;
    It is allegiance to a mortal foe.
But how can love, with all his favor shown,
    Cause in our mortal hearts conformity,
    If love is so in conflict with itself?

                                        Luís de Camões

DE QUANTAS GRAÇAS TINHA, A NATUREZA

De quantas graças tinha, a Natureza
    Fêz um belo e riquíssimo tesouro,
    E com rubis e rosas, neve e ouro,
    Formou sublime e angélica beleza.
Pôs na bôca os rubis, e na pureza
    Do belo rosto as rosas, por quem mouro;
    No cabelo o valor do metal louro;
    No peito a neve em que a alma tenho acesa.
Mas nos olhos mostrou quanto podia,
    E fêz dêles um sol, onde se apura
    A luz mais clara que a do claro dia.
Enfim, Senhora, em vossa compostura
    Ela a apurar chegou quanto sabia
    De ouro, rosas, rubis, neve e luz pura.

OF ALL THE MANY GRACES SHE POSSESSED

Of all the many graces she possessed,
  A beautiful rare treasure Nature made,
  And with rubies and roses, snow and gold,
  A lofty and angelic beauty shaped.
The rubies first she placed upon your lips,
  Upon your cheeks the roses I die for;
  Upon your head the worth of golden ore;
  Upon your breast the snow which burns my soul.
But with your eyes she showed her truest might,
  And made of them a sun whence she brings forth
  A light more bright than that of brightest day.
And last, my Lady, in your whole demean,
  She waited and then showed how much she knew
  Of rubies, roses, gold, snow, and pure light.

Luís de Camões

—QUE ESPERAIS, ESPERANÇA?—DESESPERO

—Que esperais, esperança?—Desespero.
  —Quem disso a causa foi?—Uma mudança.
  —Vós, vida, como estais?—Sem esperança.
  —Que dizeis, coração?—Que muito quero.
—Que sentes, alma, vós?—Que amor é fero.
  —E, enfim, como viveis?—Sem confiança.
  —Quem vos sustenta, logo?—Uma lembrança.
  —E só nela esperais?—Só nela espero.
—Em que podeis parar?—Nisto em que estou.
  —E em que estais vós?—Em acabar a vida.
  —E tende-lo por bem?—Amor o quere.
—Quem vos obriga assim?—Saber quem sou.
  —E quem sois?—Quem de todo está rendida.
  —A quem rendida estais?—A um só querer.

WHAT DO YOU HOPE FOR, HOPE?
—"I HOPE FOR NAUGHT"

—What do you hope for, hope?—"I hope for naught."
  —What brought you to this pass?—"Inconstancy."
  —And you, life, how fare you?—"Bereft of hope."
  —And you, my heart, say what?—"I truly love."

—My soul, what do you feel?—"That love is cruel."
—How do you live then?—"Without confidence."
—Then what sustains you?—"Just a memory."
—In that alone you hope?—"In that alone."
—Where can you take your stand?—"Where I am now."
—And where is that, pray tell?—"The end of life."
—You hold death then a boon?—"Love wills it so."
—What so obliges you?—"That which I am."
—And what are you?—"One shorn of everything."
—By whom?—"By her alone whom I do love."

Luís de Camões

§ *Polish*

NA OCZY KRÓLEWNY ANGIELSKIEJ,
KTÓRA BYŁA ZA FRYDERYKIEM,
FALCGRAFEM RENSKIM,
OBRANYM KRÓLEM CZESKIM

Twe oczy, skąd Kupido na wsze ziemskie kraje,
    Córo możnego króla, harde prawa daje,
Nie oczy, lecz pochodnie dwie nielitościwe,
    Które palą na popiół serca nieszczęśliwe.
Nie pochodnie, lecz gwiazdy, których jasne zorze
    Błagają nagłym wiatrem rozgniewane morze.
Nie gwiazdy, ale słońca palające różno,
    Których blask śmiertelnemu oku pojąć próżno.
Nie słońca, ale nieba, bo swój obrot mają
    I swoją śliczną barwą niebu wprzód nie dają.
Nie nieba, ale dziwnej mocy są bogowie,
    Przed którymi padają ziemscy monarchowie.
Nie bogowie też zgoła, bo azaż bogowie
    Pastwią się tak nad sercy ludzkimi surowie?
Nie nieba: niebo torem jednostajnym chodzi;
    Nie słońca: słońce jedno wschodzi i zachodzi;
Nie gwiazdy, bo te tylko w ciemności panują;
    Nie pochodnie, bo lada wiatrom te hołdują.
Lecz się wszytko zamyka w jednym oka słowie:
    Pochodnie, gwiazdy, słońca, nieba i bogowie.

ON THE EYES OF
THE ENGLISH PRINCESS WHO STOOD BEHIND
FRIEDRICH OF THE RHINE
WHEN HE WAS ELECTED
KING OF THE BOHEMIANS

Your eyes, O daughter of a mighty king,
  Whence Cupid grants proud rights to all the world,
Not eyes are, but two torches merciless,
  Whose flame makes ashes of unlucky hearts.
Not torches, stars instead, whose radiant dawns
  Implore the angered sea with sudden wind.
Not stars, but variously burning suns,
  Whose blaze no mortal eye can think to grasp.
Not suns, but firmaments with their own course,
  Their lovely hue by heaven's unsurpassed.
Not firmaments, but gods of wondrous might,
  Before whom fall the monarchs of this earth.
Not gods entirely, for when do gods
  Wreak vengeance cruelly on human hearts?
Not heavens: heaven knows a single track;
  Not suns: the sun can only rise and fall;
Not stars: for stars rule only in the dark;
  Not torches, for a torch bows low to wind;
The single word of "eye" embraces all:
  The torches, stars, suns, firmaments, and gods.

Daniel Naborowski

CUDA MIŁOŚCI

Karmię frasunkiem miłość i myśleniem,
Myśl zaś pamięcią i pożądliwością.
Żądze nadzieją karmię i gładkością,
Nadzieję bajką i próżnym błądzeniem.

Napawam serce pychą, omamieniem,
Pychę zmyślonym weselem z śmiałością,
Śmiałość szaleństwem pasę z wyniosłością,
Szaleństwo gniewem i złym zajątrzeniem.

Karmię frasunkiem płaczem i wzdychaniem,
Wzdychanie ogniem, ogień wiatrem prawie,
Wiatr zasię cieniem, a cień oszukaniem,

Kto kiedy słychał o takowej sprawie,
Że i z tym o głód cudzy się staraniem
Sam przy tej wszytkiej głód ponoszę strawie.

THE WONDERS OF LOVE

I nourish love with sorrow and deep thought,
Deep thought with recollection and desire,
Desire I feed with hope and tenderness,
With fantasy and vain delusion—hope.

I swell my heart with pride, with self-deceit,
Pride with pretended mirth and boldness mixed,
Boldness I pasture with mad ecstasy,
Mad ecstasy with wrath and wicked woe.

Anxiety I feed with tears and sighs,
The sighs with fire and fire with raging wind,
The wind I sow with shade, shade with deceit.

Whoever heard of such a state wherein,
Concerned about another's famishment,
I starve myself 'midst all this nourishment.

                                        Jan Andrzej Morsztyn

CUDA MIŁOŚCI

Przebóg! Jak żyję, serca już nie mając?
Nie żyjąc, jako ogień w sobie czuję?
Jeśli tym ogniem sam się w sobie psuję,
Czemuż go pieszczę, tak się w nim kochając?

Tak w płaczu żyję, wśród ognia pałając,
Czemu wysuszyć ogniem nie próbuję
Płaczu? Czemu jak z ogniem postępuję,
Że go nie gaszę, w płaczu opływając?

Ponieważ wszytkie w oczach u dziewczyny
Pociechy, czemuż muszę od nich stronić?
Czemuż zaś na te narażam się oczy?

Cuda te czyni miłość, jej to czyny,
Którym kto by chciał rozumem się bronić,
Tym prędzej w sidło z rozumem swym wskoczy.

THE WONDERS OF LOVE

My God! I live, and yet without a heart?
Not living, yet a flame within me burns?
If with this flame I do myself destroy,
Why do I lovingly embrace it so?

If thus I live in tears, afire 'midst flame,
Why make I no attempt to dry the tears
With fire? And why, since I command the flame,
Can I not put it out with flowing tears?

Since maidens' eyes do in themselves contain
All pleasures, why must I from them take leave,
Instead of dashing boldly to those eyes?

These are the wonders worked by love, her deeds.
Who'd reason use against them in defense,
The sooner falls with reason in their net.

Jan Andrzej Morsztyn

O SWEJ PANNIE

Biały jest polerowany alabastr z Karrary,
   Białe mleko, przysłane w sitowiu z koszary,
Biała łabęć i białym okrywa się piórem,
   Biała perła, nie częstym zażywana sznurem,
Biały śnieg, świeżo spadły, nogą nie deptany,
   Biały kwiat lilijowy za świeża zerwany;
Ale bielsza mej panny płeć twarzy i szyje
   Niż marmur, mleko, łabęć, perła, śnieg, lilije.

ON HIS MISTRESS

White the polished marble of Carrara,
   White the milk from cow sheds fetched in baskets,
White the swan and covered with white plumage,
   White the pearl unspoiled by frequent stringing,
White the snow, fresh fallen, still untrampled,
   White the lily plucked in all its freshness,
But whiter still my lady's face and neck
   Than marble, milk, swan, pearl, fresh snow, and lily.

Jan Andrzej Morsztyn

DO TEJŻE

Oczy twe nie są oczy, ale słońca jaśnie
　Świecące, w których blasku każdy rozum gaśnie;
Usta twe nie są usta, lecz koral rumiany,
　Których farbą każdy zmysł zostaje związany;
Piersi twe nie są piersi, lecz nieba surowy
　Kształt, który wolą naszą zabiera w okowy;
Tak oczy, piersi, usta—rozum, zmysł i wolą
　Blaskiem, farbą i kształtem ćmią, wiążą, niewolą.

TO HIS MISTRESS

Not eyes your eyes, but brightly shining suns
　Whose brilliance brings to ruin every mind;
Not lips your lips, but coral red in hue
　Whose radiance makes captive of each sense;
Not breasts your breasts, but heaven's unworked form
　From which are fashioned fetters for the will.
'Tis thus that eyes, breasts, lips—mind, sense, and will
　By brilliance, color, form—blind, bind, imprison.

Jan Andrzej Morsztyn

DO PANNY

Twarde z wielkiem żelazo topione kłopotem,
Twardy dyjament żadnym nie pożyty młotem,
Twardy dąb wiekiem starym skamieniały,
Twarde skały, na morskie nie dbające wały;
Twardsza-ś ty, panno, której łzy me nie złamały,
Nad żelazo, dyjament, twardy dąb i skały.

TO A YOUNG LADY

Hard the iron smelted with great care,
Hard the diamond hammer never touched,
Hard the oak tree petrified with age,
Hard the cliffs aloof from ocean's waves;
Harder you, whom tears have failed to break,
Than iron, diamond, solid oak, and cliffs.

Jan Andrzej Morsztyn

NA KRZYŻYK NA PIERSIACH JEDNEJ PANNY

O, święta mego przyczyno zbawienia!
Któż cię wniósł na tę jasną Kalwaryją,
Gdzie dusze, które z łaski twojej żyją
W wolności, znowu wsadzasz do więzienia.

Z którego jeśli już oswobodzenia
Nie masz i tylko męki grzech omyją,
Proszę, niech na tym krzyżu ja pasyją
I konterfektem będę do wytchnienia.

A tam nie umrę, bo patrząc ku tobie,
Już obumarła nadzieja mi wstaje
I serce rośnie rozgrzane persiami.

Nie dziw, że zmarli podnoszą się w grobie,
Widząc, jak kiedyś ten, co żywot daje,
Krzyż miedzy dwiema wystawił łotrami.

ON THE LITTLE CROSS ON
A CERTAIN LADY'S BREAST

O holy cause of my salvation!
Who raised you to this fair Calvary
Where souls, which solely by your grace
Are free, you place again in prison?

From which, if there be no release
And only cleansing sin with torture,
I ask to rest upon this cross
Till passion and contrition drain me.

I shan't die there, for looking unto you,
A languid hope in me arises;
My heart, warmed by your breasts, revives.

'Tis no surprise the dead rise in their graves,
Seeing, how once he who gives life
A cross did place between two thieves.

                                        Jan Andrzej Morsztyn

NIESTATEK

Prędzej kto wiatr w wór zamknie, prędzej i promieni
Słonecznych drobne kąski wżenie do kieszeni,
Prędzej morze burzliwe groźbą uspokoi,
Prędzej zamknie w garść ten świat tak wielki, jak stoi,
Prędzej pięścią bez swojej obrazy ogniowi
Dobije, prędzej w sieci obłoki połowi,
Prędzej, płacząc nad Etną, łzami ją zaleje,
Prędzej niemy zaśpiewa, a ten, co szaleje,
Co mądrego przemówi; prędzej stała będzie
Fortuna i śmierć z śmiechem w jednym domu siędzie,
Prędzej prawdę poeta powie i sen płonny,
Prędzej i aniołowi płacz nie będzie płonny,
Prędzej słońce na nocleg skryje się w jaskini,
W więzieniu będzie pokój, ludzie na pustyni,
Prędzej nam zginie rozum i ustaną słowa—
Niźli będzie stateczną która białogłowa.

INCONSTANCY

The sooner will you trap the wind, small bits
Of sunbeams sooner with your pockets line,
The sooner calm the raging sea by threats,
The sooner grasp the world within a fist,
The sooner painlessly thrust hand in fire,
The sooner go in chase of clouds with nets,
The sooner drown Mt. Etna with your tears,
The sooner mutes will sing, and those insane
Speak wisely; Fortune sooner constant be,
Or death and mirth reside beneath a single roof,
The sooner poets not lie, and sleep be vain,
The sooner angels pay no heed to tears,
The sooner in a cave the sun seek rest,
Or peace in prison reign, or deserts filled,
The sooner reason perish, and words cease,
Than any woman ever constant be.

Jan Andrzej Morsztyn

NIESTATEK

Oczy są ogień, czoło jest zwierciadłem,
  Włos złotem, perła ząb, płeć mlekiem zsiadłem,
Usta koralem, purpurą jagody,
  Póki mi, panno, dotrzymujesz zgody.
Jak się zwadzimy, jagody są trądem,
  Usta czeluścią, płeć blejwasem bladem,
Ząb szkapią kością, włosy pajęczyną,
  Czoło maglownią, a oczy perzyną.

INCONSTANCY

Your eyes are fire, your brow a mirror,
  Hair—gold, pearls—teeth, skin—curdled milk,
Mouth—coral, purple-berried color,
  While we, my lady, live in peace.
But quarrel turns the berries leprous,
  Your mouth—a maw, skin—pale white lead,
Teeth—horse's bones, hair—web for spiders,
  Your brow—a mangle, eyes—burnt ash.

                              Jan Andrzej Morsztyn

DO TRUPA

Leżysz zabity i ja też zabity,
Ty strzałą śmierci, ja strzałą miłości;
Ty krwie, ja w sobie nie mam rumianości,
Ty jawne świece, ja mam płomień skryty.

Tyś na twarz suknem żałobnym nakryty,
Jam zawarł zmysły w okropnej ciemności;
Ty masz związane ręce, ja wolności
Zbywszy, mam rozum łańcuchem powity.

Ty jednak milczysz, a mój język kwili,
Ty nic nie czujesz, ja cierpię ból srodze;
Ty jak lód, a jam w piekielnej śrzeżodze.

Ty się rozsypiesz prochem w małej chwili;
Ja się nie mogę, stawszy się żywiołem
Wiecznym mych ogniów, rozsypać popiołem.

TO A CORPSE

You lie struck dead; struck dead I also am.
Death's arrow felled you, me the dart of love.
You have no blood, and I no color more.
Your candles glow, my flame hides deep within.

Your face is covered with a mourning shroud;
In dreadful darkness are my senses trapped.
Your hands are bound, while I am free
No longer, chains around my mind instead.

You are, however, silent; my tongue whines.
You feel not, while I suffer frightfully.
You are like ice; I burn in hellish fires.

Before much time, you shall go unto dust.
To scatter into ashes I cannot,
Eternal element of my own flames.

                                    Jan Andrzej Morsztyn

ODJAZD

Jadę precz, lecz bez siebie, bo bez ciebie; z sobą
    Obaczę się, kiedyć się stawię swą osobą;
Jadę, lecz połowicą, a druga zostaje
    Przy tobie—ten mię odjazd na dwie sztuce kraje.
Jadę i mnieszą siebie część biorę, mdłe ciało,
    Przy tobie lepsza, serce i z duszą zostało.
Jadę tak rozdwojony i w kupie nie będę,
    Póki do ciebie po część drugą nie przybędę,
Wtenczas skupiony wszytek w kompaniją miłą,
    Całyć już służyć będę i zupełną siłą.

DEPARTURE

I part, but without me, for without thee;
    Myself I'll greet when I am me again.
I part, but only half, the rest remains,
    With thee, departure me divides in two.
I part, taking my lesser self, frail shell;
    The better, heart and soul, remains with thee.

I part, divided so, and whole won't be,
   Till I return to claim the other half.
Then reunited in fair company,
   I shall serve whole and with full energy.

                              Jan Andrzej Morsztyn

PIEŚŃ

Kasiu, czyś chora, czy uporem,
Czy zgniewana na sołdaty,
Nie chciałaś choć z królowej dworem
Nawiedzić oboźne chaty?

Nie mogą-ć być straszne te chłody
I następujące mrozy,
Gdy może płomień twej urody
Popalić nasze obozy.

Jeśli się boisz postrzelenia,
Darmo o się chodzisz czule,
Bo ciebie, gdyś cale z kamienia,
Żadne się nie imą kule.

Masz też mocniejsze na obronę
Cekauzy swe i armaty,
Rzucając z oczu w każdą stronę
Kule ogniste, granaty.

A tym masz nad nieprzyjaciele,
Że się mu złoży żelazem
I chybia też, a ty zaś śmiele
W serca trafiasz każdym razem.

Przybądź tedy, bo w tym zaćmieniu
Słońca mego niebytności
Zda mi się, żem ja oblężeniu,
A że Toruń na wolności.

Nie kochaj się tak w swym klasztorze,
Uczyń przymierze z pacierzem.
Każdy mnich po trzecim nieszporze
Bardzo rad by był żołnierzem.

SONG

Kate, are you sick or obstinate
  Or angry with the troops?
Even though the Queen's been here in state
  Your Prettiness never stoops.

It can't be cold that keeps you there:
  The Frost won't take the blame.
If you were here, your beauty's flare
  Would set our huts aflame.

Nor should the fusillades alarm
  As some of us suggest.
Caution is needless since no harm
  Can pierce a stony breast.

Besides, for your defense, you train
  A bright artillery.
Grenades explode and bullets rain
  Where'er you cast an eye.

Then, too, your aim is surer than
  Iron's ever is.
You hit the heart of every man,
  Unlike our enemies.

Come, visit me, my little sun.
  Eclipses should be brief.
I am besieged and not Torun.*
  You must bring my relief.

Make a covenant with prayers.
  Forsake your nunnery.
Three vespers said, even monks repair,
  To join the soldiery.

                              Jan Andrzej Morsztyn
              Trans. by Jerzy Peterkiewicz and Burns Singer

* A city in northern Poland.

§ *Croatian*

AKO UZDASI MOJI OGNJENI

Ako uzdasi moji ognjeni,
Ako suze moje grozne,
Ako pogled moj ljuveni,
I ako riječi mê žalosne
Nemogoše ognjenoga
Svjedok biti moga plama,

O prelijepa, ka mê smami,
Prosti ove plačne glase,
Upisane, jaoh, suzami,
Koji iz srca moga izlaze.
Daj im vjeru kada vide
Oči moje mê beside.

One biće svjedok pravi
Od gorušta plama moga,
Koji prži, koji travi
Mene vjerna slugu tvoga.

IF MY ARDENT SIGHS

If my ardent sighs,
If my wretched tears,
If my tender glance
And my plaintive words
Witness could not claim
Of my burning flame,

Fairest, who allures,
These sad woes forgive
Now inscribed in tears,
Which my heart pours forth.
Trust them, since my eyes
See themselves my cries.

They'll true witness bear
of my ardor's flame,
Which burns and yet charms
Me, your faithful slave.

Stijepo Djordjić (Djurdjević) (1579–1632)

NEMOJ, NEMOJ, MA LJUBICE

Nemoj, nemoj, ma ljubice
Bistru viru virovati.
U kom rajsko tvoje lice
Općiš često ogledati.

Ere neće, vjeruj meni,
Dugo vrijeme kazat tebi
Medne usti, pram zlaćani
I dvije zore zgara s nebi.

Skoro, skoro promijenit će
Vas tvoj ures i svu diku,
Tebe istu tebi skrit će
Da neć' poznat tvu priliku.

Bježi mlados, dni othode
Vele brže, vele plaše
Neg' li istoga vira vode
I ka se u njim sjena kaže.

Tijekom, tijekom lete ljeta,
Sve pod suncem satire se,
I zasve dan dodje opeta,
Naša doba ne vrate se.

Odori će bit i plijeni,
Od gusara, ki sve stira,
Tvoj drag pogled, prem ljuveni,
Slatke usti, lice od lira.

Tim se mlada ne oholi.
Čim pogledaš sliku tvoju,
Neg se smili na me boli,
O ljubjeni moj pokoju!

DO NOT, PRITHEE, MY BELOVED

Do not, prithee, my beloved,
Put faith in the swirling eddy
In which often, as your wont is,
You behold your heav'nly features.

For believe me, when I tell you,
Long it will not hold before you

Lips of honey, locks' gold color,
And two dawns from heav'n descended.

Soon indeed, before you know it,
All your charms and pride will vanish,
Hiding from you this fair image
Till you recognize yourself not.

Youth flees as our days depart us
Far more suddenly and quickly
Than the water of the eddy,
Leaving nothing but a shadow.

Like a stream the years flow swiftly;
All things 'neath the sun to dust turn,
And although a new day follows,
Our life-span has no tomorrow.

Your dear look, your lovely ringlets,
Your sweet lips, your face of lily,
In the end will be the booty
Of the thief who plunders all.

Take no pride then, my young lady,
When your image you behold there,
But have pity on my torments,
O beloved source of comfort.

Džibo Bunić-Vučić (Ivan Bunić-Vučićević)
(1591–1658)

BIJELOGA ČEMINA

Bijeloga čemina za drag dar ljuveni
Vil moja jedina darova sad meni.
Rekoh joj: Diklice, za tebe toj hrani,
A meni cvjetice od prsi ne brani,
Ere su pobjelje od cvijeća tve prsi,
U kijeh me želje i život zamrsi.
To li hoć, da je moje, združit me dopusti
S njim ruse, ke goje rumene tve usti!

WHITE JASMINE

A precious gift of love of jasmine white
My one and only mistress makes me now.
I said to her: You keep it for yourself,
But hold not back the blossoms of your breasts,
For whiter than all flowers are those orbs
Which my desires, my life confusion cause.
Would you so favor me, let me unite
With them the roses which your red lips tend.

Dživo Bunić-Vučić (Ivan Bunić-Vučićević)

RAZBLUDNA MÂ VILA

Razbludna mâ vila celiva i mili
Sred draga nje krila djetešce, ke cvili,
A za me, jaoh, vaje i za me sve boli
Ništa se ne haje, ništa se ne boli.
Ne će on da pristane, čijem ma ga tješi vil,
A tijem bi me rane sama ona ozdravil';
Suze mu otire nje celov medeni,
Ma mlados umire, čim branjem jes meni.
Cvilimo eto oba s vesele nje dike,
On rana u doba, ja tužan u vike;
Nu iste darove ne primam, er uze
On sebi celove, a meni da suze.

MY LOVELY MISTRESS

My lovely mistress kisses and consoles
Beneath her precious wing the whimp'ring child,
But for my griefs and torments, sad to say,
She cares no whit at all, nor shares my pain.
The child stops not his cries, lest she stop too;
With what she comforts she could heal my wounds.
His tears she wipes away with honeyed kiss;
Denied the same, my youth is quick to wane.
Thus, we both weep because of her gay pride;
Grief mars his early years but all of mine.
The gifts the child presents I must decline:
He takes her kisses, but leaves me his tears.

Dživo Bunić-Vučić (Ivan Bunić-Vučićević)

DIJELJENJE OD GOSPOJE

Već se dijelim, ma gospoje,
Na put spravljam me stupaje,
Nu ti ostavljam srce moje,
S tobom duša ma ostaje.

Dijelit ću se, al' ne pače,
S tobom biću, dušo, u vike,
Ko da ostavim, slatki brače,
Tve ljeposti rajske dike?

Ko da živem bez života
I bez duše dijelim da se,
Srca od moga tva ljepota
Ko da ostane na po na se?

Po sred njega zlatnom strilom
Udjeljana je tva prilika,
Neka u družbi s takom vilom
Srećan živem svedj do vika.

Ali 'e sila htjenja od nebi
Poklonit te, ma gospoje,
Dijelit mi se, ah, jaoh, trijebi,
Od bolesti duh mi podje.

Huda srdžba huda udesa
Odvede me, moja draga,
Na daleče tvoga uresa,
Gdje ljudskoga nije traga.

Svedj ću smišljat tve razblude
U dne, u noći, zimi, i ljeti
Dokle u meni duh uzbude
S mislim, s srcem, iz pameti.

Kada vidim zrak sunčani
Gdi isteče iz istoči,
Pomislit ću da je izbrani
Rajski pogled tvojijeh oči.

Kad li vidim jasna zora
Da objavi lice milo,
U njoj tvoga sred pozora
Razmišljat ću rumenilo.

Razbirat ću usred cvijeća
Tvojijeh prsi lijepe bijele,
Ke ranoga primaljeća
Ures jesu pridobile.

Tako od zemlje i od nebi
Izabraću ljepše što je
Za iznać ures sličan tebi,
I dostojan dike tvoje.

Nu ko ufat mogu viku
Da će narav i nebesa
Igda iznać tvu priliku
Izvan tvoga sred uresa?

Već se dijelim, ne brani mi,
Poć gdi srjeća ma me zove,
Najpokonje veće primi
Me uzdahe i celove.

Ah, ne veće ma besjeda
Od žalosti trud da izusti,
Jaoh, izdahnuh, ne naprijeda,
Riječ mi umire posrijed usti.

PARTING FROM HIS LADY

We part, my lady, you and I,
My steps I've set upon the path,
But you I leave my heart behind,
My soul alone remains with you.

Take leave I shall, yet nonetheless,
Forever shall I be with you
For, fairest one, how can I leave
The glories of your heav'nly charm?

How can I live, deprived of life,
And so take leave, without my soul?
How can your beauty, from my heart,
Remain divided so in half?

A golden arrow 'midst the heart
Holds your fair image there transfixed;
I pray that I shall always live
With such a nymph in happiness.

If heaven's will it proves to be,
I must, my lady, bow to you
And, woe is me, be on my way;
My soul from pain shall quickly flee.

The cruel wrath of cruel fate
Leads me away, my dearest one,
Far from your loveliness' sway
To where no human steps have gone.

Your charms shall ever be in mind
The summer, winter, day and night,
So long as live my spirit stays
With mind and heart and memory.

When I behold the sun's bright rays
As from their source they usher forth,
They shall become then to my mind
The heav'nly aspect of your eyes.

And when the brilliant dawn I see
As it reveals its fair visage,
In pond'ring its reddish blush
'Tis yours before me that shall be.

Among the flowers I shall pluck
The lovely whites of your fair breasts,
Which have the conquest truly made
Of all the charms of early spring.

Thus both from heaven and from earth
The loveliest of all I'll choose
To find a beauty such as yours
And worthy truly of your praise.

Yet how can I anticipate
That nature and the heav'ns above
Will recognize your image fair
Amidst a beauty outside yours?

And so we part, prevent me not,
From following the call of fate;
Accept from me the last time now
My sighs and kisses without count.

No longer will my words express
The pain my grief but poorly stills.
Alas, I can no more, I die;
Death halts the words upon my lips.

Vladislav Menčetić (1617–66)

GOSPODJI NADALEKO

Otkad me je ostavila
Prigizdava tvâ ljepota,
Živem tužan bez života
I bez duše, dušo mila.

Ginem, sahnem, gasnem, blidim,
Ranjen tugam bezbrojnijeme
Misleć kad će doći vrijeme,
Mâ Ljubice, da te vidim.

I razmišljam da jednako
Nije biće moje i tvoje:
Ja umiram, o gospoje,
A ti uživaš dobro svako.

Ti uživaš u radosti
vode, dubja i zeleni,
A ja kunem, vajmeh meni,
Mê nezgode, mê žalosti

Ke mi skrovna sumnja uzroči,
Jesam li ti u milosti
Al' sam dalek tvôj ljeposti
Tako od srca kako od oči.

Ah da mogu krila od ptice
Po ljuvenom čudu steći
Za u tebe doć leteći,
uzdisana mâ božice!

Nu pokli mi po naravi
Nije to dano, moj pokoju,
posilam ti dušu moju
Na krilijeh od ljubavi.

TO HIS MISTRESS FAR AWAY

From the time your haughty beauty
Parted company with me,
Sadly live I, no life have I,
And without a soul, my soul.

I die, wither, fade, expire,
Wounded by a host of woes,
Thinking when the time will be here
When, my love, I'll see you next.

And I ponder how quite different
Are the lives we lead apart:
I am dying, O my lady,
While you savor every joy.

You enjoy in carefree spirit
Water, woodlands, and green meadows.
I, however, am but fated
To lament my woes and griefs

Which the secret doubt gives rise to,
If I still enjoy your love,
So far distant from your beauty
As I am from heart and sight.

Ah, but could I, by love's magic,
Wings of birds myself acquire,
Flying would I soon come to you,
Goddess whom I sigh for so.

Since, however, I'm denied this
By the law of nature, dear,
Naught I can do but to send you
Borne on wings of love my soul.

Ignjat Djordjić (Djurdjević) (1675–1735)

Index of Names and Anthologized Poems

First lines of poems are printed in ordinary roman type, *titles of poems are quoted, and excerpts from longer works are in italics.*